Investing in Collateralized Debt Obligations

Edited by

Frank J. Fabozzi, Ph.D., CFA

Laurie S. Goodman, Ph.D.

Published by Frank J. Fabozzi Associates

© 2001 By Frank J. Fabozzi Associates
except where noted.
New Hope, Pennsylvania

Table of Contents

Preface

Contributing Authors

1. *Introduction to Collateralized Debt Obligations*   1
   Charles Schorin and Steven Weinreich

2. *Structural Features of Market Value CDOs*   33
   Luigi Vacca

3. *Rating Agency Methodologies*   53
   Meredith Hill and Luigi Vacca

4. *CDO Structure and Arbitrage*   79
   Laurie S. Goodman

5. *Emerging Market CBOs*   91
   Laurie S. Goodman

6. *Mortgage Cash Flow CBOs*   101
   Laurie S. Goodman

7. *CDOs Backed by ABS and Commercial Real Estate*   115
   R. Russell Hurst

8. *Synthetic CDOs*   141
   Laurie S. Goodman

9. *Cash and Synthetic European Bank CLOs*   157
   Alexander Batchvarov, Ganesh Rajendra, William Ross, and
   Xavier De Pauw

10. *Analyzing Mezzanine Tranches of CBOs*   199
    Laurie S. Goodman and Jeffrey Ho

11. *Relative Value Framework for Collateralized Debt Obligations*   209
    Charles Schorin and Steven Weinreich

12. *Pricing Debt and Equity in a Market Value CDO*   219
    Luigi Vacca

13. *Use of Credit Derivatives in CBO/CLO Structures*   225
    Meredith Hill and Luigi Vacca

Index   233

Contributing Authors

Alexander Batchvarov	Merrill Lynch
Xavier De Pauw	Merrill Lynch
Laurie S. Goodman	UBS Warburg
Meredith Hill	Banc of America Securities
Jeffrey Ho	UBS Warburg
R. Russell Hurst	First Union Securities, Inc.
Ganesh Rajendra	Merrill Lynch
William Ross	Merrill Lynch
Charles Schorin	Morgan Stanley Dean Witter
Luigi Vacca	Banc of America Securities
Steven Weinreich	Morgan Stanley Dean Witter

Preface

The fastest growing sector of the asset-backed securities market is the collateralized debt obligation (CDO) market. CDOs are securities backed by a pool of diversified assets and are referred to as collateralized bond obligations (CBOs) when the underlying assets are bonds and as collateralized loan obligations (CLOs) when the underlying assets are bank loans. *Investing in Collateralized Debt Obligations* covers not only the fundamental features of these securities and the investment characteristics that make them attractive to a broad range of institutional investors, but also the tools for identifying relative value.

To be effective, a book of this nature should offer a broad perspective. The experience of several analysts is more informative than that of a single analyst, particularly because of the diversity of opinion with respect to some issues. We have chosen some of the best known analysts to contribute to this book. All have been actively involved in the evolution of the CDO market.

This book does not address tax issues. For a comprehensive discussion of the tax treatment of securitizations generally and of sponsors, issuers, and holders of CDOs and CBOs, see James Peaslee and David Nirenberg, *Federal Income Taxation of Securitization Transactions* (3d Ed., Frank J. Fabozzi Associates, 2001) [www.securitizationtax.com].

We wish to thank the contributors to this book and their firms — Charles Schorin and Steven Weinreich of Morgan Stanley Dean Witter, Meredith Hill and Luigi Vacca of Banc of America Securities, Russell Hurst of First Union Securities, Alexander Batchvarov, Ganesh Rajendra, William Ross, and Xavier De Pauw of Merrill Lynch, and Jeffrey Ho of UBS Warburg. We thank UBS Warburg for allowing Laurie Goodman to contribute to and coedit the book. The participation of these investment banking firms to this book is indicative of their commitment, as well as other firms, to the development of the CDO market.

We wish to thank the rating agencies — (in alphabetical order) Fitch, Moody's Investors Service, and Standard & Poor's — for permitting the contributors to use tables and graphs in the preparation of their chapters. The data in the exhibits in this book are based on the latest information available from the rating agencies. However, the reader is warned that the rating agencies continually update the statistical information that they employ to derive credit ratings and therefore the data reported in the exhibits may not reflect current data.

Finally, we thank Burton Esrig of UBS Warburg for encouraging the publication of this book.

Frank J. Fabozzi
Laurie S. Goodman

v

Chapter 1

Introduction to Collateralized Debt Obligations

Charles Schorin
Principal
Director of ABS Research
Morgan Stanley Dean Witter

Steven Weinreich
Associate
Morgan Stanley Dean Witter

The market for *collateralized debt obligations* (CDOs) is the fastest growing sector of the asset-backed securities market. From less than $3 billion originated as recently as 1995, the market for CDOs reached $57 billion in 1997 and another $30 billion in the first half of 1998. Though it is not the newest asset class — the first CDO was created in 1988 — it has become both an extremely popular instrument for investors and a very attractive vehicle for issuers. Investors have been attracted to the sector because of the relatively high yield for the highly rated paper, while issuers' motivations — among others — have been to maximize return on equity and increase assets under management.

CDOs are special purpose vehicles investing in a diversified pool of assets. The investments in the CDO are funded through the issuance of several classes of securities, the repayment of which is linked to the performance of the underlying securities that serve as collateral for the CDO liabilities. The investments are managed/serviced by an experienced investment manager/servicer, sometimes referred to as the *collateral manager*.

The securities issued by the CDO are tranched into rated and unrated classes. The rating of each class is primarily determined through the priority of interest in the cash flows generated by the collateral. The senior notes are typically rated AAA to A, may pay a fixed or floating rate coupon and have the highest priority on cash flows. The mezzanine classes are typically rated BBB to B, may pay either a fixed or floating rate coupon and have a claim on cash flows that is subordinate to the senior notes.

The subordinated notes/equity of the CDO are generally unrated and are the residual of the transaction. Subordinated noteholders receive a current coupon out of the residual interest proceeds generated by the collateral, after payment of expenses and debt service on the securities that rank senior to the subordinated notes. The coupon may be deferred or eliminated depending upon available cash flow. The subordinated notes are in a first loss position; because they represent a leveraged investment in the underlying collateral, they have a higher expected return — although with a higher volatility of return — than the underlying collateral pool.

CDOs may be characterized as *collateralized bond obligations* (CBOs), *collateralized loan obligations* (CLOs) or both. These instruments are analogous to other collateralized securities, with the collateral for a CBO being a pool of outstanding bonds or bond-like securities, while that for a CLO is a pool of loans. The collateral also may contain various types of credit derivatives, including credit linked notes (CLNs).

CDOs can further be categorized into two types: arbitrage or balance sheet transactions. In an *arbitrage transaction*, the equity investor is capturing the spread difference between the relatively high yielding collateral and the yields at which the senior liabilities of the CDO are issued. A *balance sheet transaction*, in contrast, is intended to remove loans, or in some cases, bonds, from the balance sheet of a financial institution so that it achieves capital relief, improved liquidity or a higher return on assets through redeployment of capital.

Arbitrage transactions can be divided into *cash flow transactions* or *market value transactions*. Balance sheet deals are all cash flow transactions. Cash flow deals are those that are based on the ability of the collateral to generate sufficient cash to pay interest and principal on the rated classes of securities issued by the CDO. Market value transactions, in contrast, depend upon the ability of the fund manager to maintain a collateral market value, potentially through actively trading the portfolio subject to various constraints, sufficient to generate cash upon the sale of such collateral in the collateral pool to pay the CDO securities.

The collateral manager of a CDO monitors the pool and makes ongoing trading decisions within parameters established prior to closing and defined in the transaction indenture. In fact, a trustee is hired to ensure that these covenants of the CDO are followed. The trustee assumes complete control of the release of any cash and/or securities of the transaction, and pre-approves all trading decisions.

Investors in CDO senior notes are attracted to the sector because it enables them to achieve high yields relative to other asset-backed securities for a given bond rating category.

The collateral manager/sponsor may have several motivations for the creation of a CDO. For balance sheet CLOs, sponsors can achieve capital relief by removing assets from their balance sheet. In addition, to the extent that these assets are relatively high quality and therefore low yielding, the sponsor can redeploy capital to higher yielding investments, as well as tap a relatively inexpensive or new funding source.

Exhibit 1: Generic CDO Structure

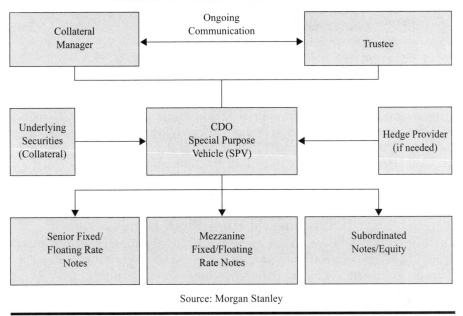

Source: Morgan Stanley

Sponsors of arbitrage transactions are motivated by the ability to increase assets under management in order to increase management fees. Equity investors are motivated by the ability to realize leveraged returns on the underlying assets, while achieving funding that is attractive relative to alternatives, such as repo financing.

This chapter begins with a description of the collateral types employed in CDO transactions and then moves to a discussion of the various CDO structures and mechanics. We include discussions of credit enhancement and coverage and quality tests, as well as present sample transactions. We next turn to the manner in which ratings agencies analyze CDO structures in terms of credit, followed by a framework in which investors should analyze the senior notes and mezzanine classes in terms of relative value. In Chapter 11 we introduce a new method to better analyze defaults and the credit protection of CDO transactions. The rating agency methodologies for rating CDO transactions are reviewed in Chapter 3.

COLLATERAL

Investors in a CDO have a perfected security interest in the underlying collateral, which may consist of a multitude of asset types. This diversity of collateral types can make the sector as a whole quite challenging to understand.

In this section we consider the most common types of assets utilized to date. These asset classes are:

- U.S. domestic high yield bonds
- emerging market debt
- U.S. domestic bank loans
- special situation loans and distressed debt
- foreign bank loans
- credit derivatives

Collateral for a CDO transaction is not limited to one of these groups. Many transactions are structured with collateral from several groups, perhaps including a combination of domestic high yield and emerging market debt, as well as domestic bank loans. While not all of these asset classes easily lend themselves to all CDO structures, there are structures that can utilize any one of these asset types. Cash flow deals require current cash paying assets, whereas market value transactions can employ distressed, non-current assets.

U.S. Domestic High Yield Bonds

Domestic high yield bonds are one of the most common forms of collateral underlying CBOs. The high coupon associated with these relatively risky assets makes them perfect candidates for use in cash flow arbitrage transactions.

The rating agencies treat different sectors of the U.S. high yield market as having different degrees of correlation, in some cases even being relatively uncorrelated. Exhibit 2 shows the classification by Moody's of the various sectors of the high yield market. The rating agencies tend to give diversity credit for multiple industrial sectors within developed economies, but group together various sectors within single countries or regions of emerging markets.

Exhibit 2: Domestic High Yield Sectors

	Industry			Industry
1	Aerospace and Defense		18	Grocery
2	Automobile		19	Healthcare, Education and Childcare
3	Banking		20	Hotels, Motels, Inns and Gaming
4	Beverage, Food and Tobacco		21	Insurance
5	Broadcasting		22	Leisure and Entertainment
6	Buildings and Real Estate		23	Machinery
7	Cargo Transport		24	Mining and Non-precious Metals
8	Chemicals, Plastics and Rubber		25	Oil and Gas
9	Containers, Packaging and Glass		26	Personal and Non-durable Consumer Prod
10	Div. Nat. Resources, Precious Metals		27	Personal Transportation
11	Diversified/Conglomerate Manufacturing		28	Personal, Food and Miscellaneous Services
12	Diversified/Conglomerate Service		29	Printing, Publishing
13	Durable Consumer Products		30	Retail Stores
14	Ecological		31	Telecommunications
15	Electronics		32	Textiles and Leather
16	Farming and Agricultural		33	Utilities
17	Finance			

Source: Moody's Investors Service

Emerging Market Debt

Emerging market collateral has been used frequently in cash flow arbitrage transactions. The relatively large yield spread between these securities and the higher rated bonds sold out of the special purpose CDO vehicle allow these bonds to be used in cash flow transactions. Their high price volatility has prevented them from being employed very often in market value transactions.

In emerging market regions, the rating agencies generally do not grant credit for sector diversification within a country. The reason for this is that the perceived high correlation between the overall emerging economy and an individual sector within that market is high enough not to warrant diversification credit in the analysis. In fact, for purposes of measuring portfolio diversification, Moody's, for instance, groups all emerging market countries into five regions, and further penalizes Latin America with a higher correlation of bonds defaulting.

When emerging market securities are used as collateral, rating agencies tend to place restrictions on the concentration a portfolio can maintain in any one geographic region. These restriction levels have typically been somewhat higher than the percentages in the actual collateral portfolios at time of origination. A large percentage of CDOs structured in the past few years have used at least some portion of emerging market debt in the collateral pool. The ratings analysis for emerging market backed CDOs is similar to that of domestic high yield CDOs.

U.S. Domestic Bank Loans

Higher quality domestic bank loans have typically been employed as collateral in balance sheet CLOs. As mentioned above, the relatively low yield of higher quality domestic bank commercial and industrial (C&I) loans makes their use impractical in arbitrage or market value CBOs. For instance, the NationsBank Commercial Loan Master Trust balance sheet CLO transaction is backed by higher quality bank loans; the objective of NationsBank was to remove these assets from its balance sheet and achieve a higher return on the assets that remained on balance sheet. The NationsBank transaction is said to be de-linked from the issuer, in that investors face credit exposure only to the assets in the trust and not to the sponsor. Similar to traditional asset-backed transactions for which the collateral was transferred to the trust in a true sale, a downgrade of the sponsor would not in and of itself result in a downgrade of the transaction.

High yield loans have also been employed in CDO collateral pools. Also referred to as HLT loans — loans from highly leveraged transactions — these high yield loans contain certain covenants that provide additional protection. This protection frequently includes a security interest. High yield loans have been used extensively as collateral for cash flow arbitrage CLOs.

Special Situation Loans and Distressed Debt

In addition to high quality C&I loans, more risky types of bank loans have also been employed as CDO collateral. These include special situation loans and distressed debt. Special situation loans are those that involve unique, individually negotiated terms, such as workout loans. Distressed debt represents loans to borrowers that already have experienced some economic difficulty and may be expected to have a higher likelihood of default. These more risky types of bank loans have been in pools backing market value arbitrage transactions.

Foreign Bank Loans

Foreign bank loans have also been used as CDO collateral. These generally have been relatively high quality loans backing balance sheet CLOs. The loans themselves may be dollar or non-dollar denominated. Examples of non-dollar loans include the British pound loans behind ROSE Funding and the French franc loans backing Credit Lyonnais Cyber Val. Foreign loans introduce special considerations for perfection of security interests owing to the differential development of the legal infrastructure pertaining to securitization in various countries.

Credit Derivatives

Credit derivatives, including credit linked swaps and linked notes (CLNs), have also been used as collateral in various CDOs. Credit derivatives have typically been used to tailor exposure to a specific credit or efficiently transfer credit risk.

The cash flows from credit derivatives are tied to the performance of anything from a single credit to a basket of corporate or sovereign credits. Investors in credit derivatives, then, achieve exposure to defined credit instruments of potentially varying credit ratings by holding a single instrument. Ratings of CLNs or credit swaps are linked not only to that of the underlying credits, but also to that of the issuing entity or swap counterparty. For example, ratings of the SBC Glacier transaction are linked to those of Swiss Bank Corporation. This is in contrast to de-linked structures, for which the assets have been sold or assigned directly into the issuing vehicle and the investor has no exposure to the issuer/sponsor, per se.

TRANSACTION STRUCTURES AND MECHANICS

Most collateralized debt obligations can be placed into either of two main groups, arbitrage or balance sheet transactions. Within the arbitrage heading, there are cash flow and market value transactions. For the most part, balance sheet transactions utilize the cash flow structure. Exhibit 3 diagrams the conceptual breakdown between arbitrage and balance sheet transactions, while Exhibit 4 shows their relative market composition over the past few years. In this section we will explore the structural nuances of these types of deals.

Arbitrage Transactions

Arbitrage transactions can be classified into cash flow and market value transactions. In this section we discuss their structural and practical differences. The primary difference relates to the manner in which the collateral asset pool generates cash to pay the transaction liabilities. Whereas cash flow transactions focus on the ability of a collateral pool to generate interest and principal sufficient to pay the CDO's liabilities with a substantial cushion to protect against defaults, market value transactions rely on the value of the underlying collateral. The collateral in a market value deal is marked to market on an ongoing basis and must maintain enough market value to pay off the fund's liabilities with substantial cushion to protect against market declines. This is the primary distinction between the two structures, although there are other differences that cause the two structures to behave and trade quite differently. Arbitrage transactions generally range in size from $100 million to as much as $1 billion or more.

Cash Flow Transactions

Cash flow arbitrage deals attempt to extract the difference between the relatively higher yield on the speculative grade and/or emerging market debt assets of the CDO and the lower cost of the relatively higher rated securities issued by the CDO structure. These transactions employ a collateral pool with a given expected loss and prioritize the underlying pool's credit exposure into several classes which, in aggregate, have credit exposure identical to the pool's, but individually have either greater or lesser risk. This differential credit exposure is achieved primarily via subordination. Added credit enhancement in the form of excess spread, overcollateralization, structural triggers, reserve accounts or insurance wraps may also be utilized.

Exhibit 3: CDO Market

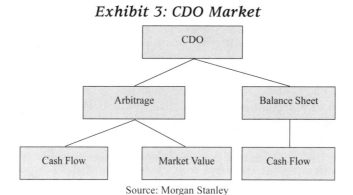

Source: Morgan Stanley

Exhibit 4: CDO Market Composition: Arbitrage versus Balance Sheet (1996, 1997, 1998 through July)

| | Volume (Billions of $) | | No. of Transactions | |
	Arbitrage	Balance Sheet	Arbitrage	Balance Sheet
1998	10.9	19.3	27	20
1997	22.2	34.9	68	18
1996	12.7	5.0	36	1

Source: Morgan Stanley

Ratings on the liabilities of cash flow CDOs are dependent upon cash flow generation and portfolio characteristics. There are no requirements to buy or sell securities of the underlying collateral pool due to adverse market value movements. The primary consideration is the default risk of the underlying collateral.

A benchmark cash flow arbitrage transaction is the $1.276 billion Van Kampen CLO I, Ltd. structure. This is backed entirely by U.S. domestic bank loans, with neither high yield bond nor emerging market collateral. It consists of an Aa2/AA rated senior secured floating rate class totaling $375 million; an Aa2/AA rated revolving credit facility that may be drawn up to $625 million; a Baa3 rated second priority senior secured note class totaling $130 million; and unrated subordinated notes of $146 million.

Collateral Because the rating of cash flow CDOs is supported by projected cash flows of the underlying collateral, the collateral pool tends to consist more of conventional debt instruments with defined principal and interest schedules than is the case with market value transactions. Securities backing cash flow CDOs may consist of a variety of assets types, such as bank loans, high yield bonds, emerging market debt (both sovereign and corporate), and securities from other structured transactions.

Generally bank loans included in such arbitrage structures would consist of sub-investment grade loans, whereas higher quality commercial and industrial loans would more likely be included in balance sheet transactions.

Structure Cash flow transactions rely on a concept similar to most asset-backed securities structured as senior/subordinate bonds. Income generated from the underlying pool of assets is used to pay first servicing and other trust fees, then interest to the senior most bondholders and then interest to the mezzanine holders. Subordinated noteholders receive distributions of residual interest by the collateral only after all other payments that are due currently have been made.

Principal payments go through the same type of cash flow waterfall after a reinvestment or revolving period. Generally, a large portion of the servicing/management fee is subordinate to the payments of the rated liabilities of the CDO.

Distributions of principal receipts from the underlying collateral are made to subordinated noteholders only after all of the senior and mezzanine securities have been paid in full.

Cash flow CDOs typically have a 3- to 6-year period — referred to as the *reinvestment period* or *revolving period* — during which principal cash flows from the collateral pool may be reinvested in new collateral, subject to certain predefined constraints. After the reinvestment period, only unscheduled principal, such as that from calls, tenders or collateral sales, may be reinvested. All other principal collections from the collateral are used first to repay the senior notes until they are retired. The basic structure and cash flow waterfall for an arbitrage CDO transaction are diagrammed in Exhibits 5 and 6.

Exhibit 5: Interest Cash Flow Waterfall of Cash Flow CDO

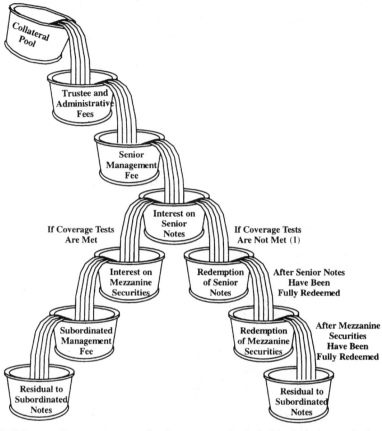

Note: (1) If Coverage Tests are not met, and to the extent not corrected with principal proceeds, the remaining interest proceeds will be used to redeem the most senior notes to bring the structure back into compliance with the Coverage Tests. Interest on the Mezzanine Securities may be deferred and compounded if cash flow is not available to pay current interest due.

Source: Morgan Stanley

In general, a certain percentage of the pool can be traded at the portfolio manager's discretion in order to take advantage of relative value opportunities that may become apparent after the transaction has been issued. To ensure that the collateral pool maintains a resemblance to its composition at issuance, the transaction's indenture will stipulate restrictions and diversification requirements that will be maintained throughout the transaction's life. These are referred to as *quality tests* and will be explained below.

Credit Enhancement Senior notes in cash flow transactions are protected by subordination and overcollateralization. The senior notes have a priority claim on all cash flows generated on the underlying collateral pool. The senior notes are further protected by coverage tests — generally par and interest coverage tests — that serve to accelerate the redemption of the senior notes if violated. Similar to home equity loan ABS senior/subordinate transactions, cash is diverted from the subordinate notes to the senior notes in the event of poor collateral performance. In the case of cash flow arbitrage CDOs, however, *interest* cash flow as well may be diverted from the more subordinate classes to pay *principal* on the senior classes if coverage tests are breached. The subordinated notes being in a first loss position, plus this redirection of cash to the senior classes in the event of weak collateral performance, are the credit enhancement features that allow the senior notes to obtain ratings significantly higher than the pool of assets underlying the transaction.

Exhibit 6: Principal Cash Flow Waterfall of Cash Flow CDO

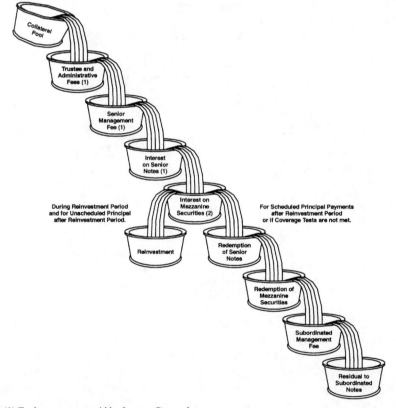

Note: (1) To the extent not paid by Interest Proceeds.
(2) To the extent Senior Note Coverage Tests are met and to the extent not already paid by Interest Proceeds. If Coverage Tests are not met, the remaining Principal Proceeds will be used to redeem the most senior notes to bring the structure back into compliance with the Coverage Tests. Interest on the Mezzanine Securities may be deferred and compounded if cash flow is not available to pay current interest due.

Source: Morgan Stanley

There are two scenarios where the senior notes may receive accelerated principal payments, other than those applied after the reinvestment period due to principal payments generated by the underlying collateral pool. One scenario would be if the senior notes are called. Cash flow CDOs usually provide for the senior notes to be callable at par or at a make-whole premium by the subordinated note holders after a stated non-call period, which usually is 2 to 5 years. The second scenario is if the interest or par value coverage tests are breached. This may occur, for instance, due to defaults within the underlying collateral portfolio. In this case, cash flow that would otherwise go to holders of the subordinate classes, and even mezzanine classes, if necessary, would be used to pay down the senior notes until coverage levels are restored. After this point, cash flow would be resumed to the mezzanine and subordinate classes, respectively.

Besides coverage tests, cash flow transactions also provide for quality tests. While the violation of a coverage test leads to the redirection of cash flows, the quality tests are put in place to ensure that the portfolio maintains similar characteristics as those at issuance.

Coverage Tests There are two types of coverage tests — par value test and interest coverage test.

1. *Par value test:* For cash flow CDOs, the *par value test* requires that rated bonds have at least a given stated percentage of collateral supporting it. This is analogous to the overcollateralization trigger in the home equity loan ABS arena. For example, if the trigger is set at 115% on a $100 million senior bond, then if at any time the par value of the assets in the collateral portfolio decreases below $115 million, the senior bonds will receive principal payments until the trigger is cured.

Lower rated CDO bonds will have lower percentage par value hurdles. For example, if the senior par value percentage were set at 115%, the mezzanine securities may have a par value test of 105%. However, in the calculation of the par coverage test for mezzanine classes, the amount of the senior bonds is included in the analysis. Consider a $20 million mezzanine class with $100 million in senior bonds above it. If the minimum par coverage level were set at 105% for the mezzanine bond, the collateral must maintain a minimum level of 105% of $120 million, or $126 million. Again, if the test were breached, the most senior notes would be redeemed until the test came back into compliance.

2. *Interest coverage test:* For cash flow CDOs, the *interest coverage test* is applied to ensure that the interest cash flow on the underlying collateral has sufficient cushion to absorb losses and still make interest payments to the rated CDO securities. This test is analogous to the debt service coverage ratio analyzed in the commercial mortgage backed securities (CMBS) market, although in the CMBS market, a decline in the debt service coverage ratio would not trigger a reprioritization of cash flow. The debt service coverage ratio in CMBS analysis is purely a

descriptive statistic. With cash flow CDOs, however, should the interest coverage test be breached, payments will be redirected to the senior bonds until the trigger is cured. An interest coverage level is generally set for each rated security at time of issuance.

Quality Tests Examples of quality tests within other sectors of the ABS market are difficult to find. The reason is due to the difference in the collateral pool composition of CDOs versus other ABS. CDO collateral pools are actively traded, in contrast to the static nature of ABS pools. In addition, ABS pools typically comprise thousands, and perhaps tens of thousands of individual loans, so that the performance of any one loan would generally not affect the transaction performance. In contrast, there are fewer loans or bonds in CDO collateral pools, so the risks are more lumpy. Poor performance of a single component of a CDO collateral pool could have a marked affect on deal performance.

The basic purpose of quality tests in CDOs is to ensure that the collateral pool does not become under-diversified or have its composition change dramatically through the normal trading activities of the manager. When quality tests are breached, there is no change to the cash flows directed to bond holders, but trading is restricted to actions that improve the collateral composition in relation to the breached quality measure. The four primary quality tests focus on diversity scores, concentrations in certain regions, the weighted average rating of the underlying collateral pool, and maturity restrictions.

1. *Minimum diversity score:* The diversity score developed by Moody's is probably the single statistic in the CDO market that is most associated with a rating agency.

A diversity score is a statistic indicating the degree of variability — or diversity — in the CDO collateral pool. It is recalculated each time the bonds in the collateral pool change. The collateral pool may change for any of several reasons, including:

- bond in the collateral pool being sold
- bond being purchased into the collateral pool
- scheduled repayment changing the percentage composition of the pool
- unscheduled payments (e.g., calls or tenders) of underlying assets
- defaults.

A portfolio manager may not execute a trade that would result in this test being breached, i.e., that would result in a diversity score below the stated minimum. If an event happens outside the control of the portfolio manager that causes the diversity score to fall below the stated minimum — for example, a bond paying down — then future trades would be restricted to actions that would improve the diversity score.

2. *Concentrations in emerging market regions:* The indenture will also formally describe certain restrictions as to the exposure of the portfolio to certain sectors and/or regions. During the ratings process, the agencies place levels on the securities based on certain assumptions as to the composition of the portfolio once the collateral pool is completely populated. For example, consider a portfolio that, when fully populated, will contain 80% domestic high yield bonds and 20% emerging markets debt, with the emerging market composition being 3% Latin America, 5% Russia, 8% non-Japan Asia and 4% Eastern Europe. The rating agencies will assign ratings based on this portfolio composition. They will, however, run stress scenarios to ensure that the rating is applicable given even higher concentrations in these emerging market regions. As such, the indenture may stipulate that the portfolio may have no more than 5% in Latin America, 8% in Russia, 10% in non-Japan Asia, and 5% in Eastern Europe. These levels would constitute the maximum representation of the given regions in the portfolio.

Defaults, amortization and call provisions may result in the maximum concentration percentages being breached. The portfolio manager is prohibited from executing a trade that would breach these levels. If these levels are breached, once again there are no implications on cash flows to the CDO noteholders. The portfolio manager's trading ability, however, would be limited to actions that would improve the representation of these regions in the underlying collateral pool.

3. *Minimum weighted average rating:* The indenture will require that the collateral pool underlying the transaction maintains a minimum average rating. The balances of the securities in the pool as well as the non-linear expected default rate of different ratings categories, derive the weighted average rating. Moody's and Fitch assign a numerical measure to each rating category, incorporating the expected default for that category. Since expected default is non-linear in the ratings categories, the numerical progression of this measure does not move one-for-one along the ratings spectrum. While S&P does not specifically employ a numerical average rating concept, its trading model does factor in the expected defaults based upon the ratings distribution of the collateral.

Exhibit 7 shows the integer value that Moody's and Fitch equate to each rating level. Averaging these values across the collateral pool, weighted by the balance of the respective security in the pool, will result in the weighted average rating. Typically the minimum average rating will be set initially at a level somewhat lower than the actual rating of the existing pool to allow for some trading flexibility after issuance.

Similar to the diversity score test described above, a portfolio manager cannot add or remove a bond from the portfolio if the resultant portfolio violates the minimum weighted average rating test. This test may be breached if assets within the portfolio are downgraded. On an ongoing basis, the trustee calculates the average rating on each remittance date. Breaches of this trigger result in similar trading restrictions as discussed above. Trading would be limited to actions that improve the collateral pool relative to this test.

Exhibit 7: Rating Factors Used to Derive Weighted Average Ratings

	Moody's	Fitch
Aaa/AAA	1	1
Aa1/AA+	10	8
Aa2/AA	20	10
Aa3/AA-	40	14
A1/A+	70	18
A2/A	120	23
A3/A-	180	36
Baa1/BBB+	260	48
Baa2/BBB	360	61
Baa3/BBB-	610	94
Ba1/BB+	940	129
Ba2/BB	1,350	165
Ba3/BB-	1,780	210
B1/B+	2,220	260
B2/B	2,720	308
B3/B-	3,490	356
CCC+	NA	463
Caa/CCC	6,500	603
CCC-	NA	782
< Ca/ <CCC-	10,000	1,555

Source: Moody's Investors Service and Fitch

4. *Maturity restrictions:* In older cash flow transactions, maturity restrictions stipulated that if the collateral manager were to sell a security, he would be constrained to purchasing another security with a maturity no longer than the security that was sold. For more recent transactions, the manager trades the portfolio within maturity buckets, so that the sale of one security could be followed by the purchase of a longer dated security, so long as there is room in the maturity bucket into which the purchased security will be placed. Maturity restrictions are used to ensure that when rated securities are scheduled to be redeemed, a large enough portion of the collateral is scheduled to mature to pay the issuing vehicle's liabilities.

Sample Transaction: Calhoun CBO, Ltd. Calhoun CBO, Ltd. is a representative cash flow arbitrage transaction. It is collateralized by a high yield/emerging market breakdown of approximately 80%/20%. The deal is summarized in Exhibit 8.

The Calhoun CBO contains the features discussed here: non-call and reinvestment periods, minimum collateral diversity score and average rating requirements. The capital structure consists of Aa2 rated senior notes, Baa3 rated second priority senior notes and unrated subordinated classes.

Exhibit 8: Representative Cash Flow Arbitrage Transaction: Calhoun CBO, Ltd.

- Manager: American Express Asset Management
- 82.2% U.S. high yield bonds, 17.8% emerging market bonds
- Fixed rate: 91.4%
- Interest rate hedge: $180 million notional
- Minimum average rating: B2
- Minimum diversity score: 40
- Reinvestment period: 5 years
- Non-call period: 3 years
- 12-year final maturity
- Aa2 rated Senior Notes, 7.7 yr AL (70.18% of transaction)
- Baa3 rated Second Priority Senior Notes, 11.0 yr AL (15.79%)
- Senior Subordinated Notes (7.02%)
- Junior Subordinated Notes (7.02%)

Source: Morgan Stanley

Rating Cash Flow Arbitrage Transactions The approach to rating cash flow arbitrage transactions differs in specifics among the three major rating agencies, but the basic methodology is essentially the same. The most important aspect of cash flow transactions in terms of rating analysis is expected loss.

Rating agencies analyze three main aspects of a cash flow CDO transaction: collateral, structure and manager. The net result is an expected loss level for each rated security. Once this expected loss level is derived, and stressed, the agencies can apply ratings to the securities based on the results of the analysis.

1. *Collateral:* The collateral underlying CDO transactions can vary across rating, industry, maturity, pay type and geographic region. As such, the analysis of this collateral is a complex and potentially arduous process. The rating agencies examine the underlying assets in terms of:

- diversity of the assets in the pool
- ratings of the underlying assets
- recovery rates associated with different asset classes
- asset/liability characteristics.

The rating agencies analyze each of these factors under various default and interest rate scenarios in order to determine the impact of each factor on the rated debt.

Diversity: The rating agencies view diversity as a positive factor. Moody's has developed a quantitative method for calculating the level of diversity within a pool of assets but each rating agency gives credit to the level of diversification in the collateral pool. The concept is analogous to the benefit — in terms of credit enhancement levels — granted securities in the CMBS market, which have a wide variety of collateral types ranging from mortgages on office buildings to retail space. In the CDO market, the rating agencies grant credit for diversity of industry, region and absolute number of issuers within an industry or region. Clearly, the marginal benefit afforded the collateral pool by including an additional issuer should decrease as the number of issuers within the sector increases. Exhibit 9 is a sample of the diversity credit granted by Moody's for various numbers of issuers within an industry.

Lack of correlation must be exhibited between sectors in order for the rating agencies to grant credit for diversity. Including two five dollar positions that exhibit 100% correlation in a pool is essentially the same as including one security representing 10 dollars in the same pool. Clearly, if the securities are 100% correlated, there should be no benefit due to diversity for including these two assets in the pool. It is not necessarily the case that two issuers within the same industry/region will exhibit 100% correlation. We will explore the calculation of diversity in more detail below. While Moody's is the only agency to publish a quantitative method for calculating the diversity of a portfolio of securities, each rating agency examines the diversity characteristics of a pool when rating a CDO.

Ratings: Each of the assets in the collateral pool must be rated, either publicly or privately, by the rating agency analyzing the pool. In the absence of such a rating, the agency may apply a shadow rating, or may take the level assigned by a different established agency and imply a rating, sometimes haircut by one or two notches. Moody's and Fitch calculate a weighted average rating on the collateral. This was discussed above in the section on Quality Tests. Ratings factors were displayed in Exhibit 7.

Exhibit 9: Moody's Diversity Scores for Firms within an Industry

Number of Firms in Same Industry	Diversity Score
1	1.00
2	1.50
3	2.00
4	2.33
5	2.67
6	3.00
7	3.25
8	3.50
9	3.75
10	4.00
>10	Evaluated on a case-by-case basis

Source: Moody's Investors Service

Exhibit 10: Sample Calculation of Weighted Average Collateral Rating

A	B	C	D	E	F
Security	% of Pool	Moody's Rating	Rating Factor	Weighting * Rating Factor (B * D)	Portfolio Average Rating
1	15	Ba1	940	141.0	
2	15	Ba3	1,780	267.0	
3	20	B1	2,220	444.0	
4	50	B3	3,490	1,745.0	
Portfolio				2,597.0	B2

Source: Moody's Investors Service, Morgan Stanley

Exhibit 11: Base Case Recovery Rate Assumptions for Various Rating Agencies

	Base Recovery Assumptions (%)		
US Debt	Moody's	S&P	Fitch
Senior Secured Bank Loans	50	50-60	60
Senior Secured Bonds	30	40-55	50
Senior Unsecured Debt	30	25-50	45
Subordinated Debt	30	15-28	25
Emerging Markets	Moody's	S&P	
Sovereign Bonds	25	25	
Corporate Bonds	10	15	

Source: Moody's Investors Service, Standard & Poor's and Fitch

Exhibit 10 works through a sample calculation based on a pool containing four rated securities. Clearly the portfolio's overall rating is skewed downward by the 50% weighting in the B3 rated asset. The non-linear relationship between ratings and expected defaults skews the aggregate rating towards the lowest rated asset in the pool. The exact rating factors used by Moody's and Fitch are different due to varying experience and data sources, but the overall methodology is essentially the same.

Recovery assumptions: The recovery rate assumed for different asset types varies across rating agencies as well as across collateral types. Exhibit 11 shows base case recovery assumptions for the three major rating agencies across various asset classes. These assumptions are intended to be conservative relative to historical recovery rates computed by the agencies. Preference in the form of higher recovery rates is awarded to more senior liens in the issuing entities' capital structure. For example, senior secured loans will exhibit higher recovery rates than unsecured senior debt.

Asset/liability characteristics: Another issue more specific to cash flow transactions is the maturity profile of the underlying collateral relative to the CDO securities. The rating agencies prefer to include securities with expected maturity dates prior to the maturity dates of the rated debt. Securities that are scheduled to mature after the rated debt may have to be liquidated in order to retire the CDO. Cash flow transactions are not based upon the actual market value of an asset, however the rating agencies will severely haircut the amount of par credit given longer dated assets in a cash flow pool.

The fixed/floating composition of the pool also becomes an issue when analyzing cash flow transactions. If the rated securities issued out of the SPV are predominantly floating rate, yet the collateral underlying the transaction is mostly fixed rate, investors would be taking on interest rate risk on top of the credit risk inherent to the CDO market. In order to achieve the desired ratings, interest rate hedges are frequently incorporated at issuance in order to mitigate this interest rate risk. These hedges may be in the form of cap or swap instruments.

2. *Structure:* Rating agencies analyze the structure of a given cash flow CDO during the ratings process. Various aspects of structure that affect the CDO ratings are:

• coverage (early-amortization) tests
• internal credit enhancement, and
• legal soundness of securitization structure.

We address the first two of these below. The target ratings of the issued debt will affect the stress levels applied on the collateral pool during the process. The higher the desired rating for a given tranche, the more rigorous the stress that has to be withstood.

Coverage and quality tests: During the rating process, the agencies evaluate the coverage and quality tests that were discussed in detail above. The levels are designed to give the CDO noteholders the necessary protection to achieve the desired rating, given the composition of the collateral pool.

Should a coverage test be breached, interest and principal proceeds are directed from the more subordinated bonds and redirected to retire the senior bonds ahead of schedule. This redirection continues until the senior bonds are retired, or the performance level is brought back into alignment. The main difference between these triggers and those often found in home equity loan ABS is that in CDOs, the subordinate bonds are completely locked out from cash flow until the trigger is cured. In home equities, the subordinate bonds do not receive principal, but do continue to receive interest. Most cash flow CDOs pay sequentially down the ratings spectrum, as opposed to pro-rata (after a stepdown date) in the HEL sector. Subordinate CDO classes are generally not scheduled to receive principal until the more senior classes are retired.[1]

Should a quality test be breached no redirection of cash flow is required, however the collateral manager's trading flexibility would be curtailed. Trading would then be restricted to actions improving the collateral pool relative to the breached test.

Internal credit enhancements: Internal credit enhancements can be provided to a CDO through methods similar to those of more traditional asset backed securities. The most common form of enhancement is provided through excess spread: the yield on the collateral is higher than the yield on the CDO securities, otherwise there would be a negative carry situation and it is unlikely that the transaction would be economically feasible for the issuer. Just as in the home equity loan, credit card, auto and manufactured housing sectors of the ABS market, excess spread in CDOs represents the first loss position in the structure. Somewhat lower than the better performing master trusts in the credit card arena, it is not uncommon to see excess spread values near 200 basis points.

The rating agencies tend to shock interest rates substantially during the rating process. As a result, it is often the case that some form of interest rate hedge is employed in the CDO structure at issuance. This hedge may be in the form of caps or swaps and would depend on the performance of the specific collateral pool in various environments.

3. *Manager:* One of the fundamental manners in which CDOs differ from other asset backed transactions is the active trading of the CDO collateral pool, in contrast to the static nature of asset backed collateral pools. As such, the primary responsibility of the portfolio manager in a cash flow CDO is to minimize defaults in the collateral pool. As part of the ratings process, the agencies will perform due diligence on the manager's performance history as well as back office capabilities. An adequate infrastructure is required by the rating agencies and can greatly affect ratings. The track record of the manager, specifically a proven ability to perform well in adverse market conditions, is also considered important. Clearly, the CDO structure is not suited to all managers.

The manager of a cash flow transaction is typically permitted to actively trade a percentage of the portfolio per year, in what is called a "discretionary trading basket." The manager is always permitted to sell defaulted, equity or perceived credit risk securities. Securities that have been upgraded, or are on watch to be upgraded, can also be sold subject to certain constraints. In no case may a portfolio manager exercise a transaction resulting in a portfolio that violates any of the coverage or quality tests as specified in the transaction's indenture.

---

[1] To be technical, deferred interest on mezzanine tranches added to principal can be paid down early.

Exhibit 12: Capital Structure of a Market Value Arbitrage Transaction

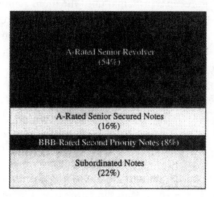

A-Rated Senior Revolver
(54%)

A-Rated Senior Secured Notes
(16%)

BBB-Rated Second Priority Notes (8%)

Subordinated Notes
(22%)

Source: Morgan Stanley

Market Value Transactions

Market value transactions actually predated cash flow structures, and after a bit of a lull, have made a major resurgence recently. It has become an attractive capital structure due to the greater flexibility afforded the portfolio manager in terms of trading ability, and the types of collateral that can be included in the asset pool. Because the actual cash flows provided by the collateral pool do not necessarily affect the rated securities, a portfolio manager can include a wider selection of asset types in the pool.

Market value transactions require that the securities in the collateral pool be marked to market by the collateral manager on a frequent basis. Therefore, investors who prefer a marked-to-market discipline may be more comfortable with this type of structure. Further, the expertise of the portfolio manager can be maximized because the capital structure can be changed post-securitization and additional leverage can be employed to invest in perceived relative value opportunities. Exhibit 12 diagrams the basic structure of a market value arbitrage transaction.

In a market value transaction, the bond classes are paid down from the sale — as opposed to the maturity — of underlying collateral, based upon either a soft bullet or controlled amortization payment schedule. The frequent marking to market of the collateral pool, mentioned above, is necessary to ensure the ability of the CDO to pay down the rated debt on schedule. As such, the primary considerations in evaluating a market value transaction are the price volatility and liquidity of the underlying assets.

Collateral The primary consideration in a market value CDO is the price volatility of the underlying collateral. Price volatility, as measured by the rating agencies, dictates an advance rate for each pre-approved category of collateral. Since the rating of the bond classes is based upon market value overcollateralization, market value CDOs lend themselves to a wider array of collateral types than cash flow CDOs. Virtually any security that can be valued in the capital markets and have its price volatility estimated may be employed in these structures. The collateral pool for a market value CDO may consist of securities includable in cash flow CDOs, mezzanine debt, convertible debt, preferreds/convertible preferreds, distressed debt, and equities.

Large percentages of emerging market debt tend to be difficult to manage in the collateral pool. The high price volatility of these asset classes results in low advance rates, making them somewhat unruly in a market value transaction. Advance rates will be discussed more completely in the credit enhancement section.

Structure Market value transactions generally include a revolver in the capital structure. This revolver is obtained by the CDO to allow the portfolio manager to increase or decrease the amount of funding in order to adjust the leverage as investments are shifted among asset classes with different advances rates and/or as the market value of the collateral changes. Additionally, to the extent that the revolver is not fully funded, payments to the liabilities may be paid by drawing down on the revolver. Market value deals tend to be more actively managed — subject to predefined constraints — than cash flow transactions. These constraints would include:

- concentration limits based on issuer, industry, geography and asset quality, and
- minimum market value of the asset pool relative to the face amount of outstanding bonds.

Exhibit 13 is a time line of the phases through which a typical market value transaction will go during its life. The transaction generally begins with a ramp-up phase, during which the manager fills the collateral pool by purchasing assets in the capital markets. This phase can last as long as six months to a year.

Exhibit 13: Time Line of Events of a Typical Market Value Arbitrage Transaction

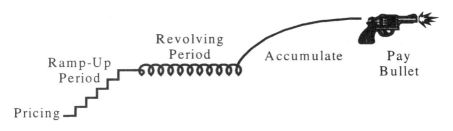

Source: Morgan Stanley

Similar to credit card ABS, there is an extensive revolving or reinvestment period during which cash flow from the underlying collateral due to maturities, whole or partial calls, amortization or any other cash flow or sale proceeds are reinvested. During the reinvestment period, the collateral manager has the ability to increase the debt exposure of the trust through the bank line established at issuance. The manager can also decrease debt exposure through the same means. Following the reinvestment period, principal collections from the collateral would be either accumulated to pay out a bullet payment, used to delever the deal and pay down the revolving line of credit or passed through to bond or equity holders, depending on the details of the structure.

Price volatility and asset liquidity are of primary importance in market value transactions. The actual weighted average rating of the underlying collateral is not important in market value structures, but a lower rating of a specific asset may result in a lower advance rate. Managers of market value transactions attempt to maximize the total value of the underlying portfolio while minimizing the volatility in that value.

Credit Enhancement The rating agencies assign advance rates to different types of collateral. This advance rate is the percentage of the market value of a particular asset that is allowed to be issued as rated debt. Analogous to net interest margin transactions in the home equity and manufactured housing ABS sectors, this percentage would be less than 100% and would move inversely with the perceived riskiness of the asset. Advance rates depend upon the return volatility of the assets, availability and quality of price/return data and liquidity of assets. The higher volatility of lower rated securities will result in generally lower advance rates. For example, equity-type securities would have a lower advance rate than high yield domestic bank loans. Additionally, this percentage will move with the target rating of the security being analyzed.

Exhibit 14 shows a sample table of advance rates that Fitch would apply to several types of collateral and target ratings. While specific levels will differ based on the actual pool of collateral, the relative difference in the levels for a given asset's expected losses, and a particular bond's target rating, can be seen.

These advance rates represent the primary form of credit enhancement employed in the structure. Therefore, the coverage test utilized in these structures relates to the market value of the assets relative to the liabilities of the issuing vehicle. A collateral manager must ensure that this market value test is not violated due to fluctuations in the price of the underlying securities.

Coverage and Quality Tests A major difference between market value and cash flow CBOs lies in the treatment of the quality tests. In cash flow deals, trades that would result in a breach of a quality test *cannot* be executed. In market value transactions, the quality tests are used in conjunction with the coverage tests. A manager can breach a quality test, but is penalized for doing so when calculating coverage tests. An example of this is provided below.

Exhibit 14: Sample Advance Rates for Indicated Asset Type and Liabilities

Asset Category	AA	A	BBB	BB	B
Cash and Equivalents	100%	100%	100%	100%	100%
Certificates of Deposit, Commercial Paper	95	95	95	100	100
Senior Secured Bank Loans	85	90	91	93	96
BB- High Yield Debt	71	80	87	90	92
<BB- High Yield Debt	69	75	85	87	89
Convertible Bonds	64	70	81	85	87
Convertible Preferred Stock	59	65	77	83	86
Mezzanine Debt, Distressed, Emerging Market	55	60	73	80	85
Equity, Illiquid Debt	40	50	73	80	85

Source: Fitch

1. *Market value test:* A common trigger found in market value deals is that the collateral must be valued at some multiple of the outstanding bond balance. For example, a $400 million collateral pool may support $320 million of rated debt. If the indenture stipulated that the market value of the collateral, haircut by the appropriate advance rate, must represent 125% of the par value of the outstanding debt, then this transaction would pass this test. If, however, the market value were later reported to be only $380 million, the portfolio manager must cure the situation either by trading collateral to improve quality and thereby advance rates or by liquidating collateral in order to reduce the outstanding debt, de-lever the transaction, and raise the collateral-to-bond ratio.

2. *Minimum net worth test:* Another common trigger found in market value transactions is a minimum net worth test. This test is designed to ensure that a minimum amount of equity is maintained in the structure. It is calculated as the market value of the collateral minus the sum of the par value of all the rated debt, as a share of the subordinated debt. Breaching the minimum net worth test is considered an event of default. Control of the transaction is passed from the equity holders to senior bondholders. The senior bondholders then can decide whether to continue the transaction or liquidate collateral and early amortize the deal.

Trading Constraints Market value transactions do not contain a minimum weighted average rating condition at all, and the concentration limits that are employed behave differently. Portfolio managers are allowed to exceed concentration requirements in issuers, industries or regions, but they are penalized in the calculation of coverage tests if they violate the quality limits.

As an example, consider a manager with a maximum concentration of $25 million permitted in the telecom industry. The manager currently holds a $15 million position in that sector, but wants to purchase an additional $15 million. The manager of a cash flow transaction would be allowed to purchase only $10 million, but a market value manager can execute the entire $15 million order. For the purposes of calculating the overcollateralization of the rated debt in the market value structure, only $25 million of collateral can be considered. If the advance rate for the particular security were 0.80, then this position would represent only 0.80 times $25 million, or $20 million for the purposes of calculating overcollateralization. Without the concentration constraint, the same $30 million security would provide 0.80 times $30 million, or $24 million, of market value.

If there is a breach of a performance trigger, the manager has a period of time, generally two weeks, to cure the breach, either by trading collateral to improve quality or by liquidating collateral from the pool in order to redeem senior bonds and bring the structure back into compliance with the coverage test. The possible need to liquidate collateral subjects market value transactions to liquidity risk. Exhibit 15 details the generic trading constraints, i.e., quality and coverage tests, for market value transactions.

Sample Transaction: AG Capital Funding Partners, L.P. The AG Capital Funding transaction is actually a hybrid cash flow/market value transaction, but the market value aspect is representative of the sector. It is summarized in Exhibit 16.

The transaction is backed by HLT and special situation loans. While the HLT portion is subject to cash flow transaction standards, the special situation basket follows market value transaction rules. The market value aspects are necessary because the special situation loans do not generate predictable cash flows.

Exhibit 15: Generalized Trading Restrictions

Issuer Diversification
- Up to Three Issuers May Each Have   7%
- Subsequent Issuers   4%

Industry Diversification
- Single Industry   15%
- Any Three Industries   40%

Other Parameters
- Emerging Markets Investments   5%
- Unquoted Investments   5%

Source: Morgan Stanley

Exhibit 16: Representative Market Value Transaction: AG Capital Funding Partners

- Manager: Angelo Gordon
- 60% HLT loans, 40% special situations
- A rated senior notes, revolver, 6.7 yr maturity, extendible to 9.7 yr (69% of transaction)
- BBB rated second priority senior notes, 7.0 yr, extendible to 10.0 yr (9%)
- Subordinates notes, 7.0 yr extendible to 10.0 yr (22%)
- Rated by Fitch Investors Service.

Source: Morgan Stanley

Rating Market Value Arbitrage Transactions Market value transactions are analyzed much the same way as cash flow transactions. The fundamental difference in the rating process is the need to analyze price volatilities and liquidity when rating a market value transaction. Principal payments to CDO securities are funded primarily through the liquidation of assets. Therefore, steep decreases in the value of the underlying collateral can result in losses to the rated CDO securities.

The primary means by which rating agencies establish acceptable over-collateralization levels is through the use of advance rates. Exhibit 14 is a sample table of advance rates applied by Fitch to various collateral type and target rating combinations. Clearly, the higher the target rating on a security, the larger the cushion required to satisfy the rating agencies, and the lower the advance rate. Similarly, the perceived riskiness or volatility of the underlying asset is inversely proportional to the advance rate, i.e., higher risk assets will be given lower advance rates.

The main difference in the performance triggers associated with market value versus cash flow transactions is in the reliance on the marked-to-market value of the underlying assets. Cash flow transactions focus on the par amount of underlying assets, whereas market value transactions rely on just that, the market value. Estimates of price volatility have been calculated by each rating agency individually. The results of these analyses are, not surprisingly, somewhat different, resulting in somewhat different advance rates across agencies. In principal, however, the methodology is similar.

The role of the manager in market value transactions is somewhat different than in cash flow deals. A market value manager attempts to maximize total returns while minimizing portfolio price fluctuations. The agencies consider the resources, as well as analyze the investment style, of the manager. Greater emphasis is placed on the infrastructure the manager has in place, as well as historical performance. In evaluating managers, the agencies will place particular emphasis on the amount of assets under management and the number of years managing the major asset classes included in market value CDOs, as well as historical performance and experience during market downturns. Both credit and trading expertise are vital, because poor credit decisions can lead to spread widening, price depreciation and defaults, and will result in overall poor performance. Clearly, a market value transaction is not designed to be issued by every portfolio manager.

The analysis of the manager is a somewhat subjective process relative to the analytic approach to quantifying price volatility, advance rates, and diversity scores.

Cash Flow and Market Value Arbitrage Transactions Comparison

Exhibit 17 summarizes the primary differences and similarities between cash flow and market value arbitrage CDOs, for each of several criteria.

Exhibit 17: Summary Comparison of Cash Flow and Market Value Arbitrage Transactions

	Cash Flow	Market Value
General Features		
Security	Secured by collateral portfolio cash flow generation	Secured by collateral portfolio market value
Rating Criteria	Based upon stressed default scenarios and expected recovery of the collateral	Based upon stressed price volatility assumptions of the collateral
Collateral Manager	Attempts to minimize defaults	Attempts to maximize total return and minimize portfolio price volatility
Credit Protection	If coverage tests are failed, cash flow is diverted from mezzanine and subordinate classes to senior notes. There are no forced liquidations	If overcollateralization tests are failed, liquidations of collateral may be required to pay down senior classes and bring overcollateralization levels back into line
Funding	Generally term floating rate note, but may be fixed. Could have revolver	Some portion of senior notes in the form of revolving credit facility or commercial paper conduit program
Maturity and Amortization	10- to 15-year final maturity • Average life expected to be 6 to 8 years for senior-most class; other classes longer • Amortizations usually begin in years 3 to 5, after the reinvestment period, as underlying collateral amortizes or is redeemed	5- to 8-year final maturity • Drawn amount of credit facility varies based on portfolio market value • Amortizations of term notes not very likely
Leverage	Generally 10-20% subordination below investment grade classes	Generally 20-25% subordination below investment grade classes
Structural Credit Protection		
Overcollateralization	• Measured on basis of portfolio par value and contractual interest payments to be received • Monitored at least monthly	• Measured on basis of portfolio market value adjusted by advance rates • Monitored weekly or bi-weekly using third party valuations from independent sources
Key Ratios	• Par value ratio • Interest coverage ratio	• Market value overcollateralization • Minimum net worth of equity
Remedies	• Collateral interest and principal diverted to redeem senior debt. No portfolio liquidations are ever required. • No stated cure period	• Ratios must be restored with two-week cure period via portfolio trading and/or liquidations

Exhibit 17 (Continued)

	Cash Flow	Market Value
Restrictions on Underlying Portfolio		
Ratings	• All collateral securities must be rated, but may be public or private • Minimum rating should be maintained • If breached, future portfolio switches must maintain or improve average rating	• Ratings not essential for all assets, but may affect advance rates • No minimum average rating required
Diversity	• Industry and geographic concentrations are monitored and must be maintained by issuer • Breaches remedied through restrictions on future trading	• Industry and geographic concentrations are monitored and must be maintained by issuer • Breaches not included in overcollateralization calculations
Type of Securities	• Limited to mostly current pay debt instruments	• May include distressed debt, preferred stock, equity and other "special situation" assets
Liquidity	• No specific requirements	• Majority of securities must be readily marketable, with easily available objective valuations • Price volatility data on target portfolio assets must be available
Trading Constraints		
Management Restrictions	• Maximum or minimum asset composition limits (e.g., bank loans, high yield bonds, emerging market debt) • Maximum or minimum limits on floating rate and fixed rate securities • Maximum fixed maturities of assets • Minimum asset ratings • Minimum average portfolio rating • Diversification requirements • Maintenance of portfolio par value and interest coverage • Reinvestments restricted after stated reinvestment period (usually 3 to 5 years) • Interest rate hedges established upfront; generally cannot be actively managed	• Maintenance of market value overcollateralization • Diversification requirements • Asset liquidity requirements • Maximum or minimum asset composition limits • No maturity restrictions

Source: Morgan Stanley

Balance Sheet Transactions

Balance sheet deals are generally the securitization of lower yielding, borderline investment grade loans, for the purpose of gaining capital relief, obtaining alternative funding or increasing the issuing entity's return on equity by removing lower yielding assets from its balance sheet. In the past year, many Japanese banks have structured balance sheet transactions to improve their capital usage, gain off-balance sheet treatment of assets and obtain term funding. In general, the Japanese banks have securitized dollar-, rather than yen-, denominated loans, although there have been some yen-based transactions. Concerns about Asian credit, as well as the lack of a financial and legal structure in Japan defining terms crucial to securitization, have thus far prevented wholesale securitization of yen-based loans.[2] Balance sheet transactions generally range in size from $1 billion to as much as $5 billion.

From an investor's point of view, balance sheet CLOs have begun to be viewed as credit card substitutes, and this trend is likely to continue. Balance sheet CLOs offer investors in credit card ABS diversification away from consumer credit into heavily diversified corporate credit with similar structure.

Collateral

Cash flow balance sheet transactions rely on the ability of the collateral to generate sufficient principal and interest to redeem the structured notes. CLOs of this type would generally contain high grade C&I loans. The relatively low coupon on these assets versus typical high yield and emerging market securities results in a much smaller excess spread cushion than in most arbitrage deals. However, the higher quality of the balance sheet CLOs requires less subordination than in arbitrage deals.

Structure

Balance sheet transactions are structured very similarly to credit card ABS, even employing the master trust structure as the primary vehicle for securitization. Loans, and from time to time bonds, are sold into a trust as collateral to support the issuance of credit- and time-tranched securities. In the credit card arena, issuers that themselves are rated BBB at best are able to remove receivables from their balance sheet and finance their assets at near AAA levels. The need to tranche credit exposure among different rating levels within a senior/subordinate structure, or purchase an insurance wrap, prevents the issuing entity from obtaining completely AAA rated all-in funding levels.

Balance sheet CLOs work in a similar manner. The trust will issue several securities prioritizing payments sufficiently to garner the desired rating. The

---

[2] For example, the concepts of bankruptcy remoteness, true sale and perfected security interest had not been addressed in the Japanese legal system. More recently, however, steps have been taken to facilitate securitization. Recent legislation in Japan provides for perfecting assignment of certain assets without notifying the obligors.

most subordinate piece of the structure is the unrated equity piece, which would be exposed to the greatest amount of risk, with the highest potential returns. The senior and mezzanine tranches are generally structured with soft bullet maturities. The basic structure of a cash flow balance sheet transaction is as follows

AAA rated senior class (95%)
A rated class   2%
BBB rated class   3%

Similar to arbitrage cash flow deals, the indenture would specify a formal cash flow waterfall defining the priority of cash flows to the respective bond classes.[3] The documents would also stipulate trigger events that would cause changes in the waterfall should the triggers be breached. Common triggers will be described in more detail below. These may include, but are not limited to, an interest coverage ratio test and a par value ratio test for each rated security. The payment waterfalls are similar to those found in arbitrage cash flow transactions, which were diagrammed in Exhibits 5 and 6. The effect on the cash flow of breaching the performance triggers is indicated.

Unlike arbitrage CDOs, where there can be extensive trading by the collateral manager, with balance sheet CLOs, there is no active trading of loans already in the portfolio. Active trading or control over the portfolio would imply that the sponsor has recourse to the pool and thus violate true sale provisions. If so, the assets would have to go back on the sponsor's balance sheet and negate any capital advantage from the transaction.

The master trust structure allows portfolio managers to add newly originated loans, or loans purchased in the secondary market, to the trust for the purpose of issuing future debt. Similar to credit card ABS, transactions are most commonly structured as soft bullets with an accumulation period, in addition to credit and time tranching.

Linked versus De-linked If the loans are transferred into the issuing trust in a true sale, then the investor's exposure is limited to that of the performance of the assets and is divorced — or de-linked — from the fortunes of the sponsor. On the other hand, if the assets have not been sold, the investor retains exposure to the sponsor. A downgrade of the sponsor, or poor performance of the portion of its loan portfolio that is not included in the particular transaction, could result in a ratings action against the CLO owing to its relationship to the sponsoring institution. This is referred to as a linked transaction.

---

[3] Some earlier transactions, for example, the NationsBank CLO, issued certificates through a master trust structure, the cash flows of which are typically governed by a pooling and servicing agreement.

The benchmark transactions in the bank balance sheet CLO sector are those from the NationsBank Commercial Loan Master Trust for de-linked structures and SBC Glacier Finance for linked transactions. The NationsBank de-linked transaction was priced at a spread that was only 6 bp wider than credit card ABS and currently trades about 10 bp behind credit cards.

Credit Enhancement

Credit enhancement in the form of overcollateralization and subordination is employed in order to attain the high rating on senior notes. Similar to other ABS sectors, cash flows from the underlying collateral are prioritized to protect the higher rated bonds in the capital structure. This tranching of cash flows effectively distributes the credit exposure unevenly across the rated and unrated securities.

Early Amortization Triggers: Coverage Tests

The balance sheet CLO sector has two primary coverage tests, the failure of which would trigger an early amortization of the transaction. These are similar to early amortization triggers pertaining to excess spread and minimum seller's interest in credit card ABS transactions. In the CLO sector, these are the par value test and interest coverage test.

The early amortization concept in the balance sheet CLO sector is similar to that in the credit card ABS arena, in that it provides a credit put from the investor back to the issuer in the event that a transaction performs poorly. Unlike in the credit card sector, however, if a trigger is breached, there is a cure period during which the trust can attempt to rectify the performance problem. If the breach is not cured, principal payments will be directed to bond holders in order of seniority until either the bonds are fully redeemed or the trigger is cured.

The difference in early amortization between balance sheet CLOs and credit cards lies in the treatment of interest and the extent of the amortization. With balance sheet CLOs, subordinate bonds are completely locked out from receiving both principal and interest payments until either the trigger is cured or the senior bonds are fully paid down. Interest is used to turbo the senior bonds to speed their paydown. In contrast, in the credit card sector, only principal payments are directed to the senior bonds, while subordinate classes continue to receive interest to the extent that funds are available.

In addition, in CLOs, a partial early amortization is possible if the trigger is cured through the early amortization process, whereas credit card securities do not allow for partial early amortization.

The par value test and interest coverage tests were discussed above in the analogous section on cash flow arbitrage transactions. The function of these tests is the same for balance sheet transactions as for cash flow arbitrage deals.

Quality Tests

Balance sheet transactions employ quality tests similar to those of the cash flow arbitrage deals. These tests would include, but are not limited to:

- minimum diversity score
- minimum weighted average rating
- concentration limits in regions and industries.

These tests were discussed above in the section on quality tests for cash flow arbitrage transactions and function similarly. Rather than redirecting the cash flow in the event that a quality test is failed, the activities of the collateral manager are restricted to trading activities that would enhance the quality of the portfolio with respect to the violated trigger.

Rating Balance Sheet Transactions
The discussion in the section on rating agency approaches to cash flow arbitrage transactions is directly applicable to balance sheet deals.

CONCLUSION

Collateralized debt obligations comprise the fastest growing sector of the asset backed securities market. Because the potential collateral for these transactions runs the gamut from unsecured corporate loans and high yield bonds to distressed loans and emerging market debt, analysis of these transactions can be extremely complicated and somewhat forbidding. To compensate for this, CDOs offer wider spreads than comparably rated paper from other ABS sectors. In this chapter we discussed the differences between the various structures.

Chapter 2

Structural Features of Market Value CDOs

Luigi Vacca, Ph.D.
Vice President
Structured Credit Products
Banc of America Securities

M arket value deals are special purpose vehicles (SPVs) designed to purchase and actively manage a diversified pool of financial assets for the benefit of debt and equity investors (see Exhibit 1). From a structural standpoint, market value CDOs share some similarities with other asset-backed securities (ABS), such as cash flow CDOs, as their capital structures consist of a series of debt and equity tranches. However, the structural covenants that regulate market value CDOs are based on the market value of the assets rather than the par value of the assets (as with cash flow CDOs).

Exhibit 1: Market Value CDOs: Assets, Structure, and Participants

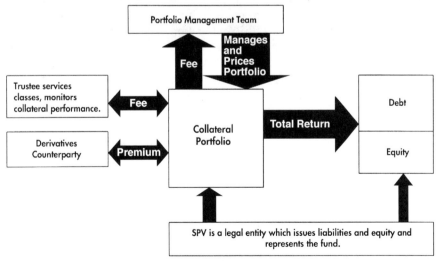

Source: Banc of America Securities LLC.

Exhibit 2: Market Value CDOs —
Sample Time Evolution of a Transaction

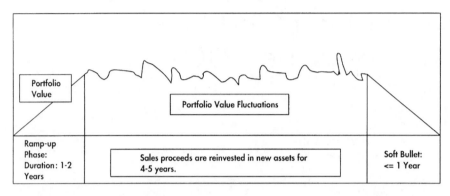

Source: Banc of America Securities LLC.

The proceeds from the sale of the debt and equity tranches of a market value CDO and borrowings under a senior lending facility are generally used by the portfolio manager to purchase a diversified portfolio of debt investments and, to a lesser extent, private equity and mezzanine investments and interest-rate derivatives. The period during which the portfolio manager purchases the assets of the initial portfolio is called the "ramp-up" period, and usually lasts one to two years.

During and after the ramp-up period, the cash flows generated by the assets of the portfolio are typically used to purchase additional investments including interest-rate hedges, pay down interest on the debt and cover fees. This period typically extends for five or more years. If structural covenants are failed and not remedied, the assets may be sold and proceeds paid out to debt holders and equity holders according to a set of rules that reflect their seniority in the capital structure. During the last phase of the deal, a period that usually lasts for one year but can be as short as a few months, the portfolio manager will sell the portfolio assets and repay all the debt, with excess proceeds paid to equity holders. Market value CDOs usually mature in five to seven years, but can be extended up to two years by the debt holders (see Exhibit 2).

In this chapter, we discuss the structural features of market value CDOs (excluding those backed by mortgage instruments) in detail to understand the risk and return behavior at all levels in the capital structure. Among the reasons why we believe that market value CDOs represent an attractive asset class are that debt from such transactions benefits from significant credit protection given by the market value tests and subordination. The market value structure is designed to allow the portfolio manager to generate attractive equity returns through active portfolio management.

Exhibit 3: Sample Capital Structure at Closing versus a Fully Leveraged Capital Structure in a Market Value CDO

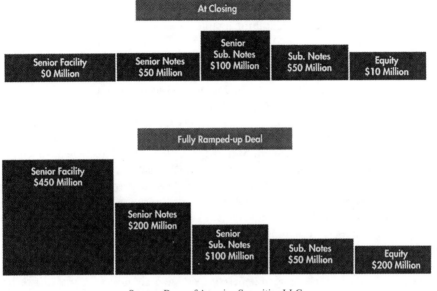

Source: Banc of America Securities LLC.

THE RAMP-UP PERIOD

The ramp-up period commences at the closing date of a market value CDO transaction, and usually ends more than one year later for the majority of such deals. The senior-subordinated and subordinated tranches are usually sold entirely at closing, with the net proceeds immediately available to the fund manager. The senior and the lowest parts of the capital structure of a CDO are drawn in stages during the ramp-up period. Both senior lenders and equity investors typically commit to transfer funds according to a ramp-up schedule. To maintain an adequate level of protection to the rated debt tranches, equity is funded so that the outstanding leverage ratio is lower or equal to the targeted leverage ratio at the end of the ramp-up period. That is, the ramp-up criterion is

$$\frac{\text{Outstanding senior debt}}{\text{Committed senior debt}} \leq \frac{\text{Drawn equity amount}}{\text{Committed equity amount}}$$

Using a sample $1 billion structure, in Exhibit 3 we illustrate for a market value CDO an example of a capital structure at closing versus a fully leveraged capital structure.

CAPITALIZATION[1]

The capitalization of any market value CDO structure is determined by borrowing base advance rates provided by one or more rating agencies. The starting point for sizing a capital structure is identifying a target asset mix by a fund's portfolio manager. A portfolio manager and the fund's equity investors generally seek to capitalize on the opportunity to leverage returns in the manager's traditional area of expertise. A target asset mix is created based on the portfolio manager's investment strategy for the fund and future outlook for targeted sectors of the financial markets. Rating agency advance rates are applied against this target asset mix to calculate a series of expected weighted average advance rates. Depending on the manager's particular preference for flexibility in managing the rating agency covenants, borrowing base "cushions" are generally added to each weighted average advance rate to afford the manager some "room for error." These cushions enable the manager to act more dynamically and opportunistically with less concern for running too close to the margin and ultimately failing OC tests during periods of price volatility.

Although a CDO may have been structured to withstand a certain target asset mix, markets are dynamic and can affect a portfolio manager's investment strategy and portfolio mix during ramp-up. Thus, a manager may have to deviate from the original base case target asset mix, causing the fund to become either underleveraged or overleveraged depending on the asset profile. Supply of collateral is a leading cause for such actions. Underleveraging is generally a temporary inconvenience, potentially affecting the equity investor's rate of return.

Overleveraging is a more serious condition that can result in the failure of OC tests and the forced selling of assets into unknown market conditions. The majority of market value funds generally are structured with some level of conservatism to prevent such events from occurring.

THE CASH FLOW WATERFALL IN MARKET VALUE CDOS

The priority of payments in market value CDOs share similarities with the "waterfall" payment structure of cash flow CDOs, the structure of which shown in Exhibit 4.

THE ASSETS OF A MARKET VALUE CDO
AND THEIR COVENANTS

A market value CDO portfolio is a diversified pool of financial assets in multiple asset categories that can range from corporate bonds and loans to private and public equity and distressed securities or emerging markets investments. Cash and money market instruments are also included on the list of possible assets,

---

[1] The Capitalization section of this chapter was prepared with the assistance of Michael Mancini of Banc of America Securities LLC.

although a portfolio manager likely will manage cash through a revolving facility rather than paying for negative carry.

Market value CDOs are total return vehicles, whose portfolio cash flows are generated from a combination of coupon, dividend, principal payments, and realized capital gains and losses. Market value CDOs are structured to allow portfolio managers to manage assets more actively and freely than in cash flow CDOs. Market value CDO portfolios can experience either significant trading activity or remain fairly static, depending on the investment style of the portfolio manager. To yield attractive equity returns, the assets of the portfolio may include high-yield assets that do not normally produce predictable cash flows but can generate much higher returns than callable debt instruments (such as distressed securities as well as private and public equity).

Exhibit 4: Market-Value CDOs — Payment Structure

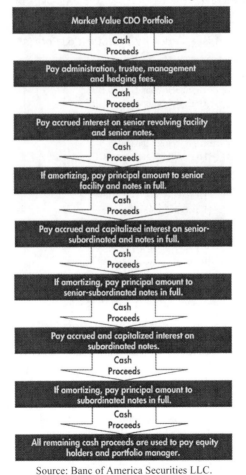

Source: Banc of America Securities LLC.

Exhibit 5: Asset Types by Rating Agencies

a. Asset Type by Moody's Investors Service*

> • Performing bank loans valued at $0.9 or above.
> • Distressed bank loans valued at $0.85 or above.
> • Performing high yield bonds rated Ba.
> • Performing high yield bonds rated B.
> • Distressed bank loans valued below $0.85.
> • Performing high yield bonds rated Caa.
> • Distressed bonds.
> • Reorganized equities.

From Table A1 (Advance Rates) in Yvonne Falcone and Jeremy Gluck, *Moody's Approach to Rating Market-Value CDOs*, Moody's Investors Service, Inc., p. 12.

Copyright 1998, Moody's Investors Service, Inc. Used With Permission. This table contains historical information and may not set forth current data.

b. Asset Types by Standard & Poor's**

> • High yields bonds rated BB+.
> • High yields bonds rated BB.
> • High yields bonds rated BB-.
> • High yields bonds rated B+.
> • High yields bonds rated B.
> • High yields bonds rated B-.
> • High yields bonds rated CCC+.
> • High yields bonds rated CCC.
> • High yields bonds rated CCC-.
> • Distressed bonds.
> • Emerging markets.
> • Public small-cap. equity.
> • Public mid–cap. equity.
> • Public large-cap. equity.
> • Performing loans priced above $0.9.
> • Performing loans priced at $0.9 or below.
> • Distressed loans priced above $0.85.
> • Distressed loans priced $0.85 or below.

** Standard & Poor's.

All individual portfolio assets fall into defined asset categories. These categories are defined by rating agencies that assign ratings to the debt tranches of the market value deal. The asset category classification is critical from a ratings standpoint, as it determines allowable leverage and defines asset concentration limits and associated risks. To introduce the various asset categories that are included in market value CDOs, we list some of the more prevalent asset categories as reported by the rating agencies in Exhibit 5.

Exhibit 5 (Continued)
c. Asset Types by Fitch***

> • Cash and equivalents.
> • Certificates of deposit and commercial paper.
> • AAA corporate bonds.
> • AA corporate bonds.
> • A corporate bonds.
> • BBB corporate bonds.
> • BB– high yield debt.
> • < BB– high yield debt.
> • Investment grade convertibles.
> • High-yield convertibles, payment-in-kind, zeros, step-up.
> • Mezzanine, distressed debt.
> • Emerging market.
> • Equity, illiquid debt.

*** Fitch

The asset categories listed in Exhibit 5 are often found in large market value CDO transactions, but do not include all types of assets in this class. Some market value CDO managers have recently purchased structured product transactions from the CDO market itself. In addition, an important class of market value deals exists called mortgage market value CDOs, whose underlying asset portfolio primarily consists of mortgage instruments and their derivatives. For purposes of this chapter, we focus on market value CDOs backed by corporate debt and equity investments.

PORTFOLIO LIMITATIONS

Portfolio limitations are asset covenants that help ensure the diversification of a collateral portfolio sufficiently to validate rating agency risk methodologies based on the volatility of market portfolios or indices as market proxies. Portfolio limitations are formulated in terms of maximum concentrations of issuers, industries and sectors. Concentrations generally are computed as a ratio between the market value of assets and the value of total outstanding liabilities; therefore, the actual portfolio may be less diversified than the computed ratio suggests. In particular, during the ramp-up period, the portfolio probably will be not diversified given that the portfolio manager likely has purchased the most liquid assets in the early stages of the deal. The portfolio limitations will be computed on the basis of an adjusted deal capitalization during the ramp-up period to allow the portfolio manager to purchase the collateral portfolio without exceeding limitations.

Common portfolio limitations are outlined in Exhibit 6.

Exhibit 6: Common Asset Covenants

- Maximum allowed market value concentration in any single issuer; concentrations vary from 3% to 8%.
- Maximum allowed total market value concentration in any three issuers (excluding illiquid investments); concentrations vary from 10% to 20%.
- Maximum allowed total market value concentration in any single industry; concentrations vary from 10% to 20%.
- Maximum allowed total market value concentration in any three industries; concentrations vary from 30% to 50%.
- Maximum allowed total market value concentration in semi-illiquid and illiquid investments; concentrations vary from 0% to 30%.
- Maximum allowed total market value concentration in illiquid investments; concentrations vary from 0% to 15%.
- Maximum allowed total market value concentration in special situations investments; concentrations vary from 0% to 30%..
- Maximum allowed total market value concentration in foreign investments; concentrations vary from 0% to 35%.
- Maximum allowed total market value concentration in emerging markets; concentrations vary from 0% to 20%.
- Maximum allowed total market value concentration in mezzanine investments; concentrations vary from 0% to 20%.
- Maximum allowed total market value concentration in convertible stocks; concentrations vary from 0% to 15%.
- Maximum allowed total market value concentration in non-cash pay investments; concentrations vary from 5% to 20%.
- Maximum allowed total market value concentration in foreign currency investments; concentrations vary from 0% to 10%.

Sources: Banc of America Securities LLC.

Several of the terms used in Exhibit 6 require a precise definition. Semi-illiquid investments are investments for which no quote is available from an approved source and whose ratings are higher or equal to B3 by Moody's Investors Service and B– by Standard & Poor's (S&P) and Fitch. All other investments that are not quoted and do not enter the definition of semi-illiquid investments are automatically considered illiquid. Special situations investments in the market value CDO lexicon are usually nonperforming loans (NPLs) and bonds, mezzanine investments, and equity or a more esoteric asset class.

Portfolio limitations affect the capital structure of a market value CDO, as more stringent limitations lead to a more diversified portfolio and imply smaller risk. In practice, portfolio limitations are chosen as a compromise between achieving diversification and maximizing returns.

PORTFOLIO DIVERSIFICATION, MARKET VALUE CDO PERFORMANCE, AND EXCLUDED INVESTMENTS

Portfolio limitations are important risk-management tools to ensure that the portfolio meets a minimum standard of diversification. In practice, the collateral portfolio will always be subject to a non-negligible amount of non-systemic risk or non-market risk. There are several reasons for the presence of this type of risk: the more issuers in the portfolio, the higher the cost of research and trading, and the less likely that the portfolio manager will outperform index benchmarks. More important, portfolio managers are strongly motivated to maximize portfolio returns to profit from their equity participation.

There are two common strategies that a market value CDO manager may use to attempt to deliver above-market CDO equity returns:

- To increase issuer concentration risk, which occurs when the portfolio has a large market value exposure to a single issuer or few issuers. This strategy is usually employed by managers who prefer a bottom-up approach and are supported by corporate research teams.
- To increase industry or sector concentration risk, which occurs when the portfolio is concentrated in only one or (at most) several industries. This strategy is taken by portfolio managers who employ both a macroeconomic and microeconomic analysis, or both bottom-up and top-down analysis.

Both strategies are constrained by their respective portfolio limitations for the benefit of the debt holders, who are generally risk-averse. However, CDO portfolio managers are permitted to exceed the portfolio limitations if they exclude those investments with concentrations above the portfolio limitations from the OC test calculations. OC tests are designed to ensure that the debt is protected by the market value of the portfolio at all times.

For example, assume a scenario in which a $1 billion market value CDO fund is actively managed by a portfolio manager who has identified the issuer XYZ for outstanding earnings and price growth. For this example, the maximum issuer concentration that the covenants allow is 5% (or $50 million). If the CDO portfolio has excess borrowing base capacity and passes all the tests, the portfolio manager may draw available funds from the revolving facility and purchase $100 million in XYZ equity, in anticipation that capital gains can be monetized if the stock price performance meets expectations. In this example, market value covenants allow the portfolio to include only up to $50 million of XYZ's market value in the OC test calculations, although the senior debt amount has increased by $100 million. This exclusion implies that the manager will be able to exceed portfolio limitations only if the discounted market value of the collateral portfolio exceeds the liabilities before the trade by an amount equal to $100 minus $50 times the advance rate of XYZ's equity position.

In summary, aggressive managers are not prohibited from purchasing investments that exceed portfolio limitations if the OC tests are met after investment exclusion; however, they will do so at the cost of reducing the portfolio diversification and may be forced to sell their positions if the market moves against them. Other types of investments may be excluded altogether from OC test calculations — namely, investments that have been borrowed, certain emerging market investments in foreign currencies, and in general any investments that are not subject to a perfected security interest for the benefit of the rated debt according to the structural priorities of the market value CDO.

THE ASSET VALUATION PROCESS AND ITS RULES

The process of marking the collateral CDO portfolio to market is crucial in validating the structural credit protection. The credit enhancements provided by discounting the collateral market value and comparing it with the obligations' value is effective only to the extent that the marks reflect the true market value of the assets. For this reason, the marking-to-market process is conducted in a manner to ensure that portfolio valuation information is reliable and accurate.

The assets of market value CDOs are priced periodically. The frequency of the marking process is a function of their liquidity, market-makers' coverage and the complexity of the instrument. Most liquid assets in a CDO portfolio such as government securities and high quality corporate bonds can be marked on a daily or weekly basis. On the other side of the spectrum, assets included in the special situations category are often marked only on a monthly or quarterly basis.

The market value of securities traded on stock exchanges is simply the closing bid price on the date when the tests are computed. A considerable number of the portfolio assets in a market value CDO are private placements or Rule 144A investments and can be purchased only by institutional and well capitalized investors; therefore, the CDO manager must rely on bid prices given by a limited number of dealers.

In general, rating agencies require that CDO investments are quoted by at least two rating agency-approved broker/dealers, and the market value of those assets is usually computed as the average of all available bid prices. When quotes from approved sources are not available, the manager will mark the unquoted assets up to a predefined individual investment amount. Investments in excess of $25 million generally are subject to a valuation from an approved investment bank; investments exceeding $50 million require an independent third-party appraisal.

Portfolio limitations restrict the amount of assets for which no available bids exist in the market. If the value of the unquoted assets marked by the manager exceeds the limitations, the excess may not be included in the OC test calculations. If no external quote for a determined asset is available, the market value will be the lower of the portfolio manager's quote and the cost of the asset.

Exhibit 7: Select Asset Categories and Respective Advance Ratings

Asset	Advance Rates			
Category	AA/Aa	A/A	BBB/Baa	BB/Ba
A	100%	100%	100%	100%
B	94	96	96	100
C	85	91	92	93
D	84	90	91	92
E	72	82	86	90
F	68	75	84	86
G	52	60	73	80

Source: Banc of America Securities LLC.

Exhibit 8: List of Some Asset Classes Included in Each Category

Asset Category	Asset Classes
A	Cash and short-term government securities.
B	Longer-term government securities, commercial paper and CDs.
C	Performing loans.
D	Performing BBB1/Baa3 rated or better high yield debt.
E	BB-/Ba3 rated or better high yield and performing loans priced between 80 and 90.
F	B rated high yield and mezzanine debt.
G	CCC+/Caa1 rated or lower high yield and mezzanine debt.

Source: Banc of America Securities LLC.

ADVANCE RATES

An *advance rate* is a positive number less than or equal to one assigned to an asset category and is a function of a rating on a debt tranche. Advance rates are a measure of risk to a given asset category in the event of a significant market downturn. The example in Exhibit 7 shows typical advance rates as a function of asset category and CDO debt rating.

Exhibit 8 describes the asset categories using a listing of all the types of assets included in each category.

The example in Exhibit 7 reflects Moody's and Fitch's rating methodologies, which bundle multiple asset classes together for advance rate calculations. S&P's advance rates are more specific in their asset category classification. Advance rates are a function of the length of time that the assets are subject to market volatility before a cure is required, the level of diversification in the portfolio, and the risk exposure of all asset categories. In general, the longer the exposure, the lower the advance rate. In addition, advance rates are assigned based on the desired rating on the CDO debt tranches — the higher the desired rating, the lower the advance rate.

Exhibit 9: Sample $1 Billion Market Value Transaction (Dollars in Millions)

Collateral Portfolio Composition			Target Deal Capitalization			
	Amt.	Pct.	Tranche	Rating	Amt.	Structure Mix
Bank Loans	$200	20%	Senior Facility	AA	$450	45%
High Yield	600	60	Senior Notes	AA	200	20
Mezzanine	100	10	Senior Sub.	A	100	10
Equity Investments	100	10	Sub. Notes	BBB	50	5
			Equity	NR	200	20
Total	$1,000	100%	Total		$1,000	100%

Source: Banc of America Securities LLC.

THE OVERCOLLATERALIZATION TESTS

The OC tests are designed to provide credit protection to the rated debt tranches by utilizing a minimum collateral value to protect each rated tranche. Market value CDOs usually have multiple OC tests that are assigned according to each seniority level in the capital structure. For each test, the overcollateralization amount is computed by taking the difference between the advance amount and the value of the debt obligations covered by the test. The advance amount is the sum of the market value of all eligible portfolio assets multiplied by their respective advance rate. The OC test is passed when the aggregate advance amount is larger than the value of the debt obligations and, conversely, is failed when the value of the debt obligations exceeds the aggregate advance amount.

To illustrate how these tests are applied in practice, we introduce a sample $1 billion market value deal in Exhibit 9. The portfolio and capital structure assume a 100% fully ramped-up portfolio.

In this example, the senior facility is a revolving credit line rated AA, the senior notes can be fixed or floaters (or a combination thereof), and they are *pari passu* with the senior facility. Because both debt tranches carry the same level of seniority in the capital structure, only one senior OC test compares the senior advance amount to the sum of the face values of each senior tranche. Accrued interest on the liability tranches is excluded from the OC tests of many existing market value CDOs; however, it is included in the price of the assets.

Under this scenario, the senior advance amount exceeds the total senior debt by $149 million, which is defined as the borrowing amount surplus (see Exhibit 10). How much market value loss can the fund withstand before the senior OC test is tripped? This is a function of the amount of loss per each asset category, as market losses are discounted by the respective advance rates. The lower the advance rate, the larger the market value drop required to violate the OC test, all other factors equal.

Exhibit 10: Senior Overcollateralization Test

	Asset Market Value	Asset Mix Pct.	Sr. Advance Rate	Sr. Advance Amount
Bank Loans	$200	20%	91%	$182
High Yield	600	60	82	492
Mezzanine	100	10	75	75
Equity Inv.	100	10	50	50
Total Value	$1,000	100%		$799
Total Senior Debt Face Value				$650
Borrowing Amount Surplus				$149

Source: Banc of America Securities LLC.

Exhibit 11: Senior Subordinated Overcollateralization Test

	Asset Market Value	Asset Mix Pct.	Senior-Sub. Advance Rate	Senior-Sub. Advance Amount
Bank Loans	$200	20%	92%	$184
High Yield	600	60	86	516
Mezzanine	100	10	84	84
Equity Inv.	100	10	73	73
Total	$1,000	100%		$857
Total Senior Debt Plus Senior Subordinated Debt				$750
Borrowing Amount Surplus				$107

Source: Banc of America Securities LLC.

Exhibit 12: Subordinated Overcollateralization Test

	Asset Market Value	Asset Mix Pct.	Sub. Advance Rate	Sub. Advance Amount
Bank Loans	$200	20%	93%	$186
High Yield	600	60	90	540
Mezzanine	100	10	86	86
Equity Inv.	100	10	80	80
Total	$1,000	100%		$892
Total Debt				$800
Borrowing Amount Surplus				$92

Source: Banc of America Securities LLC.

We outline the OC tests for the senior-subordinated and subordinated debt in Exhibits 11 and 12.

The failure of one or multiple OC tests represents a serious adverse event in the life of a market value deal, and must be remedied by the portfolio manager within a "cure" period that usually extends for two weeks or ten business days. The manager has two primary courses of action to cure an OC test failure:

• Sell portfolio assets with lower advance rates and use the proceeds to buy assets that have higher advance rates. This action increases the average advance rate while keeping the structure fully leveraged. This strategy is effective when transaction costs do not dramatically affect the total market value of the assets and the OC test is only slightly out of compliance.

• Sell portfolio assets and use proceeds to repay the debt tranches beginning with the senior debt down to the lower rated debt tranche until all OC tests are passed. The early partial or full deal amortization is a drastic (but conservative) cure of an OC test failure. This action is taken when the market value of the assets has fallen to a level where the portfolio manager has no choice but to repay debt. The partial deleveraging of the transaction, combined with large market losses, can lead to diminished equity returns as the CDO asset-liability arbitrage may no longer exist.

If the manager cannot bring the portfolio into compliance to pass the OC test during this cure period, the debt holders have the ability to seize control of the fund and liquidate the portfolio in an event of default. Debt holders will have the power to instruct the trustee to liquidate the fund in a commercially reasonable manner and use the proceeds to pay all interest and principal to the debt tranches according to the structural priorities. In practice, the full and sudden liquidation of a large portfolio in an illiquid market may not be in the best interest of the debt holders. Market value deal covenants are often written to allow the majority of debt holders to permit an extension of the cure period in order to avoid a "fire sale."

MINIMUM NET WORTH TESTS

Minimum net worth tests are also designed to offer credit protection to the rated market value CDO debt tranches, by ensuring a minimum equity cushion in the transaction. Minimum net worth tests are computed on a quarterly basis. These tests compare the net worth — namely, the excess of the portfolio market value over the total value of the debt obligations — to a given percentage of the face value of the equity tranche. The net worth at the beginning of the deal is generally lower than the equity investment because of issuance costs; thus, the net worth may be adjusted to reflect those costs.

For example, in a typical senior net worth test, the minimum net worth must be equal to, or greater than, 60% of the equity face value (see Exhibit 13). Moving down the capital structure, the minimum net worth becomes smaller. For subordinated debt, the minimum net worth can be as low as 30% of the equity face value. With regard to market value CDOs with preferred equity classes, these liabilities are included in the minimum net worth test calculation both at the fraction numerator and denominator. The preferred equity classes are typically issued as single B rated notes with contingent interest.

At the commencement of a transaction, the stringent nature of the senior minimum net worth test will override all other subordinated tests. When the senior debt is entirely retired, the senior net worth ceases to be applicable and the senior-subordinated net worth test is activated. Minimum net worth tests may add an additional layer of protection to the rated debt; as a result, their presence will lead to higher advance rates than those in a CDO without net worth tests, all other factors equal.

If a minimum net worth is failed, the portfolio manager has usually one month to bring the fund into compliance. While this cure period is longer than for the OC tests, it may be harder to find a resolution as there are no advance rates. Essentially two courses of action exist for the portfolio manager:

- Redeem the senior debt down to subordinated debt to render the senior net worth test inapplicable. This results in a lower minimum for the net worth. This solution is possible when the test is failed by a marginal amount.
- Generate enough unrealized capital gains to cure the minimum net worth test within one month's time. This is the better course of action, in our view, as it does not deleverage the deal, although it may be challenging to achieve in a bear market.

If the minimum net worth test is failed and is not cured for one month or longer, an event of default will occur and the debt holders have the right to call the deal. How does the OC test compare in terms of severity to the minimum net worth tests? One test can be more onerous than the other depending on the structure, asset mix, minimum net worth amount, and advance rates. A simple estimation can be made assuming one rated debt tranche. For example, assuming D and E are the face values of the debt and equity, AR is the average advance rate and P is the minimum percentage of equity required by the minimum net worth test (MNW), we can easily determine which test is more stringent.

OC test:	$MV > D/AR$
MNW test:	$MV > D + P \times E$
OC dominates if:	$1/AR > 1 + P \times (E/D)$
MNW dominates if:	$1/AR < 1 + P \times (E/D)$

Exhibit 13: Senior Minimum Net Worth Test

Asset Categories	Market Value
Bank Loans	$200
High Yield	600
Mezzanine	100
Equity	100
Total	$1,000
Minus Debt	800
Net Worth	200
Minimum Net Worth (60% * $200)	120
Test is Met	200>120

Source: Banc of America Securities LLC.

EVENTS OF DEFAULT

An event of default is the most serious event in the life of a market value deal and its outcome may result in the early termination of the fund by portfolio liquidation. Although such events are highly unlikely, they are addressed by each fund's covenants. In practice, an event of default is triggered by a negative occurrence that seriously comprises the performance of the fund and the credit protection of the fund's debt. The following events are generally considered events of default but may differ across CDO deals:

- Failure to comply with the OC and net worth tests within their respective cure times;
- Failure to meet interest (except when interest is deferrable) and principal payments on any rated debt note when due;
- Failure to comply with any regulations of the fund as described by the indenture document and any other legal agreements between the fund and its lenders;
- Bankruptcy of the market value CDO issuing entity;
- Certain changes in legal and tax status of the fund; and
- The departure of the portfolio manager and his staff, if no suitable replacement is available.

LIMITATIONS ON PAYMENTS

Equity dividend payments and contingent interest payments are restricted by the occurrence of an event of default and when the net worth of the portfolio falls below the equity face value less upfront costs deducted from debt and equity sales. The rationale behind these limitations is to maintain credit protection to the debt by prohibiting cash distributions to preferred equity or equity tranches unless the portfolio is performing and has retained sufficient market value to justify such distributions.

LIMITATIONS ON DEBT

Market value CDOs are leveraged funds whose debt to equity ratio will fluctuate during its lifetime. In a normal course of operation, the fund manager will borrow funds under the senior revolving facility to increase the fund's market exposure or repay the facility to reduce the exposure. Market value deals are structured to maximize the amount of leverage allowable at any one time.

In general, no additional debt or liability can be underwritten by the fund beyond the target structure — with the exception of those that are part of the business and trading operation. In some transactions, a limited amount of short positions can be taken not to exceed 1% of the portfolio market value.

FEES

Two types of fees exist in market value CDOs: upfront fees and current fees. Upfront fees originate from structuring, underwriting, legal, and rating expenses. These fees are paid directly from the deal sale proceeds; therefore, they reduce the cash available to purchase assets. In some cases, a portion of these fees are amortized for the life of the deal. Current fees are periodically paid by the fund, and they are senior to all the notes in the capital structure.

Some standard current fees include the following:

- *Trustee fees*, which pay expenses associated with monitoring and servicing the fund, are small (usually a few basis points of the portfolio value on an annual basis);
- *Primary management fees*, which are paid to the manager in an amount to cover management team expenses, are in the 50-100 basis point range of the portfolio value on an annual basis; and
- *Hedging fees* are paid to a derivative counterparty to match the duration of the assets with the duration of the liabilities.

INTEREST PAYMENTS TO THE SENIOR FACILITY AND SENIOR NOTES

The senior facility is a floating revolving loan priced at a spread to LIBOR or some other market reference interest rate. Interest accrues on the withdrawn amount of the revolver and a commitment fee of 10-30 basis points per annum may be payable on the unused portion of the committed line. The basis count for the senior facility is based on the actual number of days in a 360-day year. The senior facility can be prepaid without additional premium. The senior notes are pari passu to the senior facility; therefore, their interest payments are prorated with the senior facility interest payments. The senior notes can be floaters or fixed, and interest is paid on a quarterly or semiannual basis proportionally to the outstanding par amount on the notes.

PRINCIPAL PAYMENT TO THE SENIOR FACILITY AND SENIOR NOTES

Principal payments are made to the senior facility and senior notes in the following events: (1) mandatory redemption due to an OC or minimum net worth test failure (payments are usually made repaying the senior facility first); (2) optional redemption by a majority of equity holders (payments are made pro rata to the senior facility and senior notes); and (3) default and/or fund liquidation (payments are made pro rata to the senior facility and senior notes).

INTEREST PAYMENTS TO SENIOR-SUBORDINATED NOTES AND SUBORDINATED NOTES

Interest payments to senior-subordinated notes and subordinated notes are subordinated to interest and principal payments (if any) to all senior debt. Senior-subordinated notes and subordinated notes can be floaters, fixed or a combination thereof. Interest on the floating notes is paid quarterly on an actual/360 day basis, while fixed notes are paid semiannually on a 30/360 day basis. Notes are not generally paid in kind (PIK), with the exception of a subordinated tranche issued as a PIK note. If the senior facility and senior notes are being prepaid in the event of mandatory redemption, interest on the senior-subordinated and subordinated debt can be deferred and paid later.

Deferred interest will also accrue interest at the same rate as the underlying note. Deferred interest and corresponding accrued interest can be repaid at any time in full prior to any principal payment on the underlying note. In the event of an optional redemption, notes can be redeemed at their principal value plus accrued interest and, when applicable, a make-whole premium that is intended to compensate fixed-rate note investors for prepayment risk.

PRINCIPAL PAYMENT TO SENIOR-SUBORDINATED NOTES AND SUBORDINATED NOTES

Principal payments can be made to the senior-subordinated and subordinated notes only when the senior debt has been fully redeemed, interest payment on these notes have been made, or in the event of one or more of the following: (1) a mandatory redemption due to an OC or minimum net worth test failure; (2) an optional redemption by the majority of equity holders; or (3) a default and fund liquidation.

Senior-subordinated notes will be redeemed before subordinated notes receive any principal payment. If the notes are issued in two pari passu tranches, principal payments are made pro rata. Some CDOs have subordinated notes that receive contingent interest payments based on the performance of the fund.

EQUITY PAYMENTS AND INCENTIVE FEES

Equity holders have a residual interest in the fund; therefore, they are located at the bottom of the "waterfall." While rules vary from fund to fund, the manager is allowed to make a distribution to equity holders when all OC and net worth tests are passed, all scheduled debt payments have been made and the net worth is at least equal to the equity face value. Market value CDOs also have portfolio management incentive fees based on the performance of the equity interests. For example, some funds have hurdle rates for equity returns that are set at the beginning of a deal.

If equity distributions have been made to achieve an implied rate of return on the equity investment equal to the hurdle rate, the portfolio manager usually receives 20% of the prorated future equity distributions with the remaining 80% to equity holders. In most market value CDOs, the largest equity distributions are concentrated at the end of the deal when the portfolio is liquidated and the debt is fully repaid.

OPTIONAL REDEMPTION AND DEAL REFINANCING

The portfolio manager can repay the debt tranches at any time by notifying the debt holders 30 days prior to redemption. The price of the redeemed notes is the sum of the face value of the notes plus any accrued interest and prepayment premiums. A debt note can be redeemed only if the senior debt above it has been fully redeemed consistent with the capital structure. This repayment can be partial or full and is provided by either collateral portfolio sales or refinancing. If notes are refinanced, the new class of notes will carry a lower interest rate or spread than the original notes. Optional redemption and refinancing are usually considered if the deal is performing well and in the case of a ratings upgrade by the rating agencies, an event that is extremely unlikely given the structure's embedded flexibility.

STRUCTURAL DIFFERENCES BETWEEN MARKET VALUE AND CASH FLOW CDOS

The following are important structural differences between market value and cash flow CDOs:

- Market value deal assets are marked-to-market, while cash flow CDO assets generally are not required to be marked for test purposes.
- Cash proceeds in market value deals originate from coupon payments, dividends and sales proceeds, and market value CDO waterfalls do not separate cash proceeds in interest and principal payments as in cashflow CDOs.
- Interest coverage tests are not present in standard market value deals.
- Market value CDOs have multiple asset classes and include assets that do not pay cash, while cashflow CDOs portfolios are usually limited to cash-paying instruments such as high yield bonds and loans.
- Market value deal tests are based on the market value of the portfolio assets rather than their nominal value as in cashflow CDOs.
- The cure period for OC tests is usually ten business days, while that of cashflow CDOs is undetermined and may last for the life of the deal so as not to subject the cashflow CDO to liquidity risk.

Chapter 3

Rating Agency Methodologies

Meredith Hill
Head of ABS Research
Banc of America Securities

Luigi Vacca, Ph.D.
Vice President
Structured Credit Products
Banc of America Securities

I n this chapter we explain the rating agency methodologies for cash flow CBOs and market value CBOs.

RATING METHODOLOGIES FOR CASH FLOW CBOS

Moody's, S&P, and Fitch all command a solid market share for rating cash flow CBOs. In this section, we discuss each agency's methodology for rating cash flow transactions.

Moody's Methodology

Credit Risk and Default Correlation

In rating cash flow CBOs, Moody's compares the amount of credit risk present in the collateral pool to the credit protection offered by the structure. Estimating credit risk of the collateral pool starts with estimating the probability of default and recovery rate of each issue in the collateral portfolio. Thus, Moody's natural course of action is to use the credit ratings of each security in the collateral pool.

However, Moody's believes that the rating information is not sufficient to quantify the portfolio's aggregate credit exposure. While the credit rating of one security is an expression of the expected probability of default, assessing the credit risk of a portfolio of securities involves another calculation — that is, default correlation. Historical default data suggest that the probability of default of a single security is correlated with the probability that other securities may default. According to Moody's, the 1981–91 period was characterized by a 21.2% default rate of Ba rated bonds versus a 6.1% default rate of similarly rated bonds in the 1974–84 period. This large difference in average default rates is explained by the presence of default correlation in the high yield market. Moody's believes that default correlation is due to macroeconomic factors such as the state of the domestic economy and industry concentration. Default correlation increases the portfolio credit risk to levels higher than the one implied by its average rating. For this reason, in the rating assignment process, Moody's will ensure that sufficient CBO structural protection exists to deal with additional defaults arising from correlation effects.

Weighted Average Credit Rating

In the CBO rating process, Moody's calculates a weighted average credit rating for a given pool of securities. Securities in the pool that are not rated by Moody's will be assigned a "shadow rating." For each credit rating, Moody's has a corresponding rating factor. The average portfolio rating is calculated by adding all the products obtained by multiplying the par value of each security by its corresponding rating factor and dividing the result by the total portfolio par. The relationship between ratings and corresponding factors is nonlinear, because the average historical default rate increases much faster than a straight line for decreasing ratings. Exhibit 1 lists Moody's rating factors.

Exhibit 1: Moody's Investors Service —
Rating Factors Used in Computing Average Ratings

Rating Category	Rating Factor
Aaa	1
Aa1	10
Aa2	20
Aa3	40
A1	70
A2	120
A3	180
Baa1	260
Baa2	360
Baa3	610
Ba1	940
Ba2	1,350
Ba3	1,780
B1	2,220
B2	2,720
B3	3,490
Caa	6,500
Ca	10,000
C	10,000

From Table 8 (Rating Factor Equivalents) in Alan Backman and Gerard O'Connor, *Rating Cash Flow Transactions Backed by Corporate Debt 1995 Update*, Moody's Investors Service, Inc., p. 18.

Diversity Score

Moody's assesses the risk of default correlation through its requirement of a minimum diversity score, as default correlation is inversely related to portfolio diversification. The diversity score measures the number of uncorrelated securities in a portfolio that would exhibit the same degree of default risk of a correlated CBO portfolio. Diversity is a quality factor: the higher the diversity score, the less volatile the portfolio. Furthermore, the diversity score is always equal to, or smaller than, the total number of securities comprising the collateral portfolio.

The diversity score is a function of how many issuers and industries comprise the collateral portfolio and the degree of correlation among them. Moody's employs a 33-industry classification system listed in Exhibit 2.

Once the credit quality and diversity characteristics are computed, Moody's estimates the portfolio credit risk as the amount of loss that the structure can withstand before the rated debt experiences default. The expected loss is the average loss computed by considering all possible loss scenarios weighted by corresponding default probabilities. Computing the portfolio credit risk entails solving an equation of the following form:

Default Probability × [(1 − Recovery Rate) − Credit Protection]
  = Expected Loss

The expected loss in this formula is the average percentage loss suffered by the rated CBO debt tranche that is consistent with its rating. The recovery rate is the estimated collateral recovery rate. For example, assume that the collateral has a 30% probability of defaulting and a 40% recovery rate, and the rated CBO tranche is an investment grade bond with an expected loss of 5%. Incorporating these numbers into the formula yields a required credit protection of 43.33%.

In practice, the computation of the credit protection is more complex than the formula may suggest. Moody's runs a binomial branch method to simulate defaults occurring throughout the life of the deal. This method starts with an initial "state" in which all securities are performing. In turn, a single state can evolve into two states: one in which default occurs with probability P and one in which the security is still performing with probability $1 − P$. The process is iterated to the next period until all possible events are simulated. If the life of the deal is split into N periods, the binomial method will produce 2 to the Mth final outcomes.

The default probabilities are computed on the basis of historical default rates and adjusted for macroeconomic shocks and undiversifiable correlation. Exhibit 3 summarizes the assumed 10-year default rates and corresponding historical rates for comparative purposes.

The recovery rates are also simulated using a distribution with an average recovery rate of 30% and a range of 0%–60%. The expected losses on CBO rated debt are calculated using historical default rates and are generally lower than the ones computed only on the basis of historical data. This conservative methodology accounts for macroeconomic shocks, and leads to extra credit enhancement built into the structure. A 40% recovery rate is assumed for the CBO debt tranche, which is a higher recovery rate than the one used for the collateral portfolio. Exhibit 4 lists the assumed loss on a B2 rated collateral portfolio as a function of the desired rating and collateral portfolio diversity score for debt rating purposes.

Exhibit 2: Moody's Investors Service — Industry Classifications

Listing	Sector
1	Aerospace & Defense
2	Automobile
3	Banking
4	Beverage, Food & Tobacco
5	Buildings and Real Estate
6	Chemicals, Plastics & Rubber
7	Containers, Packaging and Glass
8	Manufacturing
9	Diversified/Conglomerate Manufacturing
10	Diversified/Conglomerate Service
11	Metals & Minerals
12	Ecological
13	Electronics
14	Finance
15	Farming and Agriculture
16	Grocery
17	Healthcare, Education and Childcare
18	Home and Office Furnishings, Housewares and Durable Consumer Products
19	Hotels, Inns and Gaming
20	Insurance
21	Leisure, Amusement, Motion Picture, Entertainment
22	Machinery
23	Mining, Steel, Iron and Nonprecious Metals
24	Oil and Gas
25	Personal, Food and Miscellaneous Services
26	Printing and Publishing
27	Cargo Transport
28	Retail Stores
29	Telecommunications
30	Textiles and Leather
31	Personal Transportation
32	Utilities
33	Broadcasting

From Table 6 (Industry Classifications) in Alan Backman and Gerard O'Connor, *Rating Cash Flow Transactions Backed by Corporate Debt 1995 Update*, Moody's Investors Service, Inc., p. 13.

Exhibit 3: Moody's Investors Service —
Historic and Assumed 10-Year Default Rate

Rating	10-Year Default Rate	
	Historic	Assumed
Aaa	1.0%	1.8%
Aa1	1.2	1.9
Aa2	1.4	2.0
Aa3	1.5	2.2
A1	1.7	2.5
A2	1.8	3.0
A3	2.3	3.6
Baa1	3.5	4.4
Baa2	4.4	5.4
Baa3	7.5	7.9
Ba1	11.9	17.4
Ba2	16.1	21.5
Ba3	20.6	26.0
B1	25.9	32.1
B2	31.6	37.9
B3	39.6	45.8

From Table 3 (Default Rates) in Alan Backman and Gerard O'Connor, *Rating Cash Flow Transactions Backed by Corporate Debt 1995 Update*, Moody's Investors Service, Inc., p. 10
Copyright 1995, Moody's Investors Service, Inc. Used With Permission. This table contains historical information and may not set forth current data.

Exhibit 4: Moody's Investors Service —
Portfolio Loss by Diversity Score and Desired Debt Rating

Score	Aaa	Aa1	Aa2	Aa3	A1	A2	A3	Baa1	Baa2	Baa3
2	100%	92%	89%	84%	79%	77%	71%	66%	59%	49%
3	98	82	78	72	66	65	59	55	50	43
4	92	74	69	64	60	58	53	49	44	38
5	87	68	64	60	55	53	49	46	41	36
7	77	61	57	53	49	48	44	41	37	32
10	69	54	51	48	45	43	40	38	34	30
15	60	48	45	43	40	39	37	34	32	28
20	56	45	43	40	38	37	35	33	30	27
25	53	43	40	38	36	35	33	32	29	26
30	51	41	39	37	35	34	32	31	29	26
35	48	40	38	36	34	33	32	30	28	25
40	47	39	37	35	33	32	31	30	28	25

From Table 7 (Portfolio Credit Risk Tables) in Alan Backman and Gerard O'Connor, *Rating Cash Flow Transactions Backed by Corporate Debt 1995 Update*, Moody's Investors Service, Inc., p. 14
Copyright 1995, Moody's Investors Service, Inc. Used With Permission. This table contains historical information and may not set forth current data.

Once the portfolio credit risk is estimated, a structure is designed based on the desired rating sought on the CBO debt and the collateral composition. The structure must contain enough credit protection to withstand the expected losses. To test the structure protection, Moody's runs a cash flow model that accurately describes the behavior of the structure in a series of default simulations and stress scenarios. Moody's adopts a conservative timing schedule for defaults under a stress scenario: 50% of the total defaults occur in the first year of the deal and 10% of the total defaults every following year up to six years of the transaction's life. This schedule is equivalent to adding two standard deviations to the historical loss patterns.

Qualitative Factors in the Rating Methodology

In its rating of cash flow CBO deals, Moody's examines other risk factors in addition to collateral risk and structural analysis. Legal risk serves a major role in the rating process, and important components of this type of risk include the following:

- bankruptcy remoteness
- asset transfer
- substantive consolidation
- subordination and enforceability

Another important source of risk in cash flow CBOs is the "ramp-up" risk. During the ramp-up period, the portfolio manager purchases the collateral portfolio. Moody's estimates the likelihood and effect of the following adverse events which may occur during a structure's ramp-up period:

- collateral will be more expensive and the price effect more significant on the liabilities
- the collateral portfolio will have a lower rating than originally assumed
- the collateral portfolio will have a lower weighted average coupon than originally assumed
- the collateral portfolio will have a lower diversity score than originally assumed

Standard & Poor's Methodology

Standard & Poor's (S&P) approach to rating cash flow CBO/CLO transactions consists of three types of analyses: credit analysis of the collateral portfolio, structural analysis, and legal analysis of the transaction. While general rating criteria apply to transactions backed by high yield bonds and high yield loans, S&P believes distinctions must be made in the rating process of these two types of deals. The loan market is less liquid than the high yield bond market; thus, this lack of liquidity increases the ramp-up risk in CLOs. Collateral loan participations make it difficult to protect the CLO rights on the collateral assets in the event of bankruptcy of the lead bank. Another important difference between bonds and loans is that loans have amortization schedules (compared with bullet payments in bonds), lower coupons and higher recovery rates with respect to bonds issued by the same company.

Credit risk analysis is the most important component of S&P's analysis. Similar to Moody's approach, S&P examines the credit rating of the borrowers and the consequent probability of default. S&P employs a proprietary computer model to estimate the potential default rate in a collateral portfolio. This technique uses historical default information collected by S&P since 1981 to compute a default frequency as a function of the debt rating and its maturity.

The S&P computer model calculates a gross default rate for the pool of collateral using bond specific probability of default dependent on the rating and tenor of each debt obligation. The model provides an expected gross default rate for the asset pool for each rating level, as shown in Exhibit 5. S&P does not offer diversification guidelines, but stresses the importance of a diversified collateral portfolio with a large number of names and industry concentration below 8%. The S&P model, which includes a 39-industry classification, makes no adjustment for industry concentrations below 8% (see Exhibit 6).

The collateral composition information is needed to calculate the aggregate default rate of the portfolio — in particular, the model requires the following inputs:

- rating of each issuer
- number of rated issuers
- par amount of each instrument
- maturity date of each instrument
- amortization schedules in the case of loans

Exhibit 5: Standard & Poor's — Structuring Model Output

Total Principal Balance: 100
WAM: 6.5 years
Number of Bonds/Loans: 20
Number of Obligors: 15

Rating Requested	AAA	AA	A	BBB	BB
Loss Rate in Percent	33.10	29.32	24.30	20.22	16.03

Scenario Loss Rates for each rating scenario
From *Global CBO/CLO Criteria*, Structured Finance Group, Standard & Poor's Corporation, 1999.
Copyright 1999, Standard & Poor's Corporation. Used With Permission. This table contains historical information and may not set forth current data.

Exhibit 6: Standard & Poor's Industry Classification

Listing	Sector
1	Aerospace and Defense
2	Air Transport
3	Automotive
4	Beverage and Tobacco
5	Broadcast Radio and TV
6	Brokerages
7	Building and Development
8	Business Equipment and Services
9	Cable TV
10	Chemical/Plastics
11	Clothing/Textiles
12	Conglomerates
13	Containers and Glass Products
14	Cosmetics/Toiletries
15	Drugs
16	Ecological Services and Equipment
17	Electronics/Electric
18	Equipment Leasing
19	Farming/Agriculture
20	Financial Intermediaries
21	Food/Drug retailers
22	Food Products
23	Food Service
24	Forest Products
25	Healthcare
26	Home Furnishings
27	Hotels/Motels/Inns and Casinos
28	Industrial Equipment
29	Insurance
30	Leisure
31	Nonferrous Metals/Minerals
32	Oil and Gas
33	Publishing
34	Rail Industries
35	Retailers
36	Steel
37	Surface Transport
38	Telecommunications
39	Utilities

From *Global CBO/CLO Criteria*, Structured Finance Group, Standard & Poor's Corporation, 1999.
Copyright 1999, Standard & Poor's Corporation. Used With Permission. This table contains historical information and may not set forth current data.

If an issuer is not rated, S&P will perform a rating estimate based on the analysis of three to five years of the issuer's financial statements. The timing of defaults is an important component in estimating the amount of credit protection needed to withstand losses. A conservative assumption is to model defaults in the early years of the transaction, because the defaults will decrease the interest generated in future payments. Another conservative assumption is to model defaults near the close of a transaction when little time is left to benefit from recoveries. S&P uses a number of default scenarios that vary the amounts of defaults occurring every year and the year when defaults start. Transactions that are similar are analyzed using the same default scenarios. However, depending on characteristics of the transactions, new scenarios may be used. Examples of S&P default scenarios are outlined in Exhibit 7.

S&P uses the recovery rates shown in Exhibit 8, on the basis of extensive historical research.

S&P assumes that recoveries on high yield bonds will occur one year after default. For high yield loans, the recovery time is longer: three years with half of the recovered amount at the end of the second year and the rest at the end of the third year.

With regard to structural analysis, S&P examines five types of credit enhancement:

- overcollateralization/subordination
- cash collateral/reserve account
- excess spread/interest
- amortization
- bond insurance

Exhibit 7: Standard & Poor's — Examples of Default Scenarios Assumed Percent of Default Amount for Original Collateral Pool*

Year	1	2	3	4	5	6	7	8-10
Scenario 1	20.0	20.0	20.0	20.0	20.0	0.0	0.0	0.0
Scenario 2	15.0	30.0	30.0	15.0	10.0	0.0	0.0	0.0
Scenario 3	0.0	0.0	20.0	20.0	20.0	20.0	20.0	0.0
Scenario 4	0.0	0.0	15.0	30.0	30.0	15.0	10.0	0.0
Scenario 5	40.0	20.0	10.0	10.0	10.0	10.0	0.0	0.0
Scenario 6	40.0	20.0	20.0	10.0	10.0	0.0	0.0	0.0
Scenario 7**	33.0	33.0	34.0	0.0	0.0	0.0	0.0	0.0
Scenario 8**	25.0	25.0	25.0	25.0	0.0	0.0	0.0	0.0
Scenario 9**	0.0	0.0	33.0	33.0	34.0	0.0	0.0	0.0

* The default percentages in the table are a percent of the default amount which the transaction should withstand, as calculated by the Standard & Poor's Default Model. Assumed default amounts are calculated as a percent of the original collateral balance, namely the aggregate principal balance of the initial collateral pool. For example, for a $1 billion collateral pool with a 10% scenario default rate, or $100 million assumed default amount, $20 million in annual defaults would be modeled in default scenario 1. Actual default scenarios will depend on the collateral pool.

** Scenarios 7 through 9 are typically run in balance sheet CLO transactions, which are typically shorter in tenor than arbitrage transactions. Default runs are tailored to the revolving period, legal final maturity and structure of the transaction.

From *Global CBO/CLO Criteria*, Structured Finance Group, Standard & Poor's Corporation, 1999. Copyright 1999, Standard & Poor's Corporation. Used With Permission. This table contains historical information and may not set forth current data.

Exhibit 8: Standard & Poor's — Recovery Range Assumptions as a Percent of Default Amount*

Loans	Recovery range assumptions (%)	Recovery Timing
Senior secured bank loans	50 to 60	2-3 years after default
Senior unsecured bank loans	25 to 50	2-3 years after default
Subordinated loans	15 to 28	2-3 years after default
Bonds	Recovery range assumptions (%)	Recovery Timing
Senior secured bonds	40 to 55	1 year after default
Senior unsecured bonds	25 to 44	1 year after default
Subordinated bonds	15 to 28	1 year after default

* Using the example from Exhibit 4, the default amount is assumed to equal $100 million in collateral. If all collateral consisted of senior secured bonds, then the assumed total recovery amount could range from $40 million to $55 million, depending on the recovery time period and sponsor workout history.
From *Global CBO/CLO Criteria*, Structured Finance Group, Standard & Poor's Corporation, 1999.
Copyright 1999, Standard & Poor's Corporation. Used With Permission. This table contains historical information and may not set forth current data.

Similar to Moody's, S&P examines ramp-up risk in its rating process: the impact of negative carry generated by a slow ramp-up process; the potential lack of collateral investments; and the consequent degradation of collateral quality during the ramp-up which may extend into the life of the transaction. Most cash flow CBOs have reinvestment periods during which the principal proceeds from the collateral pool are used to buy new collateral securities. S&P considers the credit risk present in the reinvestment process by requesting that collateral managers run the S&P default model every time a new asset is added/subtracted to the collateral portfolio. S&P will allow the portfolio manager to trade the new asset only if the default model recognizes an equal or better default rate expectation on the new portfolio. S&P does not provide a standard cash flow model to run cash flow scenarios, but instead uses the exact cash flow model designed according to the payments priority. Unlike other rating agencies, S&P places a special focus on asset-liability management study — in particular, it is concerned with the interest rate mismatches that may arise because of the following factors:

- differences in payment periodicity between the assets and the liabilities
- differences in payment dates
- basis risk
- reset risk

Interest rate mismatches may cause interest shortfalls even in a zero-default scenario; for this reason, S&P requires that every transaction is modelled under different interest rate scenarios. The collateral portfolio is subject to pre-payment risk, one that increases with falling interest rates. The portfolio manager will use the prepayment proceeds to purchase new investments at lower interest rates during the reinvestment period, which will decrease the excess spread between the assets and the liabilities. On the positive side, prepayments after the reinvestment period decrease the likelihood of collateral default. S&P estimates the speed of collateral prepayment and its effect on rated debt performance.

Finally, S&P will review a transaction's legal risk based on the following factors:

- the nature of the collateral assets transfer
- the legal state of the issuer
- the pledge of the assets as security for the deal obligations
- the relationship between the seller's credit risk and the right to the collateral assets

Fitch's Methodology

For analytial purposes, Fitch divides CBO/CLOs into three basic structures: cash flow, market value, and synthetics/credit derivatives. Fitch generally makes the following assumptions in rating cash flow CBO/CLOs:

- the issuer is a bankruptcy-remote entity
- the collateral assets are ratable debt instruments
- the collateral portfolio is diversified to justify an actuarial approach to default, although ratings have been assigned to less diversified structures
- investment grade ratings can be achieved through subordination

Through its rating process, Fitch estimates the amount of credit enhancement needed for a desired rating of a specific tranche. Fitch computes the expected loss on the collateral assets based on the default frequencies and the expected recovery rates of each asset based on various Fitch studies. The computation of the expected loss is carried out using a cash flow model that includes different factors of risk, such as timing of defaults, recovery and interest rate movements. The probability of default is estimated using a default curve, which gives the cumulative amount of defaulted par in a 10-year span for a given level of collateral quality and the rating target. Fitch's default curve is the combined result of published research on bond mortality and Fitch's proprietary information.

Exhibit 9 outlines Fitch's assumptions for stressed default rates, and shows how these rates behave as a function of the average collateral rating and the desired rating on the debt tranche. For example, if a BBB pool of assets is used to back a AAA tranche of a CDO, Fitch would use a stressed default rate of 14%. Fitch then calculates an average rating for the collateral pool based on rating factors weighted by the respective par amount, as shown in Exhibit 10.

Fitch allows collateral trading if the average rating is kept above a minimum level set at the beginning of a transaction. Fitch uses, at minimum, two stress tests for each class of rated debt. The front-loaded test assumes that most defaults occur after the completion of ramp-up. The back-loaded test assumes that most defaults occur in the last three years of the transaction. Fitch assumes a front-loaded distribution of defaults as described in Exhibit 11. Additional stresses apply, as necessary, depending on the structure.

Exhibit 9: Fitch — Stressed Default Rates

Collateral Rating	B	BB	BBB	A	AA	AAA
AAA	0.00%	0.00%	0.50%	0.80%	1.00%	1.30%
AA	0.00	0.60	0.90	1.20	1.40	2.30
A	0.75	1.03	1.30	1.60	4.30	5.00
BBB	4.00	4.50	5.00	10.00	12.00	14.00
BB+	10.75	13.50	17.00	22.25	27.75	37.00
BB	16.00	18.70	21.50	27.00	32.50	43.50
BB-	17.75	20.00	23.50	31.50	37.50	46.50
B+	22.00	25.00	29.50	35.20	42.00	50.00
B	25.00	28.40	31.80	38.60	45.40	52.20
B-	27.00	30.50	38.00	45.00	53.00	65.00

Rating Criteria for Cash Flow Collateralized Debt Obligations, Fitch, November 30, 2000.
Copyright 2000, Fitch. Used With Permission. This table contains historical information and may not set forth current data.

Exhibit 10: Fitch — Rating Factors

Rating	Factor
AAA	1.3
AA+	2.0
AA	2.3
AA-	3.3
A+	4.0
A	5.0
A-	7.5
BBB+	10.0
BBB	14.0
BBB-	20.0
BB+	37.0
BB	43.5
BB-	46.5
B+	50.0
B	52.2
B-	65.0
CCC+	90.0
CCC	100.0

Rating Criteria for Cash Flow Collateralized Debt Obligations, Fitch, November 30, 2000.
Copyright 2000, Fitch. Used With Permission. This table contains historical information and may not set forth current data.

The recovery rates assumed by Fitch are based on the seniority level of the debt in the capital structure and a blend of bankruptcy research and market experience (see Exhibit 12). The recovery is assumed to occur immediately after the default event; however, under a stress scenario it can be lagged two years.

Exhibit 11: Fitch — Timing of Expected Defaults

Year	Pct. of Total Defaults
1	33%
2	25
3	16
4	13
5	13

Rating Criteria for Cash Flow Collateralized Debt Obligations, Fitch, November 30, 2000.
Copyright 2000, Fitch. Used With Permission. This table contains historical information and may not set forth current data.

Exhibit 12: Fitch — Assumed Recovery Rates

Debt Structure	Immediate	24-Month Lagged
Senior Secured Bank Loans	60%	80%
Senior Unsecured Debt	40	65
Subordinated Debt	20	25
EM Sovereigns	20	20
EM Corporate	15	15
ABS - Most Senior Investment Grade Tranche*	60	NA
ABS - All Other Investment Grade Tranches*	40	NA
ABS - Non Investment Grade Tranche*	10	NA

ABS Asset-Backed Securities. EM Emerging Markets. NA Not applicable.
Note: Recoveries may vary for European issuers depending on insolvency regime. See *Rating Criteria for European Arbitrage Collateralized Debt Obligations*, Fitch, June 2000.
* *Rating Criteria for Cash Flow ABS/MBS CDOs*, Fitch, November 2000. Note: Recoveries are for stress case equal to or less than collateral rating.
Rating Criteria for Cash Flow Collateralized Debt Obligations, Fitch, November 30, 2000.
Copyright 2000, Fitch. Used With Permission. This table contains historical information and may not set forth current data.

Exhibit 13 describes Fitch industry classifications. Fitch defines a well diversified pool of assets as a portfolio in which the industry concentration is below 10%, although the top three industries may comprise 35% of the portfolio. Fitch adjusts the default rate assumption according to the level of diversification, both with respect to industry and obligor concentrations. In addition, Fitch provides a thorough analysis of the management aspect of a CBO, which includes a review of the historical return and risk behavior of a portfolio managed by the collateral manager, its experience and credit analysis and the skills of his/her staff. In particular, the ability and desire to hold and work out defaulted assets, structure permitting, can be a critical factor.

Summary

Moody's approach to rating cash flow deals is based on the diversity factor and the binomial method to compute the expected loss on the rated debt. Both S&P and Fitch use a cash flow model combined with a default model based on historical data to estimate the expected loss on the rated debt.

Exhibit 13: Fitch — Industry Classifications.

Listing	Sector
1	Aerospace and Defense
2	Automobiles
3	Banking, Finance, and Real Estate
4	Broadcasting and Media
5	Building and Materials
6	Cable
7	Chemicals
8	Computers and Electronics
9	Consumer Products
10	Energy
11	Environmental Services
12	Farming and Agriculture
13	Food, Beverage, and Tobacco
14	Gaming, Lodging, and Restaurants
15	Healthcare and Pharmaceuticals
16	Industrial/Manufacturing
17	Insurance
18	Leisure and Entertainment
19	Metals and Mining
20	Miscellaneous
21	Paper and Forest Products
22	Retail
23	Sovereign
24	Supermarkets and Drug Stores
25	Telecommunications
26	Textiles and Furniture
27	Transportation
28	Utilities
29	Structured Finance Obligations

Rating Criteria for Cash Flow Collateralized Debt Obligations, Fitch, November 30, 2000.
Copyright 2000, Fitch. Used With Permission. This table contains historical information and may not set forth current data.

RATING METHODOLOGIES FOR MARKET VALUE CDOS

Moody's, S&P, and Fitch have each rated market value CDO deals in the past, with Fitch representing the most active rating agency in this class. The performance of market value CDOs from a ratings standpoint is excellent. Moody's has never downgraded a class of a market value CDO, and Fitch has only downgraded one subordinated tranche in the January 1996 through September 2000 period. For comparison purposes, cash flow CDOs have experienced a fairly large number of downgrades by Moody's (48 in total) involving 22 transactions in the January 1998 through December 1999 period, with a large share of downgrades (13) suffered in the second half of 1999. Market value debt tranches rated Aa/AA or higher have never experienced a downgrade.[1]

Moody's Market Value Deal Rating Methodology

The rating methodologies developed by the rating agencies are based on estimating the market, default and liquidity risks present in a market value CDO, although each uses different sources and assumptions. Once these risks are estimated, the results are used to compute the advance rates in the overcollateralization (OC) tests to protect the rated tranches at the desired level. The advance rates and the relative level of subordination are set by the rating agencies to ensure that the ratings are consistent with the credit protection assigned to each CDO rated tranche.

Main Risk Factors

The main risk affecting rated tranches in market value CDOs is a decline of the collateral market value to a level below the face value of the rated tranches. To quantify this risk, Moody's focuses on the price volatility of the underlying assets.[2] Moody's isolates the following four fundamental factors that may affect the return of debt rated below investment grade:

- changes in ratings
- defaults
- changes in interest rates
- changes in investor preferences

Rating Changes The price of debt rated below investment grade is sensitive to a ratings downgrade. The downgrade implies a higher probability of loss on the rated debt. This higher probability of loss will cause the price to fall to a level where the investor is adequately compensated for the additional risk. Probabilities of rating changes in the debt market are found in a ratings transition matrix.

Defaults Moody's publishes a monthly default report, in which it includes a transition matrix based on the latest 12 months of upgrades, downgrades and defaults. From a probabilistic standpoint, defaults can be treated as extreme downgrades and, as such, included in the transition matrix formulation. However, when a debt instrument defaults, its price is no longer tied to general levels of spreads in the market but to the expected recovery rate on that instrument.

Interest Rate Changes Changes in interest rates also contribute to price changes of high yield, fixed-rate bonds. Moody's states that a negative correlation

---

[1] See Joseph Snailer, *Rating Changes in the U.S. Asset-Backed Securities Market: 1999 Second Half Update*, Moody's Investors Service, July 2000.
[2] See Yvonne Falcone and Jeremy Gluck, *Moody's Approach to Rating Market-Value CDOs*, Moody's Investors Service, April 1998.

exists between the general level of interest rates and credit spreads. Interest rate changes may change the cost of the liabilities.

Changes in Investor Preferences Investors may avoid certain sectors of the market if anticipating fundamental shifts in the economy. As a consequence of a change in investors' preferences, debt spreads may widen even in a constant rating and interest rate environment, thus decreasing the value of the collateral.

Moody's also notes that this framework may not well describe the behavior of distressed securities, which are subject to non-systemic price shocks as investors respond to the outcomes of bankruptcy proceedings or the market assesses the value of the distressed firm.

The Portfolio Approach

Moody's employs a portfolio approach in estimating the total risk of a market value deal portfolio. Although individual securities may carry a high degree of risk, a diversified portfolio composed of these securities will be less volatile. An important factor that contributes to portfolio volatility is the degree of correlation among all investments. The amount of return correlation in a portfolio can be estimated by the sensitivity of each investment to general market conditions and interest rates as well as by industry and/or geographic portfolio concentrations. An important aspect of risk estimation is the lack of liquidity for below-investment grade financial assets and especially for distressed securities. Illiquidity is pronounced primarily in distressed markets or when large funds engage in significant portfolio sales, and represents an important element of risk in a market value deal.

How Moody's Measures Portfolio Volatility

Moody's prefers a simulation approach versus an analytic approach to measure portfolio volatility. In the context of a simulation approach, two choices are available: direct and indirect simulation. Indirect simulation consists of generating a time series of the factors that determine portfolio price changes through some analytic formula or empirical relationship. The direct approach, which is the one adopted by Moody's, consists of directly generating asset price movements. This method has the clear advantage of robustness in market downturns, periods during which the factor relationships may not realistically describe the assets' price behavior.

To generate asset price changes, Moody's uses a combination of historical data and parametric simulation (see Exhibit 14). The main emphasis is on the historical data simulation; however, when price history is not available, Moody's will make volatility and correlation assumptions on asset classes and rely on the parametric approach.

To account for lack of data in those instances in which price history is not available, Moody's multiplies returns by a *stress factor* that is a function of the desired tranche rating and the amount of data available on the underlying asset category (see Exhibit 15).

Exhibit 14: Data Sources by Asset Category

Asset Type	Data Source	Period Covered	No. of Assets
High Yield Bonds	Interactive Data Corporation	1982-97	1,500
High Yield Loans	Loan Pricing Corporation	1991-97	213
Distressed Bonds	Moody's Distressed Bond Database	1987-97	470
Distressed Loans	Loan Pricing Corporation	1991-97	106
Distressed Equity	PPM America, Inc.	1992-96	58

From Table 1 (Asset Return Data Sources) in Yvonne Falcone and Jeremy Gluck, *Moody's Approach to Rating Market-Value CDOs*, Moody's Investors Service, Inc., p. 5.
Copyright 1998, Moody's Investors Service, Inc. Used With Permission. This table contains historical information and may not set forth current data.

Exhibit 15: Moody's Investors Service: Stress Factors

Asset Type	B	Ba	Baa	A	Aa	Aaa
Performing Bank Loans	1.4	1.6	1.8	2.0	2.20	2.50
Performing HY Bonds	1.00	1.00	1.10	1.20	1.30	1.40
Distressed Bank Loans	1.05	1.10	1.20	1.30	1.40	1.60
Distressed Bonds	1.00	1.00	1.10	1.20	1.30	1.40
Distressed Equities	1.40	1.50	1.60	1.70	1.80	2.00

From Table 2 (Stress Factors) in Yvonne Falcone and Jeremy Gluck, *Moody's Approach to Rating Market-Value CDOs*, Moody's Investors Service, Inc., p. 5.
Copyright 1998, Moody's Investors Service, Inc. Used With Permission. This table contains historical information and may not set forth current data.

The stress factor will be greater for higher ratings in circumstances when less data is available. Moody's states that a higher stress factor for performing bank loans is fully justified because only a limited number of defaults are observed for bank loans. Moody's analyzes industry correlation based on historical price data. It then selects correlation levels that are lower than the highest correlation recorded in the most stressful periods and higher than the average correlation measured during longer time periods. Since the data is not accurate enough to distinguish between industries, Moody's assumes a constant same industry correlation of 55% and 40% between two different industries.

Another important factor in market value deals is portfolio liquidity, especially for the most distressed assets. Extensive bid-ask spread historical records are not available for this class; thus, Moody's relies on feedback from market practitioners to discount the illiquid assets by a constant set of liquidity "haircuts" (see Exhibit 16).

How Moody's Computes Advance Rates

Similar to cash flow CDOs, Moody's rates market value deals on an expected loss basis. To compute these expected losses, Moody's starts by assuming that the OC test is performed with a certain frequency — for example, biweekly with a cure period that extends for two weeks or ten business days. Therefore, the maximum duration of the period during which the portfolio is subject to market volatility is one month. Moody's assumes that the structure is on the boundary of tripping the OC test at the beginning of the exposure period, which is the most conservative assumption. The simulation is then started by a random selection of price returns from Moody's database. At the end of the exposure period, the total market value of the portfolio is computed and, if insufficient to repay the debt tranche, the tranche will experience a loss. This run is repeated for each month during the entire life of the deal until the portfolio undergoes full liquidation. Expected losses are averages of total losses on all possible simulated outcomes weighted by their respective probabilities.

Moody's assigns a rating to a tranche if the expected loss on the rated tranche is consistent with the historical loss experience of a pool of bonds with the same rating. The most important factors that determine the magnitude of the advance rates are as follows:

Diversification. The higher the degree of diversification in the portfolio, the lower the volatility and, thus, the greater the advance rates, all other factors equal. Moody's stresses the importance of asset diversification with respect to industry concentration limits.

Asset type limitations. In most transactions, an upper limit exists to the total market value in one single asset category. These covenants are generally beneficial and lead to higher advance rates. However, Moody's notes that a stringent set of asset type limitations does not always result in an appreciable increase in advance rates.

Subordination. In a multiple debt tranche deal, a debt tranche can benefit from its seniority to a greater level of subordinated debt and equity, all other factors equal. This increase in credit enhancement also results in higher advance rates.

Exhibit 16: Moody's Investors Service — Liquidity Haircuts by Asset Class

Asset Type	Liquidity Haircut
Performing Bank Loans	7%
Performing High Yield Bonds	5
Distressed Bank Loans	12.5
Distressed Bonds	10
Reorganized Equities/Trade Claims	20

From Table 4 (Liquidity Haircuts) in Yvonne Falcone and Jeremy Gluck, *Moody's Approach to Rating Market-Value CDOs*, Moody's Investors Service, Inc., p. 5.

A minimum net worth test. Higher advance rates can result from a minimum net worth test. This test helps to ensure that the equity receives a minimum fraction of its face value in case of liquidation. The minimum net worth test is usually performed on a quarterly basis and always at frequencies lower than those for the OC tests. Depending on the asset mix, this test can actually be more onerous than the same tranche OC test when the portfolio is comprised of assets with high advance rates.

Other important and more qualitative considerations enter the Moody's rating process. First, Moody's does not assign ratings on the portfolio manager's ability to outperform a series of benchmarks. However, it verifies that the portfolio manager's track record demonstrates a proven ability to deliver solid risk-adjusted returns. Second, the manager should also be supported in credit selection by an experienced team of credit analysts. Third, deal monitoring is an integral part of the management process — in particular, it must value the portfolio as required and calculate the OC tests independently of the trustee. Finally, the marking to market process is particularly important as a large number of investments in market value CDOs (especially in the distressed segment) are thinly quoted or sometimes not quoted by dealers. The risk that other appraisers may overestimate the actual price of illiquid assets is mitigated by the liquidity haircuts that Moody's applies to the collateral asset categories.

Fitch

Fitch's market value CDO rating methodology combines corporate analysis with structural finance techniques.[3] Historically Fitch has been the most active rating agency in market-value deals.

Main Focus

Fitch examines the following areas with particular focus:

1. Assessment of the asset manager
2. Collateral evaluation
3. Structural provision
4. Modeling and stress testing
5. Advance rates versus credit enhancement
6. Legal structure
7. Surveillance

Assessment of Asset Manager Market value CDOs allow portfolio managers to actively trade a diversified pool of assets. Thus, the role of the manager is even more important than in cashflow CDOs, where trading is restricted. Fitch stresses the importance of an experienced portfolio manager with a proven track record at

---

[3] See *Market-Value CBO/CLO Rating Criteria*, Fitch, June 1999.

managing mark-to-market portfolios and an ability to deal with market down-turns. This requirement is not confined to the portfolio manager, but extends to all members of the management team. A team of Fitch analysts interview management teams to ensure that they have the necessary credit and research skills to manage a market value CDO.

Similar to Moody's, Fitch defines as superior performance a series of solid returns on a risk-adjusted basis. This is consistent with other rating agencies, which prefer a consistent performance throughout the life of the deal rather than isolated exceptional returns. Fitch believes that an excessive required amount of diversification may actually hurt the performance of a CDO, as it can force the manager to invest in assets and industries in which he/she is unfamiliar. As evidence, Fitch has analyzed the returns of 17 of the largest high yield mutual funds and demonstrated that funds with higher-than-average industry concentrations have experienced less downside risk than more diversified funds.

Another aspect of Fitch's assessment process is the investment goal. Fitch states that aggressive managers often purchase a higher-risk asset pool, which may lead to boost returns on the manager's financial interest in the fund. The affiliation of CDO management is also taken into consideration. Larger firms often have better execution, wider access to the market and greater legal support.

An excellent track record of an outstanding portfolio manager will not result in Fitch assigning higher advance rates to the structure, but will allow the manager more flexibility in selecting the portfolio assets. Fitch may not rate a deal if the portfolio manager's skills are inadequate and do not fit into a market value CDO structure.

Collateral Evaluation Advance rates and relative OC tests are designed to protect the rated debt from substantial market drops. Fitch examines the historical volatility performance of a set of indices that represent the market behavior in the asset categories found in market value CDO deals (see Exhibit 17).

Exhibit 17: Fitch — Historical Volatility Performance of Asset Categories in Market Value Transactions

Asset Category	Average Price Change	Standard Deviation	Worst Change	Source
High-Yield Bank Loans	0.04%	0.53%	(2.46)%	BT Alex Brown HY Loan Index
BB High Yield Bonds	0.87	1.70	(5.05)	ML HY BB Master Index
Emerging Market Bonds	0.69	6.14	(28.74)	JP Morgan EMBI
Equity	1.16	4.34	(21.76)	S&P 500 Index
Distressed Debt	0.64	4.05	(18.25)	Altman Distressed Bond Index

Market-Value CBO/CLO Rating Criteria, Fitch, June 1999.
Copyright 1999, Fitch. Used With Permission. This table contains historical information and may not set forth current data.

Exhibit 18: Fitch — Stress Factors for
Monthly Market Value Changes

Rating	Stress Factor Multiple
AAA	5.0
AA	4.0
A	3.0
BBB	2.0
BB	1.5
B	1.0

Market-Value CBO/CLO Rating Criteria, Fitch, June 1999.

Other factors that affect the advance rates are liquidity and credit quality of assets. When historical information on an asset class is insufficient, Fitch will apply further discounts to the advance rates in the same respective asset classes. The advance rates are set at the single B rating level to avoid affecting the rated debt's promised return even if the collateral portfolio experiences the worst historical month price change. Exceptions to this rate setting are the equity market and emerging markets, whose stress scenarios are set lower than their worst historical changes.

Fitch applies additional discounts to the advance rates to account for non-systemic risk in the portfolio and lack of liquidity in distressed markets. The advance rates for ratings higher than single B are computed by stressing the worst monthly price changes by a stress factor (see Exhibit 18). Each rated tranche must recoup its principal and interest under a stress factor, which is a multiple of the single B stress scenario and consequent collateral liquidation.

Diversification Requirements Diversification requirements are applied to the collateral portfolio to ensure that the market value stress of the collateral portfolio will capture most of the portfolio risk in a market downturn. If the portfolio is concentrated in only a few names and/or industries, most of the risk will be non-systemic and, thus, not well represented by the behavior of market indices. Some of the most common portfolio limitations in Exhibit 19.

Modeling and Stress Testing Fitch will stress the market value transaction structure using a variety of scenarios ranging from gradual declines in market value over extended periods of time to selective asset price declines. One important scenario consists of recreating the market conditions of the 1998 Asian financial crisis, wherein investors sought out quality credits and bond spreads widened considerably. This stress assumes that all market declines occur simultaneously and that the structure is fully ramped-up. This stress test is repeated for six consecutive months, which will cause OC tests to be triggered. The tests are run for each class to be rated and, upon early prepayment, the class has to receive full and timely interest and principal payments to achieve the desired rating.

Exhibit 19: Fitch — Common Portfolio Limitations

Item	Pct. of Portfolio
Single Largest Issuer	3%-8%
Three Largest Issuers	9-22
Single Largest Industry	15-20
Three Largest Industries	40-45
Total Semi-Liquid and Illiquid Investments	0-25
Total Illiquid Investments	0-15
Total Foreign Issuers	0-35
Total Emerging Market Issuers	0-15

Market-Value CBO/CLO Rating Criteria, Fitch, June 1999.
Copyright 1999, Fitch. Used With Permission. This table contains historical information and may not set forth current data.

Other assumptions made by Fitch in these stress scenarios include the following:

- When OC tests are failed, the lower advance-rate securities are sold and the proceeds are used to buy the highest advance rate assets. This shift in asset mix usually results in a higher average advance rate for the entire portfolio.
- If this shift is unable to cure the failed OC test, the portfolio will be liquidated except for illiquid assets that are held for three months prior to liquidation.
- The minimum net worth test will take place at the latest possible time and force liquidation four months after the beginning of the stress period.
- There is no external infusion of capital into the structure.

If investors elect not to unwind the deal after a minimum net worth test is failed, Fitch may adjust its ratings to reflect the loss of credit protection.

Advance Rates versus Credit Enhancement Market value deals benefit under Fitch's methodology from the presence of an equity cushion in addition to the protection offered by the OC tests. The equity allows the structure to withstand small market corrections without experiencing accelerated prepayment or collateral sales. Fitch, when rating investment grade classes, assumes that the equity cushion is not available and relies solely on the OC test's protection. For all other classes, the protection offered by equity is important and may contribute to a higher rating.

Legal Considerations Some of the most important legal considerations that apply to market value CDOs include the following: (1) bankruptcy remoteness of the issuer; (2) perfection of security interests; and (3) enforcement of party agreements.

Surveillance Market value CDOs require the most accurate and timely monitoring of any other ABS, and include such actions as frequent OC test calculations and portfolio market value reports. Minimum net worth tests as well as audited financial statements on each collateral asset are reported on a quarterly basis.

Standard & Poor's

S&P has developed a quantitative approach to compute advance rates in a market value deal. The main factors are the exposure period during which the collateral is subject to negative market declines before any cure is applied, asset category, issuer and industry concentrations, debt rating, maturity, and the desired rating on the liabilities.[4] S&P uses the following model to calculate advance rates:

- an analytical return volatility model to adjust for issuer and industry concentrations
- a volatility model to adjust for duration
- a binomial default model for default risk
- a liquidity spread model

Advance Rates

S&P focuses on advance rates and a clear definition of exposure periods. The agency relies on portfolio theory to compute the market value deal advance rates — namely, the result that states that the more diversified portfolio, the lower the total risk of the collateral portfolio.

Price volatility is the single most important factor in S&P's methodology of determining advance rates. The higher the volatility, the lower the advance rates. Other important factors from a collateral portfolio standpoint are the asset type, target mix, maturity, coupon, and rating as well as the mark-to-market frequency of each asset. On the liabilities side, an important factor is the desired rating on the debt.

Exposure Period

S&P stresses the importance of clearly defining a market value CDO deal's exposure period. This period is defined as the number of business days between the last valuation date on which the OC tests were satisfied and the liquidation date. The exposure period consists of two periods: the mark-to-market period and the cure period. For example, if assets are marked to market every two weeks and the cure period lasts two weeks, then the exposure period is 20 business days or four weeks. Quantifying the exposure period is key in S&P's methodology, because it defines the time span during which the portfolio can be subject to market declines before the portfolio manager is forced to cure the structure due to OC failure.

---

[4] See Erkan Erturk and Soody Nelson, *Structured Market-Value Transactions: A Quantitative Enhancement Approach*, Standard & Poor's, August 1999.

Exhibit 20: Standard & Poor's —
Data Sources by Asset Category

Asset Class	Source	Period Covered
High-Yield Bond	Merrill Lynch HY US	1988-98
Distressed Bond	Altman Distressed Public Bond Index	1987-97
Emerging Markets Bond	JP Morgan EMBI	1991-98
Bank Loan	Loan Pricing Corporation	1991-93
Public Equity	S&P 400, S&P 500 and S&P 600	1984-98

Erkan Erturk and Soody Nelson, *Structured Market-Value Transactions: A Quantitative Enhancement Approach*, Standard & Poor's, August 1999.
Copyright 1999, Standard & Poor's Corporation. Used With Permission. This table contains historical information and may not set forth current data.

Exhibit 21: Standard & Poor's Corporation —
Data Sources by Asset Class

Asset Class	Source	Standard Deviation
High-Yield Bond	Merrill Lynch HY US BB Rated	1.13%
High-Yield Bond	Merrill Lynch HY US B Rated	1.71
High-Yield Bond	Merrill Lynch HY US C Rated	2.73
Distressed Bond	Altman Distressed Public Bond Index	3.58
Emerging Markets Bond	JP Morgan EMBI	4.13
Public Equity	S&P 500	4.41

Erkan Erturk and Soody Nelson, *Structured Market-Value Transactions: A Quantitative Enhancement Approach*, Standard & Poor's, August 1999.
Copyright 1999, Standard & Poor's Corporation. Used With Permission. This table contains historical information and may not set forth current data.

Data
To estimate risk in a market value CDO portfolio, S&P relies on the historical information provided by a series of broad indices based on similar asset categories (see Exhibit 20).

Risk Components and Methodology
S&P divides the total portfolio risk into three major risk components: market risk, default risk, and liquidity risk. Both default risk and liquidity risk are considered part of the non-systemic risk of the portfolio.

Market risk is defined as the worst loss that can be experienced by the portfolio over an exposure period's time. To estimate this loss, the historical performance of the broad indices is used. The market risk is further defined by S&P into the following: (1) interest rate risk; (2) credit spread risk from factors other than rating migration; (3) credit spread risk due to rating migration; and (4) liquidity risk in normal market conditions.

The monthly standard deviations shown in Exhibit 21 are computed from all indices during the periods listed in Exhibit 20. S&P believes that these standard deviations do not adequately represent the risk present in a market value CDO portfolio.

To reproduce a more realistic behavior of the portfolio, S&P makes two volatility adjustments — one to adjust for duration to create the same duration characteristics between the index and the portfolio; and the second adjustment consists of changing the index volatility to take into account the issuer and industry concentrations.

Default Risk S&P models default risk assuming that the ratings on the debt and the issuer are identical. The agency believes that a portion of the default risk component is not described by price volatility. To estimate this risk component, S&P uses a binomial distribution to describe the default event.

Liquidity Risk Liquidity risk can manifest itself as wider bid-ask spreads, market segmentation and investors' flight to quality. S&P has developed a bid-ask spread model for the high yield market that captures liquidity risk in relevant market downturns as a function of the change in yield of the 30-year-Treasury bond and return on equity. The bid-ask spread on bank loans under a forced liquidation scenario is collected from market participants. Liquidity risk for equity assets is assumed to be fully embedded in the equity index price volatility.

Total Risk S&P determines advance rates by the total risk of each asset in the collateral portfolio. This risk is the sum of market, liquidity and default risk. The market risk represents risk in normal market conditions, while default and liquidity risk account for risk in sharp market declines.

Advance Rates S&P believes that bank loans have higher advance rates than high yield bonds, a view with which we concur as losses on loan portfolios are lower than their public debt counterparts. Loans are subject to frequent monitoring and are almost insensitive to interest rate changes. High yield bonds have lower advance rates as their rating decreases. Advance rates are lower when the duration of the portfolio is longer and as the rating sought on the debt increases. Finally, advance rates will increase as the exposure period is reduced.

Chapter 4

CDO Structure and Arbitrage

Laurie S. Goodman, Ph.D.
Managing Director
UBS Warburg

Both the *pattern* of CDO issuance (such as heavy or light volume, or which type of collateral dominates) as well as the *configuration* of completed deals (are there AA or A rated tranches, or simply a larger AAA and BBB class) are dictated to a large degree by CDO arbitrage. In this chapter, we first show how to look at the CDO arbitrage, and provide a "quick and dirty" analysis for benchmarking activity levels. We then focus on how the arbitrage dictates deal structure. Spread configurations and the exact collateral used are important in determining optimal deal structure. Yet when investors are looking at the merits of one deal versus another, they often look at percent subordination or percent overcollateralization as an arbiter of tranche quality. But in fact, since the arbitrage often dictates deal structure, these measures may communicate little bout tranche quality *per se*.

BUILDING BLOCKS

In a CDO, asset purchases are financed by a combination of liabilities plus equity. The "arb" exists when those assets can be purchased, and the liabilities sold, with enough left over to provide a competitive return to equity holders. Mortgage market participants recognize this exercise for what it is — a kissing cousin to the collateralized mortgage obligations (CMO) arbitrage.

Like the CMO arbitrage, in any intended CDO arbitrage sample structures are always run to determine when this arb is "close." Dealers then act on those results to optimize deal structure so as to increase the likelihood that the deal can actually be executed. Let's look at some simplified examples of "arb" runs for bond and loan deals, then at how these deals can be fine-tuned to somewhat improve the arb's attractiveness.

Early Sketches

The basis for the arb is the "crude run." No, that doesn't mean sloshing around in unrefined oil. Where we're going, and what we look for, is whether or not return-on-equity is anywhere near the actual level needed to be attractive to potential equity buyers.

To calculate the "arb," dealers run the assets and liabilities through a large structuring model. These models first compute the period-by-period returns to the equity holders, and then calculate the internal rate of return of the equity cash flows. These models gives the underwriting dealer, working with the CDO manager, considerable flexibility in optimizing capital structure. For example, higher quality assets can be used. In that case, overcollateralization levels are lower, and less equity is necessary to support the deal. Or BB rated notes can be used in lieu of equity capital which, in turn, increases overall leverage. Greater asset diversity can be substituted for equity capital. Spreads, prices, and coupons of the assets and liabilities also play a role in determining the required amount of capital over which the excess return must be spread.

However, to compute whether or not any "arb" is close, we do not need a complex CDO structuring model. Any hand calculator, plus a dose of common sense, will do.

To illustrate our point, we use a very generic CBO deal (Exhibit 1). The assets in this representative deal consist of high-yield bonds purchased at par and with a yield equal to the yield (to worst) on the Merrill Lynch Cash pay index (which was 12.32% as of June 5, 2000). Our generic deal's $425 million of liabilities consist of $350 million senior notes paying LIBOR + 40, plus $75 million of BBB-rated mezzanine notes at LIBOR + 200. Deal structure is supported by $75 million in equity. To be realistic, we also assumed 2% in up-front expenses, and on-going expenses of 70 basis points/year.

The CBO Arb

Now look at the CBO arbitrage as of 6/5/00 (in the last column of Exhibit 1). After deleting 2% in up-front expenses from our $500 million amount, $490 million ($500 million × 0.98) remains to be invested. These assets earn 12.32%, or a total of $60,368,000, per year. We also assumed asset defaults of 3% and recoveries of 50%; so we subtracted 1.5% per year, or $7,350,000 per year, from total asset returns. Thus our initial $500 million of assets generates a return of $53,018,000 after that 1.5% loss.

We then subtracted the cost of the LIBOR-indexed liabilities. That cost would be understated, and hence, the returns to equity overstated, if we based the cost of the liabilities on current LIBOR rates. (That's because current LIBOR is lower than forward LIBOR, as the market is expecting LIBOR to be higher over the life of the note than is reflected in current rates.)

So we sidestepped that problem by using swap rates for the appropriate maturity. In our case, we used the 7.33% fixed rate on the 7.5 year swaps plus 40 basis points as the cost of the Class A notes (which is equal to 7.73%); and the 7.32% 10-year swap rate plus 200 basis points as the cost of the Class B notes (which is equal to 9.42%). Note that with the swap curve so flat, tenor assumptions are immaterial to the results. Anyway, the cost of the Class A note thus becomes [($350,000,000 of Class A notes) × (0.0773 cost)] = $27,041,525. The cost of the B Notes is [($75,000,000 of Class B notes) × (0.0932 cost)] = $6,991275.

Exhibit 1: CBO Arbitrage, 1st Half, 2000

	($M)
Assets	500,000,000
Class A Notes	350,000,000
Class B Notes	75,000,000
Equity	75,000,000
Upfront Expenses	2.0%
Investable Assets	490,000,000
Losses	1.5%
Expenses	0.7%

Date	1/31/00	2/29/00	3/31/00	4/30/00	5/31/00	6/5/00
High Yld Index	11.20%	11.31%	11.82%	12.15%	12.44%	12.32%
Class A Note Spread	55	50	46	45	42	40
Class B Note Spread	250	240	235	225	215	200
7.5-yr Swap Yield	7.49%	7.39%	7.29%	7.42%	7.63%	7.33%
10-yr Swap Yield	7.52%	7.43%	7.29%	7.41%	7.64%	7.32%
Class A Note Yield	8.04%	7.89%	7.75%	7.87%	8.05%	7.73%
Class B Note Yield	10.02%	9.83%	9.64%	9.66%	9.79%	9.32%

Arbitrage

Date	1/31/00	2/29/00	3/31/00	4/30/00	5/31/00	6/5/00
Gross Return on Assets	54,894,700	55,428,800	57,898,400	59,544,800	60,951,100	60,368,000
Losses	7,350,000	7,350,000	7,350,000	7,350,000	7,350,000	7,350,000
Net Return Assets	47,544,700	48,078,800	50,548,400	52,194,800	53,601,100	53,018,000
Cost of Class A Notes	28,147,525	27,599,775	27,113,100	27,557,425	28,187,600	27,041,525
Cost of Class B Notes	7,518,300	7,371,150	7,226,400	7,246,350	7,339,950	6,991,275
Expenses	3,430,000	3,430,000	3,430,000	3,430,000	3,430,000	3,430,000
Total Cost & Expenses	39,095,825	38,400,925	37,769,500	38,233,775	38,957,550	37,462,800
$ Return to Equity	8,448,875	9,677,875	12,778,900	13,961,025	14,643,550	15,555,200
% Yield on Equity	11.27%	12.90%	17.04%	18.61%	19.52%	20.74%

We added to these two costs the 70 basis points of expenses ($490,000,000 × 0.007) = $3,430,000. Thus total cost of the liabilities plus expenses equals $37,462,800. That leaves $15,555,200 as a dollar return-to-equity. Dividing that return by our example's $75,000,000 of equity delivers an equity yield of 20.74%.

Caveats

This is obviously a very basic calculation for the following reasons.

1. the bonds are usually not purchased at par (most are at a discount).
2. losses don't kick in immediately (as we assumed).
3. this is a one-period calculation, a simple simulation of returns we have not taken into account any asset pay-down schedule.

4. we have not assumed any ramp-up period (versus typical ramp-ups of 2-4 months).
5. we overlooked the possibility of hitting some deal triggers, even at 3% defaults (which would cause automatic deleveraging).
6. once a manager is selected, a deal gets fine-tuned to fit that firm's style and then-current market appetites for alternative liability structures (return-to-equity may rise or drop).
7. the calculation ignores the cost to the equity holders of deleveraging.

Consequently, approximate equity returns estimated in this fashion should be regarded as a very basic estimate of actual equity returns.

Changes Over Time

Applying the crude arbitrage calculator detailed above to the month of June 2000 suggests an equity return of 20.74%. That's certainly quite attractive both in absolute terms, as well as relative to other equity alternatives (such as public or private equity). In fact, when equity return is above 15% via this simple calculation, CBO structurers know that it pays to look more closely at whether structural changes can be made to make the CBO more attractive. If the "quick and dirty" analysis indicates a return lower than 15%, then that's generally a fruitless exercise. Of course, as detailed above, this calculation is certainly not omniscient, nor perfect. But it is certainly indicative.

Now let's move back to the then-current market scenario in the first quarter of 2000. Issuance was much more limited at that point, and was mostly concentrated in CLOs. At the end of January 2000, the yield-to-worst on the high-yield index was 11.20% (which was 112 basis points lower than on 6/5/00). The cost of liabilities was also higher in January 2000, as well. Class A notes required a yield of LIBOR + 55, while the cost on the Class B notes was LIBOR + 250. On a swapped basis, the Class A notes yielded 8.04% (that's 31 basis points higher than June 2000's 7.73% level). Meanwhile, the Class B notes yielded 10.02% (70 basis points higher than June's level of 9.32%). Thus the lower yield on the assets and a higher cost of the liabilities only delivered a dollar return to equity of $8,448,875. Dividing that gross amount by the $75 million (of equity) provided an equity return of only 11.27% (as seen in Exhibit 1). That is obviously not at all attractive. It also suggests that high-yield deals were quite non-economic in January 2000 — which, in fact, they were.

Ebbs and Flows

As can also be seen in Exhibit 1, the CBO arb became increasingly more attractive during the first half of 2000. Yields on high-yield bonds increased over that period, and the cost of the liabilities declined. In February, the return-on-equity was 12.90%. It then rose to 17.04% in March, 18.61% in April, 19.52% in May, reaching 20.74% (shown above) in June.

Intuitively, since equity is a levered investment, an increase in asset yield or a decrease in liability costs magnifies, gears, or levers, the impact of that specific change. *Equity returns benefit the most from an increased return on the assets.* Each 1 basis point rise in asset yield increases return-on-equity in our example by 6.53 times (490/75). So the 112 basis point rise in asset yields from January to June of 2000 increased equity yields by 732 basis points (6.53 × 112).

Correspondingly, each 1 basis point drop in liability cost in our example increases returns on equity by 4.67 times (350/75). Hence the 31 basis point drop in the cost of the liabilities added another 145 basis points to the equity return (31 × 4.67). Finally, each 1 basis point drop in the Class B notes increases the return-on-equity by an amount equal to that drop in costs (75/75). Thus, the 70 basis points drop in the cost of the Class B notes added another 70 basis points to the equity return.

Adding it all up within our simple approximation, the arb in June 2000 should look 946 basis points (732 + 144 + 70) better than it did in January 2000, based on changes in the component parts (costs and returns). That's actually quite close to the market's real life return-on-equity improvement of 947 basis points (20.74% − 11.27%).

And The CLO Arb?

The improvement in the CLO arb in the first half of calendar year 2000 has been less dramatic (as shown in Exhibit 2). We again set up a generic bank loan deal, sized at $500 million in assets. However, the capital structure differs from our earlier bond deal. In that prior deal, we had assumed $375 million Class A notes plus $75 million Class B notes plus $50 million capital. A lower capital requirement from the rating agencies stems from the fact that bank loans are often secured, and have much higher recovery rates than do high yield bonds.

Calendar year 2000 loan spreads were consistent at about LIBOR + 315 basis points. "Loan yield" converts this to a fixed rate, which is constructed by adding in the rate payable on a 10-year swap (7.32%). June's asset yield thus becomes 10.57%. We then assumed defaults are the same 3% (as on high-yield assets in our CBO deal example), but that recoveries would be higher, at 75%. Thus losses become 0.75% (= 3.0% × 0.25) per annum. We assumed liability costs identical to those on the CBO at LIBOR + 40 on the AAA rated notes, with a 7.73% yield; and LIBOR + 200 on the BBB-rated notes, for a 9.32% yield. We also assumed identical up-front expenses of 2% and ongoing expenses of 70 basis points. Based on these levels, Exhibit 2 shows that as of June 5, 2000, return to the $50 million in capital would have been 17.46%.

Some Tides Turn Slowly

The CLO arbitrage improved somewhat during the first half of calendar year 2000, but not nearly as dramatically as did the CBO arbitrage. The return-to-equity on our representative CBO was 16.03% in January 2000. But by June, that return had risen to 17.46%. That improvement stems from reduction in the cost of liabilities. The Class A notes tightened 15 basis points (from LIBOR + 55 to LIBOR + 40), while the BBB rated notes tightened by 50 basis points (from LIBOR + 250 to LIBOR + 200.)

Exhibit 2: CLO Arbitrage, 1st Half, 2000

	($M)
Assets	500,000,000
Class A Notes	375,000,000
Class B Notes	75,000,000
Equity	50,000,000
Upfront Expenses	2.0%
Investable Assets	490,000,000
Losses	0.75%
Expenses	0.7%

Date	1/31/00	2/29/00	3/31/00	4/30/00	5/31/00	6/5/00
Loan Spread	3.25%	3.25%	3.25%	3.25%	3.25%	3.25%
Loan Yield	10.77%	10.68%	10.54%	10.66%	10.89%	10.57%
Class A Note Spread	55	50	46	45	42	40
Class B Note Spread	250	240	235	225	215	200
7.5-yr Swap Yield	7.49%	7.39%	7.29%	7.42%	7.63%	7.33%
10-yr Swap Yield	7.52%	7.43%	7.29%	7.41%	7.64%	7.32%
Class A Note Yield	8.04%	7.89%	7.75%	7.87%	8.05%	7.73%
Class B Note Yield	10.02%	9.83%	9.64%	9.66%	9.79%	9.32%

Arbitrage

Date	1/31/00	2/29/00	3/31/00	4/30/00	5/31/00	6/5/00
Gross Return on Assets	52,794,560	52,323,180	51,622,480	52,242,820	53,344,340	51,801,330
Losses	3,675,000	3,675,000	3,675,000	3,675,000	3,675,000	3,675,000
Net Return Assets	49,119,560	48,648,180	47,947,480	48,567,820	49,669,340	48,126,330
Cost of Class A Notes	30,158,063	29,571,188	29,049,750	29,525,813	30,201,000	28,973,063
Cost of Class B Notes	7,518,300	7,371,150	7,226,400	7,246,350	7,339,950	6,991,275
Expenses	3,430,000	3,430,000	3,430,000	3,430,000	3,430,000	3,430,000
Total Cost & Expenses	41,106,363	40,372,338	39,706,150	40,202,163	40,970,950	39,394,338
$ Return to Equity	8,013,198	8,275,842	8,241,330	8,365,657	8,698,390	8,731,992
% Yield on Equity	16.03%	16.55%	16.48%	16.73%	17.40%	17.46%

It's quite interesting to compare Exhibits 1 and 2. The disparity is the difference in asset behavior — high-yield spreads widened in the first half of 2000, while spreads to LIBOR were roughly constant for loan deals. As a result, the CBO arbitrage improved dramatically, while the CLO arbitrage improved much less.

Activity levels bear this out. In January and February of 2000, it was difficult to do CBO deals (since return-on-equity was too low to be appealing). For example, the total volume of deals rated by Moody's in the first quarter of 2000 was $5.63 billion. Most of those were CLOs (backed exclusively by loans) or CDOs (backed primarily by loans). Few CBOs were involved. By contrast, in the second quarter of 2000, Moody's rated over $15 billion in deals, the majority of which were backed primarily by bond collateral. This reflected the fact that return-to-equity was higher on the high-yield bond deals than on the loan deals.

Exhibit 3: Effect Of Increasing Leverage

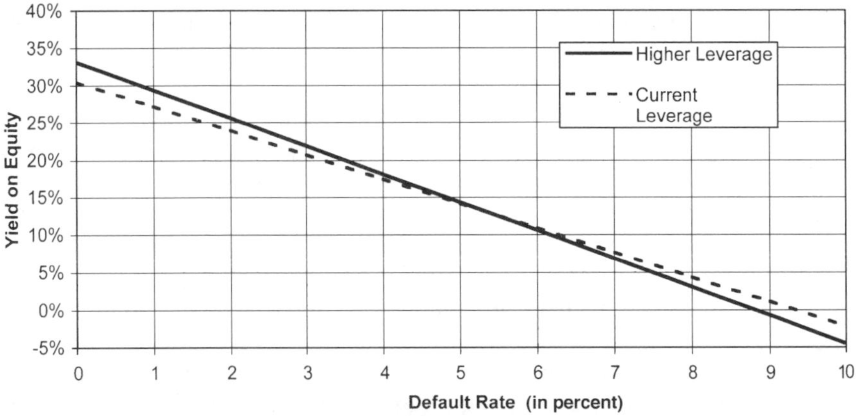

Improving the Arb

Now we know what's driving the arbitrage. And once a deal is "close," structurers can tinker and nudge it closer to the needs of equity buyers. Trade-offs can be made between leverage, the level of overcollateralization for triggering tests, asset quality, liability ratings, diversity, as well as acquisition prices and coupons. There's actually quite a basketful of structuring nuances.

Certainly, one of the ways to increase the potential equity return is to expand leverage. Greater leverage heightens yield responsiveness of the assets to default rates. To show this, we first computed yield responsiveness of our representative CBO deal (that detailed in Exhibit 1, a CBO with 15% equity, based on $75 million equity within a $500 million deal). We used June 2000 data for the calculations. The dotted line in Exhibit 3 shows the yield profile for CBO equity in our representative 15% equity deal. Note that at 3% defaults, the equity return is 20.74% (That's exactly the same number as in Exhibit 1.) At default rates below 3%, return-to-equity is greater; at higher default rates, equity returns are lower.

To assess the effects of higher leverage, we then decreased equity capital by $10 million (to $65 million) and introduced $10 million of BB rated notes (coupon of LIBOR + 550). The resultant structure has 13% equity plus 2% BB rated notes. We also recomputed return-on-equity at different default rates. Thus, as shown by the solid line in Exhibit 3 (at 3% defaults) return-to-equity is 21.84% in this "high leverage" deal. By contrast, it is 33.15% at 0% defaults and 3.00% at 8% defaults.

Effect of Higher Leverage

It is useful to compare results of an "average leverage" deal with what might evolve from one more highly levered. The net effect is that more highly leveraged deals have steeper return profiles. In our simple analysis, at default levels below

5%-6%, the more highly levered equity piece yields more; while at default levels above 5%-6%, it yields less. Specifically, at 0% defaults, a deal with "average" leverage only returns 30.44%, while that with higher leverage throws off 33.15%. At 9% defaults, the average leverage deal generates 1.04%, while the deal with high leverage yields −0.77%.

In point of fact, this analysis is too kind to the more highly geared deal. The deal with greater leverage would also have tighter overcollateralization levels, which would also hit the triggers sooner and thus de-lever more quickly. So overall, that would create a far more negative impact on returns than shown in Exhibit 3. (Remember, we used a simple one-period analysis, and ignored trigger events.)

Rating agencies ultimately dictate capital structure supportable within a deal's parameters. Any increase in leverage, all other factors constant, reduces protection for the rated classes. Therefore, any such higher leverage must be accompanied by raising the quality of assets, or by tightening overcollaterization. The latter is done by decreasing the level of overcollaterization necessary to trigger a de-leveraging.

Gauging Activity Levels

To create a CDO, two conditions are necessary. First, the arbitrage must be favorable. Second, CDO assets must be available.

Our basic calculation allows rated note buyers to gauge how favorable the CDO arbitrage is. Then, one needs to consider asset availability so as to figure activity levels. In June 2000 (at the time this chapter was written), the current return-to-equity was very attractive, as evidenced by our sample deals, and collateral was readily available. It was no surprise that there were a dozen new deals in the market.

IMPACT OF CDO ARBITRAGE ON STRUCTURE

Many decisions made in the CDO structuring process are a function of "the arb." If certain classes are more expensive than combinations of other classes, those classes more expensive are less apt to be created. The output of such structuring decisions will be bonds with different characteristics.

We make this point by looking at trade-offs inherent in deal structures. We show that greater subordination and more overcollateralization, can, at times, result in greater extension risk. It is very important for investors to examine an entire deal structure in light of their portfolio objectives.

Rules of CDO Deal Structuring

Following are two rules of CDO structuring. Rule #1 is never leave money on the table! That's un-American, to boot. If (all things being equal) a deal structure can support 80% AAA rated bonds, it is unlikely that any issuer will construct that deal with 78% AAA rated bonds. So if two tranches of different deals (both rated

AAA by the same rating agency) are in the market simultaneously — then it is likely that both contain the maximum amount of AAA bonds supportable by their structures. If one deal carries a higher percent of AAAs, then trade-offs were made elsewhere in the structure.

Rule #2 is optimize deal structure. It's survival of the fittest out there. Issuers try various deal structures, and come up with one or two that look the "best." (Structurers' trashcans generally overflow with print-outs of trials failed 'cause they were "non-optimal.") Optimal structure in CDOs is that for which each of the rated notes can receive a market-determined interest rate, with IRR maximized on the equity piece. If one dealer structures an equity return of 17% while another offers 18% off the same collateral at similar leverage then an investor will clearly run, not walk, to that higher return.

Interest Costs Drive Subordination

We now look at how the CDO arbitrage and current spread configuration dictates structure. Note that many investors (particularly at the AAA level) look at percent subordination as an indicator of protection. While it is certainly one such bellwether, it should not be used as the be-all and end-all. In fact, Rules #1 and #2 above are so powerful that if two tranches are created at the same time with the same rating, there is unlikely to be any strict dominance of one over the other.

Exhibit 4 displays five different structures, using typical combinations of mortgage-related collateral (ABS, MBS, CMBS, and REITs). The first three (labeled Deals "A," "B," and "C") are backed by exactly the same collateral. The cost of that collateral was assumed to be $97.88 (which includes the CMBS IO that is often included in these deals). The diversity score is 17 (also very typical of mortgage deals), and the weighted average rating factor is 345 (corresponds to the BBB level). The WAC on the collateral is 8.30% (again, including the effects of the CMBS IO).

Exhibit 4: Structuring Tradeoffs

	Liability	Deal				
	Spread	A	B	C	D	E
Principal Face		300	300	300	310	310
Total Cost		97.88	97.88	97.88	94.70	94.70
Rating Factor		345	345	345	320	320
WAC		8.30%	8.30%	8.30%	7.45%	7.45%
AAA	L+50	86.67%	86.67%	76.67%	70.30%	70.30%
AA	L+90	—	—	11.67%	17.25%	17.58%
A-	L+150	9.00%	—	7.33%	—	6.92%
BBB	L+250	—	10.83%	—	7.89%	—
BB	T+700	1.67%	—	1.67%	4.56%	5.21%
Equity		2.67%	2.50%	2.67%	—	—
Min AAA I/C Required		122	122	144	120	120
Min AAA O/C Required		110	110	128	130	130
Equity Yield		17.09%	17.24%	15.69%	NA	NA

In Deal A, liabilities were tranched into AAA, A−, BB rated notes and equity, proportioned 86.67%, 9.0%, 1.67%, and 2.67%, respectively. Note that this structure maximized the amount of AAA rated notes permitted (shown in the middle section of Exhibit 4). The bottom part of the exhibit shows that after paying a liability holder the spreads shown separately in Exhibit 4, the return-to-equity (assuming no defaults) is 17.09%.

Deal B has essentially the same structure. The only difference is that the A− and BB amounts are collapsed into a BBB class. Equity yield then expands to 17.24%, although that's not all that much different from Deal A's 17.09%.

In Deal C we recarved the AAA and A− cash flows into AAA, AA, and A− rated notes, holding constant the amounts of BB and equity. This structure would be considered sub-optimal, as return-to-equity drops to 15.69%, versus Deal A's 17.09%. No matter how gifted a salesperson is, they would *not* be able to sell equity at this level.

Anyway, the reason the "arb" is much less attractive in Deal C is due to the spread configuration. The deals shifted 10% of the AAA rated bonds (paying LIBOR + 50) and 1.67% of the A− bonds (paying LIBOR + 150) into the AA bucket (which pays LIBOR + 90). That raised our interest costs 25.7 basis points on 11.67% of the deal. By the way, note that there is a relative value implication here — the AA rated bonds are quite attractively priced.

Don't Look Exclusively at Subordination

You are a buyer of AAA rated paper. You are trying to decide between the bond in Deal A or that in Deal C. Which should you want in your portfolio? At first glance, the one in Deal C looks "better" because of its 23.23% subordination, rather than the 13.67% subordination in Deal A. Furthermore, the minimum I/C and O/C levels are much higher for Deal C's AAA rated bond.

But don't forget that according to Rule #1, you should "never leave money on the table." Each of the deals has already maximized the amount of AAA bonds that can be created in that structure. Thus, rating agencies consider the bonds roughly equivalent.

Many believe Deal C could never be worse than Deal A. That is wrong. The application-of-cash waterfall typically pours collateral interest and principal cash flow into AA interest payments prior to paying any AAA principal. More precisely, rating agencies will not allow a AA rated class to defer interest payments. However, if defaults are very high, cash flows in the deal will be lower. Thus, Deal C's AAA rated notes are more likely to extend than are Deal A's. Intuitively, an additional 40 basis points of interest on 10% of the deal plus the entire interest payment on 1.67% of the deal is "earmarked" to pay the AA rated noteholders, who are ahead in line of the AAA rated notes in getting principal back.

Collateral is an Important Determinant of Structure

Besides the rate configuration, type of collateral is another important determinant of the deal arbitrage and the resulting structure. We assume Deals D and E in

Exhibit 4 are backed by low dollar price collateral (with a lower WAC). This enabled more overcollateralization and less interest coverage. Thus for the same investment as in Deal A, we could buy $310 million of collateral, rather than $300 million. In Deal A we had $300 million par of collateral, at a price of $97.88, for a total investment of $293.64 million. In Deals D and E, for the same $293.64 million investment, we bought $310 million of collateral at an average price of $94.7.

This cash flow structure which utilizes collateral selling at a large discount to par lends itself to a different liability structure. Given the level of overcollaterization on the deal, no equity tranche was necessary. That's because the deal can take $10 million in losses (3%) and still pay par to the bottom (BB) tranches.[1] Assuming recoveries at 45%, then 3% losses translate into defaults of 5.5% (3/0.55). And that's an incredibly high number for BBB rated collateral.

Investors should be aware that the BB rating addresses the return of principal and a stated rate of interest. This stated rate of interest (the coupon) will generally be less than the market rate of interest in the tranche. For example, in Deals D and E, we used an 8% coupon on the BB tranche, and the bond was rated with respect to the return of principal and the 8% coupon. The coupon on this tranche is low because the BB bond serves as the equity in the deal. Like a traditional equity tranche, the BB tranche has some upside, which is not taken into account in the rating. If the deal does exceptionally well, the BB tranche captures that upside.

Moreover, both Deal D and Deal E have a relatively low percentage of AAAs (70.30%). Deal D has AAs, BBBs, and BBs, while Deal E has AAs, A–s, and BBs. The choice between the two depends on where each of the bonds can be sold.

The reason there are so few AAAs in Deals D and E is that the interest cash flow is very limited, as the WAC on the deal is 7.45%. Thus, interest cash flows in Deals D and E are roughly 90% of what they were in Deal A.

Now, remember that collateral cannot be liquidated to pay AAA interest. But if the deal can't pay the AAAs on time, those AAA holders can vote to sell deal assets to protect their interest. Thus, to protect other noteholders, the amount of AAAs is very limited.

Are all AAAs Equal?

In deciphering which AAA is better, it is clear that Deals D and E have substantially greater overcollateralization. So most investors would automatically assert that either deal's AAA is "better" than the AAA rated note in Deal A. But in reality, this is not all that clear.

Deal A has a substantial amount of excess cash flow from interest payments, which could be applied to the AAA principal. By contrast, rising defaults in Deals D and E might absorb excess interest entirely. Deals D and E would then turn to principal redemption to delever the transaction.

---

[1] losses = defaults × (1 − the recovery rate).

Let's look at some numbers. Deal A begins life with 115% overcollateralization at the AAA level. For the first year, there's $25 million total interest inflow, and $19.5 million AAA interest outflow. Thus after paying the AAAs, net interest cash flow is $5.5 million. For Deal E, with 143% initial O/C, total interest inflow is $23.1 million and the AAA and AA interest outflow is $20.6 million. Thus net interest cash flow, after paying the AAAs and AAs is only $2.5 million. (Recall that the waterfall requires that the AA rated bonds must receive all their interest in each period before the AAA rated bonds receive any principal return.) That makes for an interest cushion difference of $3.0 ($5.5 − $2.5) million. And that $3 million excess cash flow can be applied to pay down AAA principal, giving the AAA tranche in Deal A much less potential for extension risk.

CONCLUSION

In this chapter we have shown that the CDO arbitrage is the key to CDO transactions. And the arbitrage calculations also shown in this chapter allow investors to gauge activity levels. Those activity levels are especially crucial to equity buyers and to CBO managers.

Equity buyers need check the equity returns pitched by an investment bank. If that return is materially different from what you figure on your hand calculator — investors should find out what assumptions are being made about the structure, and be very sure that they are comfortable with those.

Additionally, these arbitrage calculations allow potential CBO managers to determine when they really want to press to get a deal done. Marginal arbitrage may portend that it's better to sit tight and await better timing. And deal performance is certainly important to any deal manager. It impacts future deals, plus a manager's own pocket is directly impacted, in that they typically retain a large chunk of the equity.

The CDO arbitrage is also a major determinant of deal structure. We have shown how different spread configurations and different collateral can make for very different deal structures. That is, deals are generally optimized to maximize returns to equity holders, while making sure to pay rated note holders their appropriate market levels. Yet with very dissimilar deal structures, investors are unable to figure relative value simply by looking exclusively at subordination in a deal, or exclusively at the amount of overcollateralization. That's because the benefits of higher subordination can be offset, depending on the waterfall rules. And the benefits of higher overcollaterization can be offset by lower interest coverage ratios.

Net — since deal structures have been optimized, there are always trade-offs. Investors need to be fully aware of those choices they are implicitly making.

Chapter 5

Emerging Market CBOs

Laurie S. Goodman, Ph.D.
Managing Director
UBS Warburg

Many portfolio managers have invested a substantial amount of time and energy in understanding CBO structures. Most have become comfortable with CBO deals backed by both high-yield bonds and bank loans. However, these same portfolio managers are still quite uneasy about any CBO backed primarily by sovereign emerging markets bonds, as they believe that all emerging market debt is tainted by high default experience.

In this chapter, we shed some light on the differences (that matter) between emerging markets and high-yield deals. The picture that "emerges' (pun intended!) may surprise you — positively, that is — for the following reasons:

- There have actually been few defaults on U.S. dollar denominated sovereign Emerging Market (EM) bonds. The negative bias of many investors against EM CBOs is because they do not fully appreciate the differences between EM sovereign bank loans and EM sovereign bonds.

- Rating agencies are far more conservative in their assumptions when rating emerging markets deals than in rating high-yield deals, as performance data on EM bonds is far more limited. So there's an extra credit cushion already built into comparable credit levels.

- EM CBOs generally provide much greater structural protection, as the average portfolio credit quality is higher, resulting in a lower probability of default on the underlying portfolio. Subordination on EM deals is also much higher, hence the equity itself is much less leveraged.

We discuss each of these points in turn. Indeed, we believe that EM CBOs are no more risky than high-yield CBOs, and the rated debt often yields much more.

EM SOVEREIGN BOND DEFAULTS

EM debt has developed a bad rap. This tainted reputation stems from the fact that many potential investors do not distinguish between EM sovereign foreign currency bank loans and sovereign foreign currency bonds. In fact, the historical record on EM sovereign foreign currency bonds is very favorable. Sovereigns are far more likely to default on foreign currency bank loans than on foreign currency bond debt.

Let's look at the asset record, recently compiled in a Standard and Poor's study released in December 1999, which covers both public and private debt.[1] Exhibit 1 shows that out of a universe of 201 sovereign issuers, 13.9% of the issuers are currently in default. This includes defaults on foreign currency debt (both bank loans and bonds) as well as in local currency debt. Note that 11.9% of the issuers are in default within the category of total foreign currency debt (which includes both bank loans and bonds). But a separate break-out of just the sovereign foreign currency bonds indicates that most of these issuers are in default only on their bank loans. In fact, Column (6) of Exhibit 1 shows that in 1999 only 2.5% of the issuers were in default on their foreign currency bonds! Note that the 2.5% default on foreign currency bonds is even lower than the 3.5% default on local currency debt.

This 2.5% default rate amounts to only five issuers out of 201 issuers (sovereign borrowers). They consist of Ecuador, Ukraine, the former Yugoslavia, Pakistan, and Russia.[2] Ecuador was the only new issuer to default in 1999. That country first blew the whistle that it might not meet payments on its Brady debt during the summer, and then proceeded to default on the bonds. This shook the markets, since it was the first time that Brady debt had defaulted. However, realize that there was no contagion — other Latin American countries continued to make timely payments on their Brady bonds. Investors should realize that a sovereign can default on some bonds, while remaining timely on others. This would be reflected in Exhibit 1 as a default. For example, while Russia has defaulted on some of its bonds, it has continued to service on a timely basis its large public issues, including the Russian Federation's 'CCC' rated Eurobonds. It is also keeping current four other Ministry of Finance foreign currency bonds.

Cumulatively, since 1975, Standard and Poor's has identified a total of 78 issuers (38.8% of all sovereigns) that defaulted on their foreign currency bond and bank loans since 1975. (This constitutes a much smaller percent of all foreign currency debt in default.) Defaults usually took the form of late payments of principal and/or interest on bank loans. In fact, there were 75 bank debt defaults since

---

[1] See David T. Beers and Ashok Bhatia, "Sovereign Defaults: Hiatus in 2000?" *Standard & Poor's Credit Week* (December 22, 1999).

[2] On January 6, 2000, after the S&P study was published, the Ivory Coast announced it was suspended foreign currency debt payments indefinitely. It is clear that the country's bank loans will be impacted. It is unclear if their Eurobonds would be affected as well.

1975, and some sovereigns defaulted more than once. By contrast, only 14 issuers defaulted on foreign currency bonds in that same period. In most of these cases, the defaulted bonds had been issued by smaller countries which had little total debt outstanding. The bonds that the countries defaulted on tended to be held by banks, rather than being public issues held by a broad cross sector of investors.

This has been independently confirmed in a 1995 study by Moody's rating service. The Moody's study noted that "a review of worldwide sovereign default experience since World War II shows that when sovereign nations have defaulted on any of their foreign currency obligations...they have been more likely to default on bank loans than on sovereign bonds or notes."[3]

Exhibit 1: Sovereign Default Rates

(%of all sovereign issuers)	Number of issuers	All issuers in default (%)	New Issuers in default (%)	All foreign currency debt* (%)	Foreign currency bonds (%)	Local currency (%)
1975	164	2.4	N.A.	1.2	0.6	1.2
1976	165	2.4	0.6	2.4	0.6	0.6
1977	166	2.4	0.0	1.8	0.6	0.6
1978	169	4.7	2.3	4.1	0.6	0.6
1979	173	6.4	2.3	5.8	0.6	1.2
1980	174	6.3	1.7	5.7	0.6	0.6
1981	176	10.2	6.3	9.1	0.0	1.1
1982	176	15.9	5.7	15.3	0.0	1.7
1983	177	24.9	10.2	23.7	0.0	1.1
1984	178	25.3	1.1	23.6	0.6	1.7
1985	178	24.7	2.8	24.2	0.6	1.1
1986	179	28.5	5.6	27.9	0.6	1.7
1987	179	30.7	3.3	29.1	1.1	2.2
1988	179	30.2	1.7	29.6	1.1	1.1
1989	179	30.2	1.7	29.1	2.2	1.7
1990	178	30.9	4.2	29.8	1.1	2.8
1991	198	27.3	3.0	26.8	1.0	1.5
1992	198	29.3	3.5	28.8	2.0	1.5
1993	200	27.0	0.5	26.5	1.5	2.0
1994	201	24.4	0.0	23.9	1.5	2.0
1995	201	22.9	1.5	21.9	1.5	3.0
1996	201	21.4	0.5	19.9	1.5	3.5
1997	201	15.9	0.0	14.9	1.5	2.0
1998	201	15.9	2.5	13.9	2.5	3.5
1999	201	13.9	0.5	11.9	2.5	3.5

N.A. = Not available.
* Bonds and bank debt.

Source: Standard & Poor's

[3] Vincent Truglia, David Levey and Christopher Mahoney, "Sovereign Risk: Bank Deposits Versus Bonds," Moody's Investor Service, Global Credit Research, October 1995.

WHY THE BETTER TRACK RECORD?

There are four reasons that EM sovereign bonds have a better track record than sovereign bank loans. First, there is a strong disincentive for a sovereign to default on foreign currency bonds; it will restrict capital market access going forward. The consequences of defaulting on (or rescheduling) bank loans has been more predictable, and far less detrimental to a nation's interest than defaulting on its bonds. Defaulting on bonds could essentially bar a country from the international capital markets for a considerable period of time, and will result in much higher borrowing costs when the country is finally able to enter. Most of the developing nations depend on external financing for their growth, and hampering access to capital markets could sacrifice medium-term growth.

Second, more sovereigns have access to cross-border bank financing than have access to bond issuance in the international capital markets. International bond markets have been receptive to issuance by speculative grade rated sovereign credits since the early 1990s. But relative credit sanity has prevailed, as there have been barriers to entry by sovereigns of less credit quality, notably those from sub-Saharan Africa.

Third, it is far easier to renegotiate debt held by a few banking institutions rather than a bond issuance held by large numbers of international investors. For one, identification of creditors in advance is not always easy. By definition, there are a large number of creditors, some of which may have relatively small holdings. All of which makes restructuring more complex. Also, any one of even the smallest creditors can potentially bring legal proceedings against an issuer in a number of jurisdictions, depending on the security's documentation. The possibility of asset attachments is greater, simply because of the number of potential court cases.

The fourth and final major difference between bank loans and bond debt is that banks have multi-faceted relationships with borrowers, and usually receive sizeable fees for a variety of services. Banks often keep their long-term relationship with the borrower in perspective when agreeing to reschedule. Bondholders are not relationship-driven, and there are no business consequences for the bondholders in trying to extract the last possible dollar. The net result: sovereign default rates on bonds are much lower than on bank loans. Unfortunately, many investors do not distinguish between the two, and keep looking at sovereign debt as a homogeneous category, which clearly, it is not.

CBO RATING DIFFERENCES: EM VERSUS HIGH YIELD

The rating methodology for cash flow CBOs involves looking at the expected loss on the various tranches under various default scenarios, and probability weighting the results. This in turn requires making assumptions on how diversified the collateral is, how likely it is to default, and how much will be recovered if any default occurs. It is much harder for the rating agencies to feel comfortable with the parameters that they are using for EM bonds than U.S. high-yield bonds. Lets look at why.

First, consider EM sovereign debt. Default rate statistics on EM sovereign bonds are very limited. Moreover, EM economies are subject to greater economic instability than those of more developed countries. Corporate debt in EM countries is even more problematic for the rating agencies. Clearly, there's generally less publicly available information about companies in EM countries than about issuers in developed countries. Moreover, financial reporting in many foreign countries is often not subject to uniform reporting and disclosure requirements. Finally and most importantly, the actions of local governments are far more likely to affect the ability or willingness of EM corporates to service their debt.

Given the issues that were mentioned above, the rating agencies react by rating EM assets in a more conservative manner than other collateral. As a result, additional levels of credit protection are built into EM CBOs beyond that which is structured into high-yield CBOs. We now review some major differences in those assumptions.

Recovery Rates

The rating agencies typically assume 30% recovery rates for high-yield debt and 50% on bank loans. For sovereign debt, Moody's assumes that base case recovery rates are 30% of the market value, or 25% of par, whichever is lower. For EM corporate debt, Moody's assumes that recovery rates are 20% of market value (15% of par value) if the issuer is domiciled in an investment grade country, and 15% of market value (10% of par value) if the issuer is domiciled in a non-investment grade country. Bonds of countries that face unusually adverse political or economic conditions are treated as having a lower recovery rate, which in some cases, can be as low as zero.

In point of fact, historical recovery rates on sovereign bonds have proved far more favorable. A September 1998 Standard and Poor's study showed that since 1975, the recovery rate on foreign currency bonds has been around 75%.[4] It was higher in the majority of cases in which the defaults were cured quickly though the issuance of new debt. It was lower on bonds that remained in default for longer periods of time. Even for bonds that remained in default for longer periods, most of the recovery rates were just under 50% — far higher than the recovery assumptions made by the rating agencies. And the 75% overall recovery rate on sovereign foreign currency bonds is well above the 60% recovery rate on foreign currency bank loans.

Moreover, even though the rating agencies are more generous in the recovery rates they assume for U.S. high-yield borrowers than for sovereign borrowers, actual recovery rates for sovereign borrowers have been higher. A Moody's study showed that the recovery rates on senior unsecured U.S. corporate debt in the 1977-1988 period average 51.31%.[5] Compare this with the 75% recovery rate on the sovereign bonds.

---

[4] See David T. Beers, "Sovereign Defaults Continue to Decline," Standard and Poor's, September 1998.

[5] C. Keenan, Igor Shtogrin, and Jorge Sobehart, "Historical Default Rates of Corporate Bond Issuers, 1920-1998," Moody's Investors Service, January 1999.

Exhibit 2: Moody's Diversity Score Table for CBOs

No. of Companies (Regions)	Diversity Score	Diversity Score for Latin America*
1.0	1.00	1.00
1.5	1.20	1.10
2.0	1.50	1.25
2.5	1.80	1.40
3.0	2.00	1.50
3.5	2.20	1.60
4.0	2.30	1.65
4.5	2.50	1.75
5.0	2.70	1.85
5.5	2.80	1.90
6.0	3.00	2.00

*Diversity = 1+ (Standard Diversity Score − 1) × 0.5

Source: Moody's Investors Service

Diversity Scores

Each rating agency has its own set of tools for measuring the diversity of underlying collateral. Moody's methodology has become the industry standard. This treatment reduces the pool of assets to a set of homogenous, uncorrelated assets. For CBOs backed by high-yield or bank loans, a diversity score is calculated by dividing the bonds into 1 of 33 industry groupings, and each industry group is assumed to be uncorrelated. (See Exhibit 2.)

Assumptions are more conservative for EM bonds, reflecting rating agency fears of "contagion." Countries that carry an investment-grade sovereign rating from Moody's are each treated as a separate industry. Bonds from non-investment grade EM issuers are grouped into six geographic regions. These are Latin America, The Caribbean, Eastern Europe, Africa, East Asia, and West Asia. The latter includes the Middle East. Each region constitutes a single "industry." All bonds from a region, regardless of the industry they represent, are taken as part of the same group. Thus, the value of including corporate EM borrowers, which would customarily be seen as providing greater diversity and reduced risk from that diversification, is discounted entirely. In point of fact, many EM deals include up to 20% of the portfolio in corporate form.

For all regions except Latin America, the diversity score is the standard table used by Moody's, which relies on the assumption that defaults on bonds in the same region or industry have a correlation coefficient of approximately 30%. This is shown in the first two columns of Exhibit 2. For example, if there were equal amounts of debt from each of four Caribbean countries, the diversity score is 2.3. That is, the deal would be credited as if there were 2.3 uncorrelated assets. For Latin American it is assumed the correlation is about 60%, and the diversity score is shown in the third column of Exhibit 2. If there were four Latin American issuers, the diversity score would be 1.65. Thus, combining four Caribbean issuers and four Latin American issuers in equal amounts would "count" as 3.95 uncorrelated issuers.

Exhibit 3: Cumulative Default Rates After 10 Years as a Function of Credit Quality

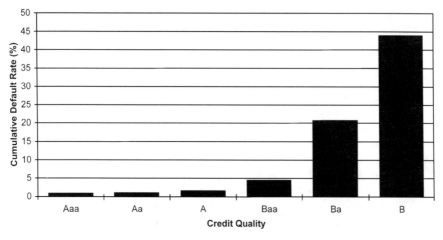

Source: Moody's Investors Service

To be even more conservative, all bonds from a particular EM country are taken as constituting one issue. Essentially, 100% correlation is assumed within each country. In effect, EM collateral does not receive diversity score "credit" for having multiple corporate issuers or industries. Thus, if one compares the diversity score on a pool of 100% emerging markets collateral with a pool of U.S. high-yield assets with similar industry diversification, the EM collateral would have a substantially lower diversity score.

Structural Protections

We have thus far focused on how Moody's deals with limited historical experience (by making more conservative assumptions). In practice, these more conservative assumptions mean several forms of additional built-in protection for the CBO buyer. First, the average credit quality is higher on a EM CBO than on a high-yield CBO. Second, subordination levels are also generally higher on an EM CBO than on a high-yield CBO.

Higher Average Credit Quality

The conservative approach used by Moody's means that average credit quality of an EM CBO deal is much higher than on a high-yield CBO. That is, CBO managers will generally choose to include higher credit quality bonds to compensate for the lower diversity scores and the more stringent recovery assumptions. Most EM deals have average credit qualities of Ba2 or Ba3. By contrast, most high-yield deals have an average credit quality of B1 or B2.

This difference is highly significant, as shown in Exhibit 3. The exhibit shows Moody's data for the average cumulative default rates by letter rating after 10 years. This groups corporate bonds with a given initial rating, and tracks those bonds through time. Data for the period 1970-1998 are included. We use the exhibit to highlight cumulative default rates after 10 years, as that roughly corresponds to the average lives of CBO deals. The findings show that default rates tend to rise exponentially as credit letter ratings fall. Of the bonds that started out life with a Baa rating, 4.39% had defaulted by the end of 10 years. Bonds with an initial rating of Ba had a cumulative default rate of 20.63%, while bonds initially rated B had a cumulative default of 43.91%. While numbers on sovereign debt are unavailable, the results are indicative that higher rated bonds actually default much less than do their lower-rated brethren. Bottom line: the higher initial portfolio quality on sovereign EM CBOs is highly significant.

Moreover, actual EM portfolio quality may be slightly higher than even that indicated by the overall rating. EM corporate bonds (generally 5%-20% of the deal) can generally receive a rating no higher than the country in which it is based.[6] This is called the "sovereign ceiling." Thus, if a company is rated Aa2 based on "stand-alone" fundamentals, but is based in a country rated Ba2, the company itself can generally only receive that same Ba2 rating. This same methodology and rating effect is reflected throughout the overall portfolio.

More Subordination

The more conservative rating methodology also means that the rating agencies require higher subordination levels. In particular, equity tranches are usually much larger on EM deals than in high-yield deals. Exhibit 4 shows a representative high-yield deal versus a representative sovereign EM deal, both brought to market at approximately the same time. Note that the equity tranche is 7.9% on the high-yield deal versus 18% on the EM deal. More generally, the investment grade bonds receive much more protection on the EM deal than they do on the high yield deal. In the EM deal, 22.2% of the deal is subordinated to the investment grade bonds, on the high-yield deal only 11.9% is subordinated.

The yields for each tranche are higher on the EM CBO than for the corresponding tranche on the high yield CBO, in spite of the fact that the rating is as high or higher on the EM debt. The AAA rated bond on the EM deal is priced at 68 discounted margin (DM), versus 57 DM on the high yield deal. The A rated EM tranche is priced at +250/10-year Treasury, versus +225/10-year Treasury for a lower rated (A-) tranche of the high yield deal. This translates into roughly a 50 b.p. differential, as the credit quality differential is worth 25 b.p. The Ba1 mezzanine bond in the EM deal is priced at +800/10-year, versus +700/10-year for the

---

[6] There have been a few CBOs backed primarily by Asian corporate bonds. These CBOs are "story bonds" driven by local investors, and have take advantage of brief "windows of opportunity." This chapter focuses on CBOs backed by diversified sovereign EM bonds. In practice, the rating agencies criteria is such that it has never been economic to include more than 20% EM corporate bonds in a sovereign EM deal.

BB- tranche of the high yield deal. Here the EM investor is receiving a 100 b.p. higher spread, as well as higher credit quality. The equity on the EM deal is the only exception to this. It may yield slightly less than on high-yield deals, as the equity is far less leveraged. The difference in the leverage can be seen by the fact that the EM equity is 18% of the deal versus 7.9% of the high-yield deal.

CONCLUSION

It is unfortunate that many investors may be reluctant to look at CBOs backed by EM collateral because of general misimpressions about the collateral. In this chapter, we have shown that there have been few actual defaults on sovereign EM bonds, which is the collateral used to back many EM CBOs. Many investors do not realize this, as they tend to clump together the experiences of both sovereign bank loans and sovereign bonds. Sovereign bank loans have clearly experienced more significant level of defaults. Moreover, when there is a default, the recovery rates are higher on the sovereign bonds than on the bank loans.

Moreover, because of the limited history of sovereign bonds, the rating agencies are far more conservative in their ratings. They are particularly harsh in the assumptions they make about recoveries and on diversity characteristics. This more conservative rating methodology means that the average credit quality of bonds is higher in the EM deal. Finally, EM CBOs have more subordination. This extra structural protection is clearly not priced in. EM CBOs trade wider than high-yield CBOs for every rated tranche.

Exhibit 4: Comparison of Emerging Market and High Yield Deal Structure

Class	Ratings Moody's/S&P/D&P	Amount ($M)	% of Deal	% Sub	Current Pricing Info
Representative Emerging Market Deal					
A1	Aaa/AAA/NR	163.00	68.6%	31.4%	+68 DM*
A2	A2/A/NR	22.00	9.3%	22.2%	+250/10yr Tsy
Mezz	Ba1/NR/NR	10.00	4.2%	18.0%	+800/10yr Tsy
Equity	NR	42.74	18.0%	—	—
Total		237.74			
Representative High Yield Deal					
A1	Aaa/AAA/AAA	344.50	68.2%	31.8%	+57 DM*
A2	NR/A-/A-	79.00	15.6%	16.2%	+225/10yr Tsy
Mezz 1	NR/NR/BBB-	22.00	4.4%	11.8%	+360/10yr Tsy
Mezz 2	NR/NR/BB-	20.00	4.0%	7.9%	+700/10yr Tsy
Equity	NR	39.79	7.9%	—	—
Total		505.29			

* DM = discounted margin

Chapter 6

Mortgage Cash Flow CBOs

Laurie S. Goodman, Ph.D.
Managing Director
UBS Warburg

M any investors consider mortgage collateralized bond obligations (CBOs) a very different animal from high-yield CBOs. But in fact, current cash flow deals utilizing mortgage assets are quite similar to those using high yield assets. The major difference is that mortgage CBOs generally hold *higher rated assets*, which permits lower equity capital. In this chapter we explore similarities and differences between cash flow deals backed by mortgage assets versus those supported by high-yield assets.

We also review some history on mortgage CBOs. Note that as late as 1999, the area was dominated by market value deals employing short duration/high-grade assets. These deals did not have a high-yield counterpart. In 2000, however, the market shifted toward cash flow structures, using combinations of BBB and BB rated asset-backed securities (ABS), commercial mortgage-backed securities (CMBS), residential mortgage-backed securities (RMBS), and real estate investment trust (REIT) securities. As we will see, these deals are similar in structure and rating methodology to their high-yield counterparts.

A PRIMER ON THE MORTGAGE CBO MARKET

The mortgage CBO market evolved in a very different fashion from the high-yield CBO market. Cash flow deals always dominated in the high-yield CBO market. By contrast, most mortgage CBOs utilized a market value structure, backed by high-grade/short duration mortgage instruments.

Exhibit 1 makes this point by listing all mortgage CBOs through the end of June, 2000. A total of $20.3 billion was raised via 37 deals.

The first mortgage CBO was created in July of 1995, with Alliance Capital Management as investment manager.[1] Over the next two years (1996-1998), the market was dominated by PaineWebber's underwriting of CBOs managed by Trust Company of the West and Alliance Capital Management. Every deal was a market value type, backed by short duration, high-grade assets.

---

[1] This deal matured in July 2000.

Exhibit 1: Mortgage CBOs (as of 6/30/2000)

Issuer	Size	Bloomberg Ticker	Dated Date	Final (years)	Investment Manager	Underwriter	Type	Assets Strategy
Pegasus I	538,000,000	PEGCAP(CORP)	7/1/95	7/20/00	Alliance Capital Mgmt	UBS	MV	short duration/high grade
Pegasus II	582,011,000	PEGCAP(CORP)	7/1/96	7/29/01	Alliance Capital Mgmt	PW	MV	short duration/high grade
Pegasus III	360,000,000	PEGCAP(CORP)	8/1/96	2/28/02	Alliance Capital Mgmt	PW	MV	short duration/high grade
Pegasus IV	640,000,000	PEGCAP(CORP)	9/1/96	7/15/02	Alliance Capital Mgmt	PW	MV	short duration/high grade
Westways I	1,000,000,000	WESFUN(CORP)	9/1/97	9/30/02	Trust Company of the West	PW	MV	short duration/high grade
Pegasus V, Series I	1,000,000,000	PEGCAP(CORP)	11/1/97	11/15/02	Alliance Capital Mgmt	PW	MV	short duration/high grade
Westways II	1,000,000,000	WESFUN(CORP)	1/1/98	1/31/03	Trust Company of the West	PW	MV	short duration/high grade
Westways III	900,000,000	WESFUN(CORP)	4/1/98	4/15/03	Trust Company of the West	PW	MV	short duration/high grade
Pegasus V, Series II	1,000,000,000	WESFUN(CORP)	4/1/98	4/30/03	Alliance Capital Mgmt	PW	MV	short duration/high grade
Aeltus III	600,000,000	AELT3(MORT)	4/15/98	4/15/03	Aeltus	BS	MV	short duration/high grade
Spinmaker	318,000,000	SPIN(MORT)	5/1/98	5/1/01	Fisher, Francis, Trees & Watts	BS	MV	market duration
Westways IV	1,400,000,000	WESFUN(CORP)	8/1/98	8/24/03	Trust Company of the West	PW	MV	short duration/high grade
ACM Libor Trust	200,900,000	—	8/1/98	8/30/03	Alliance Capital Mgmt	PW	MV	short duration/high grade
Westways V	1,000,000,000	WESFUN(CORP)	1/1/99	1/30/04	Trust Company of the West	PW	MV	short duration/high grade
Enhanced MBS I	100,000,000	—	1/1/99	11/15/08	MassMutual/David L Babson	CSFB	MV	total return neutral duration
Tribeca I	250,000,000	TRIB(MORT)	2/1/99	2/1/04	Clinton Group	BS	MV	50% mortgage derivatives neutral duration
Aeltus V	600,000,000	AELT5(MORT)	3/1/99	3/30/04	Aeltus	UBS	MV	short duration/high grade
Seneca Funding I	1,000,000,000	SENEC(CORP)	5/1/99	5/30/04	Independence Fixed Income Associates	PW	MV	short duration + mortgage overlay
Diversified REIT Trust	518,760,000	DRT(MORT)	5/21/99	3/18/11	UBS Warburg	MSDW	CF	BBB REIT
Pegasus VI	457,000,000	PEGCAP(CORP)	5/27/99	5/27/04	Alliance Capital Mgmt	BS	MV	short duration/high grade
AXES Limited	60,000,000	—	6/1/99	6/1/01	Clinton Group	Clinton Gp	MV	50% mortgage derivatives neutral duration
FORTRESS	437,500,000	FORT(MORT)	7/16/99	7/25/38	Fortress Investment Group	BS/LH	CF	BBB/BB REIT/CMBS
Pegasus VII	450,000,000	PEGCAP(CORP)	8/11/99	8/11/04	Alliance Capital Mgmt	GW/Nat	MV	short duration + mortgage overlay
Eminent	1,000,000,000	—	11/1/99	11/1/04	Trust Company of the West	ML	MV	market duration
DASH	300,000,000	DASH(MORT)	12/1/99	12/1/35	Asset Allocation	PRU	CF	BBB/BB mortgage assets
Newbury Funding I	750,000,000	NEWB(MORT)	2/15/00	2/15/05	Colonial Advisors	LH	MV	short duration/down in credit
Trainer Wortham	500,000,000	TRAIN(MORT)	2/29/00	3/1/05	Trainer Wortham	BS	MV	short duration/high grade
Bleecker	400,000,000	—	3/1/00	1/30/35	Clinton Group	PRU	CF	BBB/BB mortgage assets
DRT 2	287,150,000	DRT(MORT)	4/13/00	3/8/10	UBS Warburg	MSDW	CF	100% BBB REIT
Talon Funding	500,000,000	TALON(MORT)	4/27/00	6/5/35	West LB	LH	CF	BBB/BB MBS/ABS, no REIT
PIP I	400,000,000	—	5/15/00	5/30/35	Phoenix Investment Partners	PRU	CF	BBB/BB mortgage assets
INGRESS	300,000,000	—	5/18/00	3/30/40	Structured Credit Partners	PW	CF	BBB REIT/CMBS/ABS(MH&HEQ)
Enhanced MBS II	200,000,000	EMBS(MORT)	5/25/00	5/31/05	MassMutual/David L Babson	PW	MV	total return neutral duration
MACH 1	250,000,000	MACH(MORT)	5/25/00	5/29/30	Banc One	MSDW/GS	CF	CMBS, REIT, residential ABS
Eagle 1	500,000,000	EAGL(MORT)	6/5/00	6/30/05	Federated	LH	MV	short duration/high grade
SFA CBO I	250,000,000	—	6/22/00	6/15/35	SFA	DB	CF	BBB ABS/RMBS
PPM America	296,000,000	—	6/29/00	8/5/35	PPM	CSFB	CF	BBB ABS/CMBS/CBO
37 deals to date	20,345,321,000							

Exhibit 2: Cash Flow Deals Have Become More Important in the Mortgage Market

Date		Market Value Deals			Cash Flow Deals			Total
		# of Deals	Amount	%	# of Deals	Amount	%	Amount
1995	2nd Half	1	538,000,000	100.0%				538,000,000
1996	1st Half							
	2nd Half	3	1,582,011,000	100.0%				1,582,011,000
1997	1st Half							
	2nd Half	2	2,000,000,000	100.0%				2,000,000,000
1998	1st Half	5	3,818,000,000	100.0%				3,818,000,000
	2nd Half	2	1,600,900,000	100.0%				1,600,900,000
1999	1st Half	7	3,467,000,000	87.0%	1	518,760,000	13.0%	3,985,760,000
	2nd Half	2	1,450,000,000	66.3%	2	737,500,000	33.7%	2,187,500,000
2000	1st Half	4	1,950,000,000	42.1%	8	2,683,150,000	57.9%	4,633,150,000
Total		26	16,405,911,000	80.6%	11	3,939,410,000	19.4%	20,345,321,000

These two managers have been constant fixtures in the market. However, beginning in the Spring of 1998, the universe started expanding. New entrants included Aeltus III and Aeltus V (managed by Aeltus), Spinnaker (managed by Fisher Francis Trees & Watts), Enhanced MBS I (managed by David L. Babson, a subsidiary of Mass Mutual), and Tribeca 1 (managed by the Clinton Group). Investment bank participation also increased markedly, with Bear Stearns, Credit Suisse First Boston, and UBS joining as underwriters.

All structures done prior to the end of the first quarter of 1999 were market value deals. Most were neutral- or low-duration, with those duration targets obtained by either using short duration assets, or hedging to reduce the duration on longer instruments. These structures were backed primarily by high-grade assets.

The first *cash flow* CBO deal backed by mortgage or real estate assets was the Diversified REIT Trust managed by UBS Warburg, in May of 1999. This CBO was supported 100% by BBB REIT paper. In the second half of 1999, two more cash flow CBOs came to market — Fortress (managed by Fortress Investment Management) and DASH (managed by Asset Allocation). Even so, market value deals continued to dominate. Exhibit 2 shows that they comprised 87% of all mortgage CBOs during the first half of 1999, and 66.3% during the second half.

In 2000, mortgage CBO issuance was heavier than ever before, with $4.63 billion in the first half of 2000, alone. Cash flow deals comprised 57.9% of that total. A number of new money managers also joined, including West LB, Phoenix Investment Partners, Structured Credit Partners, Banc One, SFA, and PPM America. Dealer participation also increased. Prudential, Lehman, Bear Stearns, Morgan Stanley Dean Witter, Deutsche Bank, Credit Suisse First Boston, Goldman Sachs, and PaineWebber, have all brought at least one deal in 2000.

Cash flow CBO deals in 2000 used combinations of BBB rated CMBS, ABS, RMBS and REIT debt. A few deals also included BB rated debt.

MORTGAGE AND HIGH-YIELD CBOS

In the remainder of this chapter, we look at cash flow CBOs backed by mortgage assets. We make the case that there are many similarities between the cash flow CBOs backed by mortgage assets and those backed by high-yield assets. The reasons are

1. they are structured very similarly
2. the rating methodology is very similar
3. both share similar protections via overcollateralization and interest coverage tests

However, there are minor differences which generally stem from the fact that credit quality of the mortgage assets is much higher than in a high-yield CBO, which permits lower equity levels in mortgage CBO structures. The two effects offset, hence producing the similar expected losses at each rating level.

Deal Structure

In a cash flow CBO, ability to service the rated notes is based on the interest and principal cash flows of portfolio assets. Both high-yield and mortgage deals typically have a 5-10 year average life, and an 8-14 year expected maturity.

One small difference is that mortgage deals tend to have very long legal final maturities (2035 to 2040 in Exhibit 1) compared to high-yield deals. The legal final reflects the underlying legal final of the last cash flow in the portfolio. For example, the manager of a cash flow mortgage CBO deal done in early 2000, with a 5-year revolving period, must be able to purchase a 30-year mortgage at the end of the revolving period. That creates a 2035 legal final. By contrast, in a high-yield deal the longest securities that can be purchased are 12-14 years.

Liability structure is very similar in all cash flow deals, regardless of the underlying assets. It consists of senior notes, subordinated notes, and equity. If the underlying assets are fixed and the liabilities are floating, interest rate swaps are used in both cases. One major difference is that credit quality (average rating) of the mortgage assets tends to be considerably higher, which allows less equity in mortgage structures than in high-yield deals.

For example, a typical 100% high-yield deal will have an average rating of B1 to B2, and equity will average 13%-15% of the deal amount. By contrast, a typical mortgage deal will have average credit quality of Baa2 or Baa3, with equity averaging only 4%-6% of the deal.[2] This is shown in Exhibit 3.

---

[2] We later show that the amount of equity required is not magically pulled out of a hat. Rating agencies structure their ratings around different levels of expected losses. These expected loss numbers are derived from weighted average credit quality, diversification, and loss severity. Since the average rating is considerably higher on mortgage deals, defaults on such assets are expected to be lower. Thus, as we shall see, less subordination is required to support any given rating.

Exhibit 3: Liability Structure of Cash Flow Deals

	High-Yield Bond Deal	High-Yield Loan Deal	Mortgage Deal
Aaa	73-75	75-80	78-80
Mezzanine	10-14	10-15	15-17
Equity	13-15	8-10	4-6

It is interesting to note that while equity is much lower in the mortgage deals, the Aaa rated bonds constitute a very similar percentage of both types of deals. In a 100% high yield bond deal containing Aaa, Baa, and unrated tranches, Aaa rated bonds will constitute 73%-75% of the deal, equity will be 13%-15%, with the remainder in Baa rated bonds. In a high-yield loan deal, Aaa rated bonds will be 75%-80% of the deal, Baa rated bonds 10%-15%, and equity 8%-10%. In a mortgage deal, Aaa rated bonds will be 78%-80%, equity will be 5% and mezzanine bonds will represent the remainder. Mortgage deals typically have a number of mezzanine tranches, including a sizeable Aa rated tranche.

Rating Methodology

For all cash flow CBOs, rating methodology looks at expected losses on the various tranches under different default scenarios, and probability-weights those results. This, in turn, requires assumptions on collateral diversification, likelihood of default, and recovery rates post any defaults.

Diversification

Each rating agency has its own set of tools for measuring the diversity of underlying collateral. Moody's methodology, which has become *de facto* the industry standard, reduces the asset pool to a set of homogenous, uncorrelated assets.

For CBOs backed by mortgage assets, a diversity score is calculated by dividing the bonds into a number of different groupings, which broadly correspond to different industry sectors. For example, manufactured housing is one industry group, home equity loans are another, auto loans comprise one, and A-quality residential loans, CMBS conduit deals, CMBS credit tenant lease deals, etc. have their own groups. Every industry group is assumed to have a small correlation with each other. Two securities within the same industry group are assumed to have larger correlation to each other than would two from different industry groups. Two securities in the same deal are assumed to have 100% correlation, hence, provide zero diversification.

Note that diversification scores tend to be lower on mortgage deals than for high-yield deals, which reflect the smaller number of mortgage categories. For example, on mortgage deals diversity scores of 15-20 are typical. On a high-yield deal, scores of 50-60 (with minimum diversification requirement of 40) are more common.

Exhibit 4: Average Cumulative Default Rates from 1 to 8 Years (Percent) - 1983-1999

Years:	1	2	3	4	5	6	7	8
Aaa	0.00	0.00	0.00	0.06	0.20	0.28	0.37	0.48
Aa1	0.00	0.00	0.00	0.23	0.23	0.39	0.39	0.39
Aa2	0.00	0.00	0.06	0.20	0.45	0.55	0.66	0.79
Aa3	0.07	0.10	0.19	0.29	0.41	0.55	0.55	0.55
A1	0.00	0.03	0.33	0.52	0.66	0.82	0.89	0.97
A2	0.00	0.03	0.14	0.39	0.60	0.79	0.91	1.24
A3	0.00	0.13	0.25	0.34	0.40	0.53	0.78	0.88
Baa1	0.04	0.26	0.52	0.90	1.28	1.55	2.00	2.27
Baa2	0.07	0.33	0.60	1.18	1.80	2.45	2.79	2.93
Baa3	0.31	0.81	1.34	2.15	2.84	3.82	4.73	5.66
Ba1	0.62	2.13	3.86	6.30	8.49	10.69	12.19	13.67
Ba2	0.53	2.58	5.05	7.32	9.16	10.51	11.86	12.76
Ba3	2.52	6.96	11.89	16.47	20.98	25.05	28.71	32.61
B1	3.46	9.29	14.81	19.63	24.48	29.79	34.85	38.35
B2	6.88	13.95	20.28	24.84	28.45	31.16	32.57	34.39
B3	12.23	20.71	27.27	32.53	37.54	40.66	43.95	47.84
Caa1-C	19.09	28.37	34.23	40.07	43.37	47.73	47.73	51.33
Investment-Grade	0.04	0.15	0.33	0.59	0.82	1.08	1.27	1.46
Speculative-Grade	3.68	8.26	12.66	16.56	20.17	23.38	26.17	28.73
All Corp.	1.20	2.65	4.01	5.22	6.28	7.19	7.92	8.57

Source: Moody's Investors Service, Global Credit Research "Historical Default Rates of Corporate Bond Issuers, 1920-1999," January 2000.

Weighted Average Ratings Factor

The weighted average rating factor (WARF) is a rough guide to the asset quality of the portfolio. This factor is meant to incorporate the expected probability of default for each of the assets. Calculating the rating factor requires that each asset in the collateral pool be rated either publicly or privately by the rating agency analyzing the pool. Absent an existing rating, the agency may apply "shadow" ratings, or might take a rating assigned by another rating agency and "imply" a rating. Most commonly, any implied rating is one or two notches below the actual rating granted by the original agency.

The rationale for lowering original ratings is that an underwriter on an asset- or mortgage-backed deal will probably seek out the most lenient rating agency for any given deal. So if Rating Agency A did not rate the subordinated tranches of an asset or mortgage or CMBS deal, it was most likely because Rating Agency A would have given the deal a lower rating than the Rating Agency B (who actually rated that deal). If a security from that deal (rated only by Rating Agency B) is later contained in a CBO rated by Rating Agency A — it's reasonable that Rating Agency A assigns a lower rating than granted by Rating Agency B.

Exhibit 4 summarizes Moody's default experience by rating category. The results are definitely non-linear. In averaging data over the 1983-1999 period, at the end of eight years, among bonds initially rated A2 — 1.24% would have defaulted. Of bonds rated Baa2, 2.93% would have gone belly-up. For bonds rated Ba2, 12.76% would have defaulted, and in those rated B2, 34.39% would have stopped paying.

Since expected defaults are non-linear, and increase exponentially as ratings decline, so, too, does the WARF. This is shown in Exhibit 5 for Moody's and Fitch ratings. Look at the Moody's data. Note that a decrease in rating from A2 to Baa2 increases the rating factor from 120 to 360. A further decrease to Ba2 jumps the rating factor to 1350. Stepping down the rating factor to B2 vaults the rating factor to 2220. In short, as credit quality decreases, the probability of default, and hence the rating factor, increases.

Default Probabilities

Collateral in mortgage deals has, by and large, been BBB rated (averaging Moody's WARF of 375-500), whereas high-yield collateral tends to have average ratings between B1 and B2 (that is, WARFs of 2200-2700). Note that no cash flow mortgage deals backed by BBB assets have WARFs exceeding 500.

Exhibit 5: Rating Factors Used to Derive Weighted Average Ratings (Moody's and Fitch)

	Moody's	Fitch
Aaa/AAA	1	1.3
Aa1/AA+	10	2.0
Aa2/AA	20	2.3
Aa3/AA-	40	3.3
A1/A+	70	4.0
A2/A	120	5.0
A3/A-	180	7.5
Baa1/BBB+	260	10.0
Baa2/BBB	360	14.0
Baa3/BBB-	610	20.0
Ba1/BB+	940	37.0
Ba2/BB	1,350	43.5
Ba3/BB-	1,780	46.5
B1/B+	2,220	50.0
B2/B	2,720	52.2
B3/B-	3,490	65.0
CCC+	NA	90.0
Caa/CCC	6,500	100.0
CCC-	NA	NA
<Ca/<CCC-	10,000	NA

Source: Moody's Investors Service & Fitch.

The probability of default on any asset group is assumed to be the weighted average rating factor times a stress factor. This stress factor is different for each rating, reflecting the fact that one wants to be more conservative on the higher ratings. There is also a difference in the stress factor applied in mortgage and high-yield deals, reflecting the fact that the average ratings of the underlying collateral are different. For high-yield deals, Moody's uses a stress factor of 1.0 for the B rating, with higher stress factors for Aaa, Aa A, Baa, and Ba ratings. On mortgage CBOs, Moody's uses a stress factor of 1.0 for a Baa rating, and a higher stress factor for Aaa, Aa, and A ratings. A lower stress factor is applied to less-than-investment-grade ratings. Thus, on the example looked at later in this chapter, (of a Baa rated mortgage CBO tranche), we assumed a 390 rating factor (a very typical number for a mortgage deal) times a stress factor of 1. That implies a 3.90% default rate on each of the independent, uncorrelated assets.

Note that if WARF is higher, the default rate on an asset will be higher. Thus, a weighted average ratings factor of 2400 implies 24% default on each of the assets. It stands to reason that this would require more subordination at each level.

Recovery Rates

The recovery assumptions for ABS/RMBS/CMBS, and REIT assets are very similar to those for high-yield assets, even though the mortgage assets have collateral backing them. Let's look more closely.

Moody's recovery assumptions for ABS, MBS, and CMBS paper are based on the amount of initial capital in the subordinated tranche. Thus a BBB-rated residential tranche which represents 0.4% of the deal (40 basis points) has a recovery rate of 25% for rating purposes. A BBB rated home equity tranche comprising 4.6% of the deal would have a recovery rate of 35%. A BBB rated CMBS at 4.7% of the deal has a recovery rate of 30%.

Note that recovery rates are dependent on the bond's percentage representation of initial capital, not on the amount of subordination beneath that bond. Moody's thinking is that if the bond is a thin slice of the deal, and it gets hit, the loss severity is likely to be large, and hence the recovery rate low. (The recovery rate is simply 1 – loss severity.) By contrast, if it is a thicker slice, loss severity is likely to be more modest, and hence the recovery rate higher. (The likelihood of the bond getting hit at all is contained in the WARF.)

For most REIT debt, a 40% recovery rate is assumed, which reflects the fact the REIT debt offers strong covenant packages on "total debt-to-assets" ratios, "secured debt as a portion of total assets," "interest coverage," etc. For healthcare REITS (which carry special risks due to significant government regulation of their ownership and operation), and mortgage REITS (which tend to be highly leveraged), a 10% recovery rate is assumed.

Recovery rate assumptions on mortgage deals are very similar, if not slightly higher than, that on high-yield bond deals, where there is no collateral explicitly backing the transaction. For example, for an Aaa rating, a high-yield bond is assumed to have a recovery rate of 30%. For an A2 rating, a high-yield bond is assumed to have a recovery rate of 33%, while for Baa2, a recovery rate of 36% is assumed. On loans, many of which are secured, Moody's assumes a recovery rate of 50%.

How CBO Ratings are Derived

Moody's has an expected loss that is permissible for each CBO rating. The expected loss is derived as follows:

Expected loss

$$= \sum_{i=1}^{n} (\text{loss in default scenario } i) \times (\text{probability of scenario } i \text{ occurring})$$

A concrete example make this esoteric formula and process much clearer. Look at the Baa rated bond in a sample mortgage deal. As can be seen from Exhibit 6, this deal has a rating factor of 390, and a stress factor of 1. That implies a 3.90% default on each asset over the life of the deal. The diversity score for this mortgage deal is 17, implying equivalency of 17 independent assets. Thus, the probability of a scenario in which none of the 17 securities default is $(0.961)^{17}$, or 50.82%. The probability of a scenario in which one of the 17 securities defaults is $[17 \times (\text{probability of a default}) \times (\text{probability of no defaults})16]$. That comes out to 35.09%. The probability of 2 defaults is 11.40%, as shown in the first two columns of Exhibit 6.

Exhibit 6: Where CBO Ratings Come From

n bonds	Prob of n def	Loss	Expect Loss	DSCORE	17
0	50.8288%	0.0000%	0.0000%	AVG Rating	390
1	35.0900%	0.0000%	0.0000%	stress	1
2	11.3998%	6.5815%	0.7503%	p	0.039
3	2.3147%	31.6721%	0.7331%	Class	Baa2
4	0.3290%	58.3001%	0.1918%		
5	0.0347%	85.1766%	0.0296%		
6	0.0028%	96.8493%	0.0027%		
7	0.0002%	97.7754%	0.0002%		
8	0.0000%	97.7754%	0.0000%		
9	0.0000%	97.7754%	0.0000%		
10	0.0000%	97.7754%	0.0000%		
11	0.0000%	98.0420%	0.0000%		
12	0.0000%	98.0420%	0.0000%		
13	0.0000%	100.0000%	0.0000%		
14	0.0000%	100.0000%	0.0000%		
15	0.0000%	100.0000%	0.0000%		
16	0.0000%	100.0000%	0.0000%		
17	0.0000%	100.0000%	0.0000%		
Expect Loss			1.7077%		

The loss column in Exhibit 6 measures the loss to the bond in the event that a number of defaults occur. *Loss* is defined as the expected yield minus the actual yield. This is calculated by running the default scenario and recovery assumptions through the CBO cash flow model. Note that in this example, for zero or 1 default, there is no loss to the bond. If 2 defaults occur, the bond loss is 6.58%. However, there is only an 11.40% chance of this occurring. Thus, in this 2 default scenario, the (loss to the bond) × (the chance of the loss occurring) is 6.58% × 11.40% = 0.7503. The expected loss is then calculated by summing the probability of all default scenarios times the scenario loss. Net, this Baa rated tranche has an expected loss of 1.71%.

We can now look in Exhibit 7 to see what rating would be warranted by this bond. The average life on the bond is 8-9 years. An instrument with a 9-year average life could sustain expected losses of 1.78% (within a Baa2 rating). Since the actual number is 1.71%, the bond is awarded a Baa2 rating. For an Aaa rating, a bond with an 9-year average life could have an expected loss of 0.00451%.

Thus, ratings for any given tranche are determined by expected cumulative losses. This is, in turn, built up from the probability of (each default scenario) × (the expected loss of that particular scenario materializing).

Is it now clear why mortgage CBOs have less equity? Their higher credit quality indicates default rates will be lower. With lower default rates, less equity is requires because expected losses are lower.

MORTGAGE ASSETS' NEGATIVE CONVEXITY

Thus far, we have talked about similarities in determining expected defaults among rating methodologies. There's still a nagging concern that we missed something. It's the property of negative convexity which is potentially a problem for mortgage assets, but not for high-yield assets. In most mortgage discussions, negative convexity is front and center. Why have we not provided any discussion of this issue thus far?

The reason is that there are no cash flow "mortgage" deals to date that employ more than 33% residential MBS assets. Most of the assets used for these deals are CMBS, REIT, or ABS assets. CMBS assets have excellent call protection, and most have yield maintenance provisions, which make investors whole in the event of early redemption. Similarly, REIT debt is typically either a non-call bullet security, or call-protected by yield maintenance provisions. ABS assets include autos, credit card, franchise leases, airplane loans, and tax liens, as well as home equity paper. And we know that non-mortgage related assets have very little negative convexity. Plus home equity paper has much less negative convexity than residential mortgage paper. Over the years 1997-2000, speeds on FNCL 7.5s have ranged from 10-40 CPR (for a 30 CPR range), while speeds on home equity paper typically varied much less, between 20 and 30 CPR (a 10 CPR range).

Exhibit 7: Moody's Cumulative Expected Loss Rates (%)

Rating	Year									
	1	2	3	4	5	6	7	8	9	10
Aaa	0.00003	0.00011	0.00039	0.00099	0.00160	0.00220	0.00286	0.00363	0.00451	0.00550
Aa1	0.00031	0.00165	0.00550	0.01155	0.01705	0.02310	0.02970	0.03685	0.04510	0.05500
Aa2	0.00075	0.00440	0.01430	0.02585	0.03740	0.04895	0.06105	0.07425	0.09020	0.11000
Aa3	0.00166	0.01045	0.03245	0.05555	0.07810	0.10065	0.12485	0.14960	0.17985	0.22000
A1	0.00320	0.02035	0.06435	0.10395	0.14355	0.18150	0.22330	0.26400	0.31515	0.38500
A2	0.00598	0.03850	0.12210	0.18975	0.25685	0.32065	0.39050	0.45595	0.54010	0.66000
A3	0.02137	0.08250	0.19800	0.29700	0.40150	0.50050	0.61050	0.71500	0.83600	0.99000
Baa1	0.04950	0.15400	0.30800	0.45650	0.60500	0.75350	0.91850	1.08350	1.24850	1.43000
Baa2	0.09350	0.25850	0.45650	0.66000	0.86900	1.08350	1.32550	1.56750	1.78200	1.98000
Baa3	0.23100	0.57750	0.94050	1.30900	1.67750	2.03500	2.38150	2.73350	3.06350	3.35500
Ba1	0.47850	1.11100	1.72150	2.31000	2.90400	3.43750	3.88300	4.33950	4.77950	5.17000
Ba2	0.85800	1.90850	2.84900	3.74000	4.62550	5.37350	5.88500	6.41300	6.95750	7.42500
Ba3	1.54550	3.03050	4.32850	5.38450	6.52300	7.41950	8.04100	8.64050	9.19050	9.71300
B1	2.57400	4.60900	6.36900	7.61750	8.86600	9.83950	10.52150	11.12650	11.68200	12.21000
B2	3.93800	6.41850	8.55250	9.97150	11.39050	12.45750	13.20550	13.83250	14.42100	14.96000
B3	6.39100	9.13550	11.56650	13.22200	14.87750	16.06000	17.05000	17.91900	18.57900	19.19500
Caa1	9.55988	12.77877	15.75124	17.86336	19.97256	21.43166	22.76196	24.01133	25.11950	26.23500
Caa2	14.30000	17.87500	21.45000	24.13400	26.81250	28.60000	30.38750	32.17500	33.96250	35.75000
Caa3	28.04461	31.35482	34.34749	36.43309	38.40166	39.66106	40.88169	42.06691	43.21964	44.38500

Moreover, subordinated residential mortgage paper tends to have better call protection than does the underlying collateral. Subordinated mortgage paper typically has a 5-year lock-out and a shifting interest structure for the next five years. This paper does not actually receive a pro-rata share of prepayments until Year 10.

Finally, investors should realize that high-yield bonds and loans backing CBOs and CLOs do not have absolute call protection. High-yield bonds with a 10-year maturity typically have a lock-out for 3-5 years, then are callable at a premium, which declines over time. By Year 7, the paper is typically callable at par. Loans are generally floating rate, with little call protection. If spreads narrow, borrowers often refinance.

Modern-Day Protection

There are generally stringent indenture restrictions on the portfolio, intended to protect rated note holders. Indenture restrictions generally require that minimum average collateral rating be maintained. They also require a minimum level of diversification, so that the above analysis will continue to be valid. There are also minimum requirements on the amount of overcollateralization, as well as for interest coverage ratios.

Overcollateralization (O/C) and interest coverage tests are generally applied at the senior debt and total debt levels. Application is nearly identically for the high-yield and mortgage CBOs. Overcollateralization tests are designed to protect the rated debt from losses on the collateral, by maintaining a cushion of overcollateralization throughout the life of the CDO. If the transaction is performing well, the level of overcollateralization is maintained during the reinvestment period. It actually increases as the senior debt is paid down.

If the overcollateralization trigger is tripped, interest payable to subordinated classes or the equity is redirected to pay down the most senior classes until compliance is restored. Assets that have not defaulted are usually valued at par for the overcollateralization test. Defaulted assets are either valued at the recovery assumption for that asset class, or, the lower of the recovery assumption for that asset class or its market value.

Interest coverage tests insure that the interest thrown off by the CBO's assets are more than sufficient to cover the cost of the liabilities. This test is important for investors in rated CBO notes. It tends to be a harder hurdle in mortgage deals than in loan deals or in high-yield deals, as asset spreads are lower because average rating is much higher. As a result, it is often necessary to include CMBS IOs, which subsidizes current income, and help meet CBO interest coverage tests.

Overcollateralization and interest coverage tests are applied identically, regardless of deal type. Moreover, typical triggers for overcollateralization and interest coverage are very similar on the senior bonds, as senior bonds represent a roughly similar amount of deals in the two cases. Overcollateralization and interest coverage ratios are lower on mezzanine tranches of mortgage deals because of capital structure differences. That is, with more debt and less equity at initial launch, it stands to reason that overcollateralization and interest coverage would be lower on mezzanine tranches of CBOs supported by mortgage-related securities than on those backed by high-yield bonds.

Comparing Triggers

Exhibit 8 shows typical O/C and interest coverage ratios for the two types of deals. As can be seen, the O/C trigger on the Aaa bonds is generally 115%-125% on mortgage backed deals, while it is generally around 115-130 in high-yield deals. Initial O/C is slightly higher in high-yield deals, but the triggers are not. Since there is less equity in mortgage deals, they tend to have trigger levels closer to initial value. Similarly, interest coverage tests are very similar on Aaa tranches on all CBO deals — 115-125 in mortgage deals, and 120-130 on high-yield bond or high-yield loan deals.

At the Baa level, overcollateralization and interest coverage triggers on the mortgage deals are definitely lower — in the range of 100-105. O/C triggers on high-yield deals are generally in the 105-112 range, while interest coverage triggers are slightly higher. Again, this is not a cause for concern, it is a by-product of higher quality collateral, and hence, lower equity requirements are satisfactory.

RELATIVE VALUE

Many investors do not understand the structure and rating methodology on cash flow CBOs backed by mortgage related product. As a result of this unfamiliarity, spreads are somewhat wider than on similarly rate CBOs backed by high-yield bonds or by loans. While spread differentials are significant for all rating categories, the differences are larger the further down the credit spectrum one goes. Exhibit 9 shows a comparison of the spreads on mortgage CBOs versus high-yield CBOs. Note that all spreads are quoted over 3-month LIBOR, and are as of end-July 2000.

Exhibit 8: Overcollateralization and Interest Coverage Test

	Aaa		Baa	
	O/C	IC	O/C	IC
High Yield CBO	115-130	120-130	105-112	110-120
Mtg CBO	115-125	115-125	100-105	100-105

Exhibit 9: Comparison of Spreads over 3-Month LIBOR on Mortgage CBOs versus High-Yield CBOs

Ratings	Mortgage CBOs	High Yield CBOs
Aaa	45-50	40-45
Aa	70-90	55-75
A	125-150	105-135
Baa	225-250	185-245
Ba	650-750	525-625
B	1000	750+

In Aaa rated paper, mortgage-backed CBOs sell about 5 basis points wider than CBOs backed by high yield bonds or by loans. In A rated paper, the difference is 15-20 basis points, it is about 125 basis points on Ba rated paper. We would expect these differences to converge over time, as the investor base becomes more comfortable with CBOs backed by ABS/MBS/CMBS collateral.

CONCLUSION

Many investors view CBOs backed by mortgage collateral as completely different animals than CBOs backed by high-yield collateral. For that reason, we reviewed the history of the mortgage CBO market, and showed how the mortgage CBO market evolved. To wit, earlier structures were primarily market value deals, backed by short duration/high-grade assets that did not have a high-yield counterpart. More recent structures are primarily cash flow structures, backed by credit-sensitive ABS/RMBS/CMBS and REIT product. Structure and methodology for rating any of these securities are very similar to that used for cash flow high-yield deals.

The two major differences are that the cash flow mortgage deals tend to employ higher rated assets, and require less capital to support the liabilities. Rating methodology is exactly the same, with ratings based on cumulative expected default rates. Thus, capital required for each deal is determined objectively, based on expected default rates, loss severity assumptions, and diversification.

Chapter 7

CDOs Backed by ABS and Commercial Real Estate

R. Russell Hurst
Director
First Union Securities, Inc.

ollateralized debt obligation (CDO) structuring technology is now used to securitize the different asset classes of asset-backed securities (ABS) and commercial real estate (CRE). Although investors are beginning to embrace CDOs backed by ABS, they have more readily accepted CDOs backed by CRE. This has been due to similarities with structures in the commercial mortgage-backed securities (CMBS) market. At this early stage of development, it is useful to contrast these new products to what we know about the CDO market. To accomplish this, in this chapter we will explore the following topics:

- Motivation for issuance
- Whether these products are indeed new
- Framework for pricing the many types of CDOs
- A study by asset class on the remarkable credit quality of the ABS market
- The unique case for CDOs backed by CRE
- What is new and what is not about how each of the rating agencies rates CDOs backed by ABS and CRE

We will show that the ABS CDO is not as new as it seems. It is similar to an ABS commercial paper (CP) conduit, a special investment vehicle or, in the case of CRE, a CMBS conduit. The concept is also directly comparable to the taxable business of the monoline financial guaranty companies, which allocate their capital to each structured transaction insured. These companies must have enough capital to pay principal and interest claims when any of their insured transactions default (to an AAA level of certainty); otherwise, the monoline, and all of its guaranteed issues, will be downgraded.

Not surprisingly, motivations for issuance of these types of CDOs are similar to those for other types of CDOs. The exceptional credit quality characteristics of ABS and CRE are amplified in the CDO structure. We show that if we use historical corporate bond defaults to size any asset-backed transactions, the loss performance of the ABS will be superior to that of a corporate bond. This is a market-driven arbitrage that will allow issuance of this product for the foreseeable future. Our expectation is for exemplary credit and total-return performance of ABS CDOs and CRE CDOs.

MOTIVATION FOR ISSUANCE

There are two basic motivations for CDO issuance. The first is to transfer the collateral off the balance sheet of the issuer to achieve regulatory capital relief or manage the credit-risk profile of the issuer's balance sheet (balance-sheet-motivated). In 2000, we saw the CDO emerge as a significant balance-sheet management tool for banks. The second is a leveraged arbitrage of high-yielding collateral by insurance companies and asset-management companies (arbitrage-motivated) to generate asset-management fees and/or share in the attractive returns generated by the equity ownership. The latter group now includes the asset management arms of commercial banks.

The spreads available on mezzanine ABS and most CRE products have made the arbitrage available in securitizing these products attractive. The buy-and-hold nature of the products, or the relative illiquidity of the paper, has helped to keep the spread levels attractive. Acceptance of the CDO structure by investors and the floating-rate nature of the paper have also contributed to the arbitrage opportunity.

REINVENTING THE WHEEL —
SAME OLD STUFF IN A NEW PACKAGE

Some investors are concerned with the newness of the rules for ABS CDOs. It may seem surprising that the same rules have been used for more than 10 years to rate the structured finance securitization business of the financial guaranty firms. These rules were first developed by Financial Security Assurance Holdings Ltd. (FSA), founded in 1985, exclusively to insure ABS. The methodology has become progressively more sophisticated but is essentially the same today. As you might expect, the leverage of CDOs backed by ABS and CRE compares favorably to the leverage required by the rating agencies to support the guaranty of taxable structured financings (see Exhibit 1).

In any ABS transaction, a certain amount of subordination together with excess spread is needed to achieve a certain desired rating level. Exhibit 1 shows some of these levels. Ignoring the spread protection for the moment, our examples show higher-quality and more diverse pools of assets need less subordination or capital to achieve an AAA rating. Comparing our normal CDO with our insured CDO, an additional 18% of subordination is needed to achieve an AAA rating without the benefit of insurance. The examples also imply to be an A rated finance company you need 5% more capital than is provided in a normal CDO to achieve an investment-grade rating.

Exhibit 1: Leverage of CDOs Backed by ABS or CRE Compare Favorably to Monoline Insurers

Normal CDO (assets/liabilities)		Insured CDO (assets/liabilities)		A Rated Finance Company (assets/liabilities)		Monoline Financial Guaranty Company (assets/liabilities)		CDOs Backed by ABS or CRE (assets/liabilities)	
Below-Investment-Grade Loans and Bonds	72% AAA Tranche	Below-Investment-Grade Loans and Bonds	90% AAA Tranche	Below-Investment-Grade Loans and Bonds	65% A-1/P-1 Commercial Paper	Diversified Pool of Investment-Grade Asset-Backed and/or Commercial Real Estate-Backed Securities Pledged as Collateral	95% AAA Bonds Issued by Third Parties and Insured by a Monoline Company	Diversified Pool of Investment-Grade Asset-Backed and/or Commercial Real Estate-Backed Securities Pledged as Collateral	79% AAA Tranche
					20% A Rated Medium-Term Notes				15% AA, A, BBB Tranche
	18% AA, A, BBB Tranche								
	10% Equity Tranche—Leverage 10/1		10% Equity Tranche—Leverage 10/1		15% Equity Tranche—Leverage 6.7/1		5% Equity Tranche—Leverage 20/1		6% Equity Tranche—Leverage 16.7/1

ABS: Asset-backed securities; CDOs: Collateralized debt obligations; CRE: Commercial real estate.
Source: First Union Securities, Inc.

Why then have the rating agencies allowed insurers to lever up to 25 times capital in the structured finance business and still remain AAA rated? The agencies observed that groups of ABS classes were not correlated to each other in times of stress. This diversification reduces the probability of loss such that on average only 4% of capital is needed to provide the loss coverage necessary to upgrade a diversified investment-grade ABS portfolio to AAA. These capital charges would be less for the more homogenous asset classes and more for asset classes with wider expected loss dispersions. In the case of CDOs, the most efficient structures are requiring 4% to 10% subordination to achieve a BBB rating.

In summary, if the insurer has sufficient capital to support all of its insured transactions in a depression-like scenario, the rating will remain AAA. The subordination and excess spread protection of an ABS CDO tranche rated AAA is similar to the protection afforded the holder of an insured AAA ABS. Without the experience of regulating the financial guaranty companies over the past decade, it is unlikely the rating agencies could have created ABS CDO criteria so quickly.

Rating rationales across industrial and structured finance sectors are being modernized. A similar process of rule rationalization is occurring between structured finance market participants and regulatory and accounting bodies worldwide. We believe the capital requirements to support similar business activities across sectors will continue to converge.

STRATIFICATION OF CDO PRICING BY TYPE

The relatively young CDO market is far from being efficient. Although the first CDO was issued in 1988, significant volume has only been achieved since 1996. In 1999, CDO volume, which includes collateralized bond obligations (CBOs), collateralized loan obligations (CLOs), and hybrids (bond and loan collateral), surpassed the home equity loan (HEL) market in total public, private, and international new issuance. Using this same measure, CDOs ranked second behind HELs and before autos through the first half of 2000. Spreads on similarly rated tranches depend on many factors. We believe as the CDO market grows and becomes more efficient, investors will place more emphasis on the credit quality of the collateral. In the future, spreads over LIBOR of similarly rated tranches of CDOs should parallel the volatility of the expected losses of the collateral. Fundamentally, the volatility of credit losses depends on the type of collateral, the average rating of the collateral and its geographical mix.

Subclasses of CDOs have emerged based on the mix of collateral. There have been two new broadly defined collateral groups so far. One consists of the mezzanine tranches of one or more different ABS classes (ABS CDOs). The other is backed predominantly with CRE (CRE CDOs). As a result, we have added these two classes to Exhibit 2, which stratifies CDO types by collateral volatility. Most CDO new issuance can be grouped into the structures shown in Exhibit 2.

Exhibit 2: Collateral Volatility Characteristics by Type of CDO

Type	Acronym	% Loan Collateral	% Bond Collateral	% U.S. Collateral	% Emerging Market Collateral	% Commercial Real Estate	% ABS Collateral	Collateral Volatility Ranking
I	CLOs—BS	100	0	0–100	0	0–20	0–10	Lowest
II	CDOs—CRE	0	0	100	0	85–95	5–15	Low
III	CDOs—ABS	0	0	0–100	0–25	0–20	100	Low
IV	CLOs—BS	100	0	100	0	<5	<5	Low
V	CLOs—BS	100	0	75–85	15–25	<5	<5	Low/Moderate
VI	CDOs—Hybrid	75	20–40	100	0	<5	<5	Low/Moderate
VII	CDOs—Hybrid	75	20–40	75–85	15–25	<5	<5	Moderate
VIII	CBOs	0	100	100	0	<5	<5	Moderate
IX	CBOs	0	100	25–75	50–75	<5	<5	High

Source: First Union Securities, Inc.

ABS: Asset-backed securities; BS: Balance sheet; CBOs: Collateralized bond obligations; CDOs: Collateralized debt obligations; CLOs: Collateralized loan obligations; CRE: Commercial real estate.

Exhibit 3: Product Life Cycle of ABS

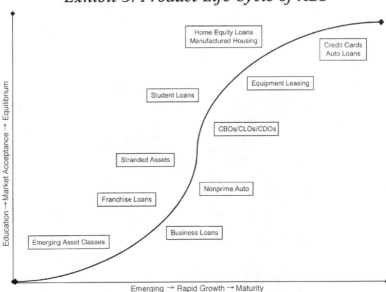

ABS: Asset-backed securities; CBOs: Collateralized bond obligations; CLOs: Collateralized loan obligations.

Source: First Union Securities, Inc.

The CDO market has been a buy-and-hold market until recently. Given the recent growth in CDO volume and the term structure of the product, CDO outstandings now rival credit cards and HELs for the top spot. Increased volume and greater investor understanding are creating greater liquidity for the product in the higher-rated classes and, as a result, secondary market activity is increasing for these classes. Once the market becomes more efficient, as has been the case with the development of markets in all asset classes (see Exhibit 3), spreads should vary with the volatility of the underlying collateral.

Decreased volatility and the ability to monitor performance should command tighter spreads to LIBOR over time as market acceptance grows. Other factors such as call protection (usually 3 to 5 years), the length of the reinvestment period, the strength of the manager, the diversity score, new issue supply, the amount of excess spread and the combination of rating agencies will affect the trading value of CDOs. In addition, CDO spreads will also be affected by the year in which the collateral was originated (a period when underwriting standards might have been aggressive versus a more restrictive environment). Expected collateral performance is still the key determinant of CDO secondary market and new issue spreads, but all of the factors mentioned above may cause CDOs to trade in wide ranges without regard for the above collateral groupings. Our approach is to start with the collateral groupings and make adjustments to the idealized spread for the other factors.

Exhibit 4: Product Life Cycle of CDOs

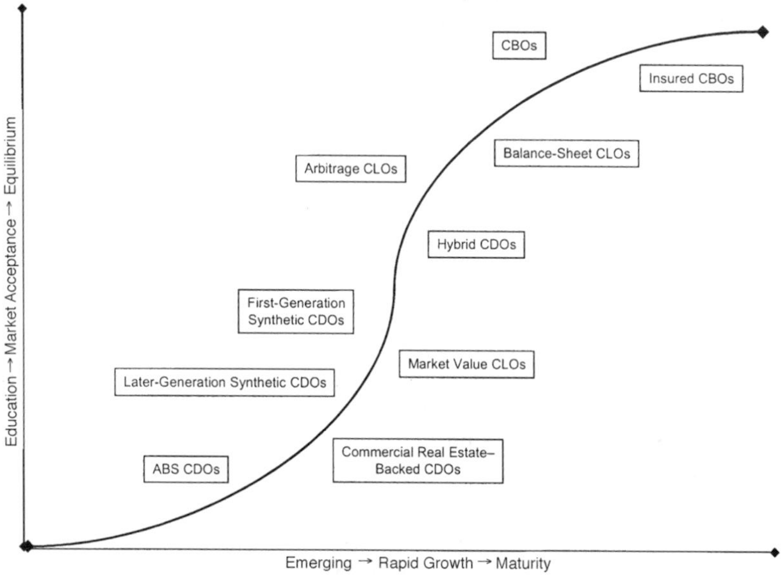

ABS: Asset-backed securities; CBOs: Collateralized bond obligations; CDOs: Collateralized debt obligations; CLOs: Collateralized loan obligations.

Source: First Union Securities, Inc.

Exhibit 3 shows CBOs/CLOs/CDOs to be in the midstage of their product life. Today, there is much greater market acceptance compared with 1988 when the first CBO was issued. Since then, the market has embraced plain vanilla CDOs and has been introduced to more innovative and complicated CDO structures. We have plotted the product life cycle of the various CDO products in Exhibit 4.

Varying spread premiums will be paid to investors for newness, complexity (story bond) and relative illiquidity. This spread premium will generally be greater the earlier the CDO product is in its product life development. As market acceptance grows over time and a greater understanding of the quality of the collateral is understood, this premium should dissipate. This has been the case with all ABS that have advanced through the ABS product life cycle.

Our view of CDO types and what their idealized spread should be (Exhibit 2) and the concept of a CDO product life cycle (Exhibit 4) allow us to differentiate and identify value when we look at current CDO new issue spreads. By identifying CDO products with low collateral volatility early in their product life cycle, a significant pickup in spread can be achieved without an increase in credit risk. Based on CDO type, current spreads should converge toward the idealized spread over time. To identify CDO sectors where we believe there is value, we examined new issue spreads for the various CDOs that have been issued through September 2000. Summary statistics that show the average, minimum and maximum spread over LIBOR of CDOs by type and the average minimum and maximum average life of the sample are shown in Exhibit 5. Exhibit 6 shows a listing of CDOs by type with notes on certain features.

The statistics show a stratification of spreads by product type that we would expect. The sample is small but representative of the diverse set of products issued in 2000. Although there were other CDO issuances, these were the ones where the pricing was disclosed. Most CDOs are private, with the exception of some balance-sheet CLOs, and pricing may not be publicly disclosed. The more mature product and low-volatility collateral types had the tightest spreads.

In our sample, balance-sheet-motivated CLOs had the tightest spread to LIBOR. A great deal of disclosure often accompanies these offerings, and the investor will look at the loan loss record of the selling bank. The tighter spreads are also partially explained by the shorter average lives of three and five years for this product. Arbitrage-motivated CLOs, CDOs with a loan/bond mix of collateral and CBOs — the three other most mature CDO types — had spreads 43 bps, 45 bps and 46 bps over LIBOR, respectively. We would expect the latter two, with collateral volatility ranked in the low/moderate and moderate categories, to trade behind CLOs, with collateral volatility ranked on the lower end of our scale. Most of the loan collateral is senior and secured, which provides high recoveries in default and results in a stable, predictable cash flow.

The data show the two newest types of CDOs, those in the earliest stages of their product life cycle, to be priced significantly wider than the more mature CDO products. CRE CDOs were issued 5 bps back of CBOs in early 2000. ABS CDOs were priced 8 bps behind CBOs on average. This is exciting because we believe the collateral volatility to be low for both types of CDOs. Once investors learn more about the superior quality and attractive characteristics of the collateral, ABS CDOs should trade in line with arbitrage CLOs.

Exhibit 5: Recent AAA Tranche CDO New Issue Spreads: 1/1/00-9/30/00

| | LIBOR Spread | | | | Average Life | | | No. of |
	Mean	Min.	Max.	SD	Mean	Min.	Max.	Tranches
CLOs—Balance Sheet	27	23	29	2.5	4.6	3.6	5.0	4
CLOs—Arbitrage	43	40	52	5.2	6.9	6.4	8.4	5
CDOs—Loan/Bond Mix	44	40	50	3.7	8.0	7.0	8.9	9
CBOs—Bonds	46	40	65	7.8	7.6	5.1	9.3	18
CLOs—CRE	51	42	58	7.0	6.8	5.2	8.2	4
CDOs—ABS	53	45	70	8.1	7.3	4.5	10.2	11
Total/Average	46	23	70	5.7	7.2	3.6	10.2	51

ABS: Asset-backed securities; CBOs: Collateralized bond obligations; CDOs: Collateralized debt obligations; CLOs: Collateralized loan obligations; CRE: Commercial real estate; SD: Standard deviation.
Source: McCarthy, Crisanti & Maffei, Inc. (MCM), and First Union Securities, Inc.

Exhibit 6: CDO New Issues 1/1/00-9/30/00(AAA tranches)

Date	Issuer	Series	AL	Spread	Index	Collateral/Comments
CBOs (predominantly bond collateral)						
1/31/00	Emerald Investment Grade CBO-II	I	7.4	48	6ML	Investment-grade and high-yield bonds
3/07/00	Juniper CBO-2	A-3I	8.9	65	6ML	High-yield debt; not rated by Moody's
3/07/00	Juniper CBO-2	A-1I	5.3	40	6ML	High-yield debt
4/05/00	South Street CBO 2000	A-1	5.1	40	6ML	North American and U.K. high-yield debt
4/05/00	South Street CBO 2000	A-2	6.9	45	6ML	North American and U.K. high-yield debt
4/05/00	South Street CBO 2000	A-3	8.7	60	6ML	North American and U.K. high-yield debt
4/18/00	American Express Centurion	Ia	7.6	42	6ML	90% U.S. high-yield bonds (guidelines provide for 10% loan bucket)
4/24/00	Gleacher CBO 2000-1 Ltd.	A	8.0	43	6ML	High-yield bonds and synthetic securities
5/22/00	Federated CBO II Ltd.	A-1	8.0	42	6ML	U.S. high-yield debt with a starting WARF of 2,587 and a ceiling of 2,720 (B2/B)
5/23/00	Eaton Vance CBO	A	7.2	43	6ML	80% high-yield bonds, 20% loan bucket
6/14/00	Rainier CBO 2000-1	A-1L	5.2	40	6ML	U.S. high-yield debt
6/14/00	Rainier CBO 2000-1	A-3L	9.3	60	6ML	U.S. high-yield debt
6/14/00	Rainier CBO 2000-1	A-2L	7.7	43	6ML	U.S. high-yield debt
6/21/00	Arlington Street	A1	8.5	40	1ML	High-yield debt (maximum 10% bank loan bucket)
6/21/00	Arlington Street	A2	8.9	52	6ML	High-yield debt (maximum 10% bank loan bucket)
6/27/00	(J.& W. Seligman) JWS CBO 2000-1	A-2	8.0	43	6ML	High-yield bonds (2,650 rating factor)
6/29/00	Magnetite CBO II	A-1	7.6	43	3ML	90% bonds, with up to a 10% loan bucket
7/21/00	FC CBO IV	A	7.7	41	6ML	85%–90% high-yield bonds and 10%–15% loans; no emerging markets
	Average		7.6	46		

Exhibit 6 (Continued)

Date	Issuer	Series	AL	Spread	Index	Collateral/Comments
CDOs—ABS (collateral includes a significant amount of ABS or other structured products)						
5/11/00	Phoenix CDO 2	A-1	7.5	51	3ML	95% investment-grade ABS and CMBS collateral with Baa2 average rating
4/27/00	Talon Funding Ltd.	A1	7.0	49	3ML	ABS, CMBS, REIT debt
3/15/00	Zais Investment Grade Ltd.	A1	8.0	45	6ML	CDOs, ABS
3/15/00	Zais Investment Grade Ltd.	A2	8.0	65	6ML	CDOs, ABS
6/08/00	SFA Collateralized Asset-Backed Securitization Trust	A1	5.4	60	3ML	CDOs, ABS
8/29/00	Beacon Hill CBO	A1	7.7	45	3ML	CDOs, ABS
8/30/00	Beacon Hill CBO	A2	7.7	50	3ML	CDOs, ABS
9/12/00	St. George Funding CBO	A	4.5	50	3ML	CDOs, ABS
6/28/00	ClearWater Funding CBO 2000-A	A	7.2	53	6ML	Project finance, equipment trust, ABS; 30% emerging market; MBIA insured
6/28/00	North Street Referenced Linked Notes 2000-1 Ltd.	A	10.2	70	3ML	UBS synthetic CDO; ABS 60%, REITs, corporates; Fitch-only rating
8/17/00	Diversified Asset Securitization Holdings (D-A-S-H)-2	A-1L	7.5	49	3ML	ABS
Average			7.3	53		
CDOs—CRE (collateral includes a significant amount of CRE collateral)						
4/07/00	Diversified REIT Trust 2000-1	A-1	5.8	42	3ML	23 investment-grade bonds
4/07/00	Diversified REIT Trust 2000-1	A-2	7.9	58	3ML	23 investment-grade bonds
5/12/00	Ingress I Ltd.	A-1	5.2	50	3ML	ABS, CMBS, REIT debt
5/12/00	Ingress I Ltd.	A-2	8.2	55	3ML	ABS, CMBS, REIT debt
Average			6.8	51		

Exhibit 6: CDO New Issues Year-to-Date 2000 (AAA tranches) (continued)

Date	Issuer	Series	AL	Spread	Index	Collateral/Comments
CDOs—Loan/Bond Mix						
3/07/00	Harch Capital Management	A	8.2	50	3ML	70% loans, 30% high-yield debt
3/28/00	Muzinich & Co.	A	7.6	47	6ML	U.S. high yield (95% loan bucket)
4/06/00	Greenwich Street Partners	1-A, Senior	8.9	40	6ML	Loans, bonds
4/20/00	Stanfield-RMF TransAtlantic Ltd.	A-1	7.6	49	3ML	U.S. and European senior secured loans, 30% bonds
5/09/00	Black Diamond CLO 2000-1 Ltd.	A	8.7	43	3ML	Senior secured loans, high-yield bonds
5/12/00	Katonah CLO	A	8.0	43	3ML	85%–95% bank loans; balance in high-yield debt; MBIA insured
5/19/00	Avalon II Capital Ltd.	A	8.0	45	3ML	Senior secured loans
6/16/00	Harbor View CBO	A	7.0	42	3ML	70% senior secured loans and 30% high-7/
21/00	Madison Avenue CDO	A	7.9	40	6ML	High-yield debt, senior bank loans, synthetic securities, and structured finance securities
	Average		8.0	44		
CLOs—Arbitrage						
3/24/00	Columbus Loan Funding Ltd.	A-1	8.4	52	3ML	Senior secured loans
5/26/00	ELC 2000-1 CDO	A-2	6.6	40	3ML	Senior secured loans
5/26/00	ELC 2000-1 CDO	A-1	6.6	40	3ML	Senior secured loans
6/07/00	Franklin CLO-I	A-1	6.4	42	3ML	Senior secured loans
7/27/00	Eaton Vance CDO III	A-1	6.6	40	3ML	European loans
	Average		6.9	43		
CLOs—Balance Sheet						
1/20/00	Chase Loan Obligations USA Trust 2000-1	A	3.6	27	1ML	Investment-grade loans
4/18/00	Clover Funding No. 1 PLC	A	5.0	27	3ML	100% loans
5/30/00	Sundial Finance Ltd.	A	5.0	23	3ML	100% loans
6/23/00	Olan Enterprises II Plc	A	5.0	29	3ML	100% loans
	Average		4.6	27		

ABS: Asset-backed securities; AL: Average life; CBOs: Collateralized bond obligations; CDOs: Collateralized debt obligations; CLOs: Collateralized loan obligations; CMBS: Commercial mortgage-backed securities; MBIA: Municipal Bond Insurance Association; MBS: Mortgage-backed securities; REITs: Real estate investment trusts; WARF: Weighted average rating factor.

Source: McCarthy, Crisanti & Maffei, Inc. (MCM), Bloomberg, Moody's Investors Service, Inc., Fitch, Inc., and First Union Securities, Inc.

For CRE CDOs, we expect the paper to trade inside of arbitrage CLOs but modestly behind bank-sponsored CMBS conduit issuers. Similar to CMBS, CRE CDOs are passively managed. With 10-year bullet maturities and the substantial call protection of the underlying collateral, there is little need for active management. Additional spread protection is created by not paying the 25 bps to 50 bps management fee required by actively managed transactions. This spread protection more than compensates for any increased optionality of the CRE CDO structure versus a normal CMBS structure. With passive management, the designated manager can only sell collateral if there is a risk of credit impairment. These structural features result in tranching similar to that of a CMBS deal, tighter payment windows than ABS CDOs and pricing that should move closer to that of CMBS over time.

CRE CDOs have also adopted disclosure practices similar to those of CMBS transactions. This disclosure enhances the liquidity of the CRE CDO market. These disclosure practices include

- *Transparency and availability of information.* When traders are asked to bid, information is readily available on the collateral and deal performance (besides the trustee report).
- *Dealers behind the transaction.* One or more dealers understand and are ready to trade the secondary paper.
- *Analytics.* Deals are modeled by third-party services such as Intex Group and Charter Communications, L.P.

ABS COLLATERAL QUALITY

We expect the performance of ABS CDOs, as part of a spread sector portfolio, to outperform. This is true because spread will tighten as more investors understand that the ABS collateral is less volatile. ABS collateral is less volatile because:

- ABS have been largely event-risk-free.
- ABS produce only marginal losses in the worst case.
- ABS have been default-free for more than 12 years.

The value added of an ABS CDO or a CRE CDO is the risk-tranching for those that understand the risk of the collateral. The arbitrage in an ABS CDO is allowed in part by the understatement of the credit quality of ABS and CRE-backed securities by the rating agencies. The investment-grade collateral quality found in ABS CDOs and CRE CDOs is superior to the high-yield-bond and leveraged-loan collateral of a normal CDO. The predictability of cash flows and freedom from collateral event risk should result in less volatile returns.

ABS continue to outperform the Moody's Investors Service, Inc. rated universe of corporate bonds when measured in terms of defaults and downgrades. The track record is amazing and should lead to a redefinition of how ABS ratings are stratified.

Exhibit 7: Credit Stability of ABS versus Comparable Corporates

Original Rating	Cumulative Five-Year Default Rate		Yearly Downgrades			Yearly Upgrades		
	CORP	ABS	1999 CORP	ABS Three-Year Avg.	ABS Five-Year Avg.	1999 CORP	ABS Three-Year Avg.	ABS Five-Year Avg.
Aaa	0.00%	0.00%	2.75%	0.00%	0.00%	0.00%	0.00%	0.00%
Aa	0.00%	0.00%	5.38%	0.42%	0.00%	1.99%	0.01%	3.33%
A	0.00%	0.00%	6.31%	0.50%	0.00%	2.28%	2.50%	3.67%
Baa	1.55%	0.00%	6.47%	3.83%	2.32%	5.27%	0.01%	1.83%
Ba	6.48%	0.00%	11.26%	2.83%	0.00%	7.50%	5.00%	2.50%
B	17.47%	0.00%	11.96%	1.00%	0.00%	4.53%	0.00%	0.00%
Investment Grade	0.41%	0.00%	5.23%	1.14%	0.53%	2.39%	1.90%	2.91%
Speculative Grade	12.98%	0.00%	11.61%	5.75%	0.00%	6.02%	3.00%	1.11%
All Corporates/ABS	4.07%	0.00%	7.36%	1.27%	0.37%	3.60%	0.89%	2.39%

ABS: All public and private asset-backed securities rated by Moody's; CORP: All public corporate bonds rated by Moody's.
Note: Data as of Dec. 31, 1999.
Source: Moody's Investors Service, Inc., and First Union Securities, Inc.

The underwriting criteria for ABS crafted by the rating agencies uses historical default studies to define loss tolerance for a like-rated ABS tranche. In other words, for Moody's, the expected loss of an A rated corporate is the same as an A rated ABS tranche. Standard and Poor's Corp. (S&P) would say the two A rated issues have the same probability of default. Although we are beginning to see more downgrades and will certainly see some defaults over the next decade, it is worthwhile pointing out just how dramatically ABS have outperformed corporates.

- The cumulative 5-year default rate (total defaults on debt outstanding five years ago) for all corporates as of December 31, 1999, was 4.07% versus zero for ABS.
- BBB corporates had a 1.55% 5-year cumulative default rate versus zero for BBB ABS.
- Corporate investment-grade downgrades in 1999 exceeded the ABS 3-year average for investment-grade ABS downgrades by five times and the 5-year average by 20 times.

Exhibit 7 includes downgrades of ABS that resulted from corporate downgrades. The data did not allow separating the collateral performance downgrades from the corporate credit-related downgrades for this analysis. In Exhibit 8, where we measure downgrades by asset class in a different way, contrasts collateral performance downgrades against corporate downgrades. Because the default levels and downgrade levels are so disparate, we believe guidelines for rating ABS will be adjusted over time.

Exhibit 8: Moody's Investors Service, Inc., Summary of ABS Rating Changes (1986-1999)

Asset Type	Upgrade of CE Total	Strong Performance Total	Grand Total	Percent of Total	Downgrade of CE Total	Weak Performance Total	Grand Total	Percent of Total	Upgrades Net of Downgrades
Agricultural Industrial Equipment	0	7	7	2.36%	0	0	0	0.00%	2.36%
Airline Tickets	1	0	1	0.34%	0	0	0	0.00%	0.34%
Auto Floor Plans	0	1	1	0.34%	0	0	0	0.00%	0.34%
Autos—Prime	0	26	26	8.78%	34	0	34	9.50%	-0.71%
Autos—Subprime	0	13	13	4.39%	0	34	34	9.50%	-5.11%
CBOs/CLOs	1	2	3	1.01%	3	45	48	13.41%	-12.39%
Charged-Off Credit Cards	0	0	0	0.00%	0	6	6	1.68%	-1.68%
Consumer Loans	0	0	0	0.00%	3	0	3	0.84%	-0.84%
Credit Cards	0	80	80	27.03%	27	0	27	7.54%	19.49%
Equipment Loans	1	0	1	0.34%	0	0	0	0.00%	0.34%
Home Equities	19	20	39	13.18%	39	16	55	15.36%	-2.19%
Manufactured Housing	53	59	112	37.84%	93	49	142	39.66%	-1.83%
Marine Loans	0	0	0	0.00%	2	0	2	0.56%	-0.56%
Motorcycles	1	0	1	0.34%	0	0	0	0.00%	0.34%
Oil Contracts	1	0	1	0.34%	0	0	0	0.00%	0.34%
Recreational Vehicles and Equipment	0	4	4	1.35%	6	0	6	1.68%	-0.32%
Small Business Loans	0	3	3	1.01%	0	0	0	0.00%	1.01%
Trucks	0	4	4	1.35%	0	0	0	0.00%	1.35%
Structured Loans	0	0	0	0.00%	1	0	1	0.28%	-0.28%
Total	77	219	296	100.00%	208	150	358	100.00%	0.00%
No. Outstanding as of Jan. 1, 2000			22,651				22,651		
Percentage Upgraded/Downgraded per Year			1.31%				1.58%		

ABS: Asset-backed securities; CE: Credit enhancer; CBOs: Collateralized bond obligations; CLOs: Collateralized loan obligations.

Source: Moody's Investors Service, Inc., and First Union Securities, Inc.

Eventually, corporates and ABS with the same rating will have similar default and downgrade statistics. The arbitrage in an ABS CDO or a CRE CDO is allowed in part by the understatement of the credit quality of ABS. Until the rating agencies adjust their underwriting standards, the arbitrage will continue to exist and ABS will continue to outperform corporates.

The most important aspect of analyzing an ABS is a thorough understanding of the collateral. With ABS, this entails understanding the collateral's payment characteristics; the security's structural features, particularly those that redirect cash flow; and the legal risk. Germane to all ABS is the predictability of cash flows and a certain freedom from event risk.

More loss protection will be required in the structure of an ABS when there is a greater uncertainty of cash flows. Absent fraud, when a mistake is made in the estimation of cash flows for an ABS, some of the lower-rated tranches may be downgraded a notch or two. In this case, the economic return to the equity holder may be diminished and a marginal loss may develop at the lower-rated tranches. It differs from the circumstances surrounding a default on a corporate bond, where the bankruptcy process may take two or three years or longer to determine what the recovery might be on a claim. To date, in more than 12 years, there has not been a default on any public or private ABS rated by Moody's.

To learn more about the credit quality of ABS, we compiled a list of all ABS upgraded or downgraded by Moody's since the agency began rating ABS in 1986. We then grouped downgrades together and upgrades together. Rating changes were then labeled in one of two ways — those that were a result of collateral performance or those that resulted from the upgrade or downgrade of a corporate guarantor or credit enhancer. The total number of downgrades and upgrades in each year was then compared with the number of ABS outstanding at the beginning of that same year. The result was a year-by-year percentage rate of downgrades and upgrades by asset class.

We calculated the contribution of performance-based changes to each year's rating and that of corporate-based rating changes to each year's total. We were unable to determine from the data provided by Moody's what portion of the ABS outstanding at the beginning of each year was performance-based or credit-enhanced. Thus, the rating change data incorporates some corporate bond rating volatility into the numbers below. True ABS are not dependent on corporate ratings to maintain their rating but are dependent on collateral performance and structural integrity. The results may be modestly overstated in years where corporate- or credit-based changes exceeded performance downgrades. The results, however, are informative and conservative and provide valuable information on what rating migration might be expected in each asset class. The results are summarized in Exhibit 8.

Exhibiting remarkable stability, ABS tranches have had 296 upgrades and 358 downgrades over the past 14 years. However, the rating agencies have become much more active in making rating changes in the ABS market over the past two years. All but two of the 654 rating changes occurred in 1998 and 1999. This is partly due to the remarkable growth in the asset-backed market and partly due to the financial turmoil in the credit markets in 1998 and 1999.

Securitizations of certain asset classes are structured to improve over time and others are structured with self-correcting mechanisms to avoid downgrades. It is worthwhile to briefly discuss upgrades and downgrades in this context.

Upgrades

There were 77 ABS upgrades over these 14 years due to the upgrading of a credit enhancer or the upgrading of a key party to the transaction. Specialty finance companies have often guaranteed lower-rated tranches of a home equity or manufactured housing securitization, or an interest-only (I/O) strip, to achieve a better execution on the financing. When the specialty finance company is upgraded or downgraded, the guaranteed tranche is upgraded or downgraded accordingly. This kind of rating change accounted for 72 of the 77 upgrades due to upgrades of credit enhancers.

There were 219 upgrades due to an improvement in the collateral performance of the transaction. Autos, credit cards, home equities and manufactured housing have features that allow for a buildup of credit protection. These asset classes accounted for 198 of the collateral performance upgrades. Autos will amortize over time so that debt service coverage increases on the mezzanine and subordinate tranches. Credit cards are often structured with spread accounts that build up over time, increasing credit protection. Collateral performance in general has been excellent for the industry over the past year. Home equities and manufactured housing have features that will capture spread in a reserve account for a certain period of time or until certain performance criteria are met. In addition, real estate values improve over time, which increases credit protection as excess spread is used to deleverage the transaction. This effectively increases the loss protection to the bondholder. CDOs also have features that cause the transactions to strengthen. For CDOs, this occurs once the reinvestment period has ended. At this point, the transaction delevers, with excess cash flow used to pay down tranches sequentially. This mechanism causes collateral coverage to increase at all tranche levels. As the recent surge in CDO volume has occurred from 1996 through 2000, the reinvestment period for most products has not yet expired.

Downgrades

The 358 downgrades consisted of 208 downgrades where the credit enhancer was downgraded and 150 downgrades for weaker-than-expected collateral performance. Again, finance companies and specialty finance companies accounted for almost all of the credit-enhancer downgrades. The analysis of these transactions requires an understanding of the underlying ABS and the finance company's credit standing.

CBOs, not CLOs, accounted for many of the downgrades due to weak performance as the result of exposure to emerging markets and, more recently, four or five troubled industries in the U.S. high-yield market. Somewhat surprisingly, CLOs were largely spared in this spate of downgrades. Subprime autos, manufacturing housing and home equities accounted for the balance of down-grades during the 14-year period. All of the specialty finance companies have been recovering from an industry shakeout that occurred due to intense competition. As a result, some of the collateral generated was underwritten aggressively and priced inappropriately for the risk. A moderate number of downgrades ensued.

A 10-year downgrade average of 2.28% for all ABS is still remarkable compared with a 7.36% average last year for corporates. We believe ABS will continue to outperform corporates, largely due to the structure of ABS. The solid credit-quality characteristics of ABS and CRE are amplified in the CDO structure.

DISTINGUISHING CRE CDOS FROM ABS CDOS

Real estate investment trusts (REITs) issue unsecured corporate bonds that are not considered ABS. CMBS are considered structured products and are not usually grouped with ABS. Home equities, manufactured housing and franchise loans are usually secured by real estate and are considered ABS. A predominant mix of REIT and CMBS collateral in a CDO structure would not be an ABS CDO. We prefer the nomenclature that more correctly describes such collateral — a CRE CDO.

The most efficient structure for any ABS typically parallels the cash flow characteristics of its underlying collateral. Depending on whether ABS CDOs are passively or actively managed, the diversity, average credit rating of the collateral and recovery rate assumptions (real estate asset classes have higher recovery rates), ABS CDOs will have different capital structures.

The collateral in a CRE CDO includes mostly investment-grade REIT bonds and the mezzanine pieces of a CMBS. A small amount of real-estate-themed ABS such as manufactured housing, franchise loans or HELs may also be included. Although we do not refer to CRE CDOs as ABS CDOs, the addition of this category will add depth and breadth to the CDO market.

To facilitate the issuance of CRE CDOs, Moody's has created 11 industry classifications for use in the agency's alternative diversity score model (see Exhibit 9).

Moody's has three categories of CMBS for use in a CDO — a CMBS conduit, a credit tenant lease (CTL), and a large loan. Most CMBS conduits are large and have a large number of property-type and geographically diversified commercial mortgage loans. Large loans might finance trophy properties or large office buildings; by definition, they are not diversified. The Empire State Build-ing or the Saks Fifth Avenue building might be considered trophy properties. A CTL depends on the creditworthiness of the tenant. In general, the tenant, almost always investment-grade, guarantees the lease payment on a commercial property used in its business. In a CDO, this would be categorized using the rating agency's standard industry classifications.

Exhibit 9: Commercial Real Estate (CRE) Classifications for CDOs

CDO	Classification
CMBS Conduits	1
CMBS Credit Tenant Leases	2
CMBS Large Loans	3
Hotel REITs	4
Multifamily REITs	5
Office REITs	6
Retail REITs	7
Industrial REITs	8
Healthcare REITs	9
Diversified REITs	10
Self-Storage REITs	11

CDOs: Collateralized debt obligations; CMBS: Commercial mortgage-backed securities; REITs: Real estate investment trusts.

Source: Moody's Investors Service, Inc.

S&P rated 1,622 tranches in 565 CMBS transactions. Of the 1,622 rated tranches, 331 (20.4%) were initially rated in the BBB category. Of all tranches rated in the BBB category by S&P, 18 experienced upgrades (5.4%) and 21 experienced downgrades (6.3%). None have defaulted. A similar study by Fitch, Inc., found the default rate over the past 10 years to be 0.09% by principal balance. Again, none of the BBB rated CMBS defaulted.

Mortgages in a CMBS conduit will have loan-to-values (LTVs) of underlying mortgages ranging up to 90%. The underlying collateral in a typical CMBS securitization will have some kind of prepayment protection. This protection most often takes the form of a lockout or make-whole provision. CMBS also benefit from a special servicer who will make advances for any missed mortgage payments as long as that payment is deemed by the servicer to be recoverable by an eventual sale of the property. This protection helps smooth the lumpiness of cash flows in the transaction. CRE CDOs will mostly invest in the BBB range of CMBS tranches. This range has the highest spread over the all-in cost of a CDO execution. A BBB CMBS also benefits from the loss protection provided by an additional 10% to 20% subordination, depending on the overall quality of the commercial mortgage pool. In a typical transaction, the real estate underlying the commercial mortgages would have to lose more than 30% of its value before an investor in the BBB tranche of a CMBS conduit would be in danger of principal impairment. This scenario is unlikely on a diversified and carefully selected CMBS portfolio. This level of protection explains in part the sector's excellent credit performance.

REITs are exempt from income taxes at the corporate level if they meet a number of specific Internal Revenue Service (IRS) rules, the most important of which are as follows:

- Ninety-five percent of a REIT's ordinary income must be distributed to shareholders.
- At least 75% of the value of a REIT's total assets must be represented by real estate.
- No more than 30% of gross income may come from selling properties held fewer than four years.

Because REITs pay out 95% of their cash flow, it is difficult for them to grow through earnings retention. Therefore, REITs must maintain access to public capital markets. This necessity gives rise to an exceptional level of security by the investing public and the rating agencies. These characteristics of REITs lead to superior management and better-quality properties in any commercial property market.

The various REIT sectors include

Healthcare: hospitals; congregate care, assisted living and long-term care facilities; and skilled-nursing facility properties

Hotel and leisure: lodging, resort, golf course and other hospitality properties, as well as leisure facilities

Industrial: industrial, manufacturing, warehouse or distribution and flex properties; triple-net-leased industrial properties; and industrial self-storage facilities

Office: central business district properties, suburban office properties and triple-net-leased office properties

Retail: restaurants, community shopping centers, regional malls, strip malls, outlet centers and triple-net-leased retail properties

Residential: apartments and multifamily and manufactured housing properties

Self-storage: self-storage facilities for residential needs or small commercial storage

An investment by a CDO in a REIT will technically be a senior unsecured corporate bond. Again, as with CMBS, the bond will be rated in the BBB range. The senior debt of a REIT, because of its covenants, is similar to a BBB CMBS conduit investment. Typical covenants would be that total debt cannot exceed 60% of total assets, secured debt cannot exceed 40% of total assets, interest coverage must exceed 1.5× and unencumbered assets must represent at least 150% of unsecured debt. An LTV of at least 60% is implied, which is comparable to the protection afforded the investor in a BBB CMBS tranche. Other features of the bonds include make-whole provisions and bullet maturities. As a result, the credit performance of REITs has been excellent.

The collateral features of CMBS and REITs have resulted in a CRE CDO structure similar to that of a CMBS securitization. The average-life stability results in a smaller tranche-by-tranche payment window than a CDO backed by ABS. In addition, CMBS with five-year and 10-year soft bullet maturities and 10-year REIT debt with bullet maturities allow the structuring of one Aaa tranche with a shorter average life and one with a longer average life. Due to the tighter payment windows, investment-grade or better collateral and a structure similar to that of a CMBS transaction, the pricing of a CRE CDO should continue to be inside that of an ABS CDO. The CRE CDO should also move closer over time to the pricing of CMBS tranches with similar ratings and average lives as investors better understand the underlying collateral performance. Aside from the structural considerations, CRE CDO spread levels have benefited from a broader investment base than other CDOs. So far, CRE CDOs have attracted investors from the CMBS and ABS markets.

Although there is little need to actively manage collateral in either a CMBS or a CRE CDO, the latter does not require a special servicer. This is primarily due to the buy-and-hold nature of the collateral. Another benefit of the new structure is the diversification of servicing risk. The sponsor of the CDO can sell collateral only in a stressed situation. To date, CRE CDOs have been passively managed.

RATING AGENCY APPROACH TO RATING ABS CDOS AND CRE CDOS

The rating agencies have allowed CDOs backed by ABS and CRE to be rated and issued by creating more industry classifications. The rating of CDOs by the rating agencies has to date been largely derivative of losses that are predicted from the agencies' respective historical default studies. These studies have not included ABS due to the difficulty of comparing ABS with corporates. Until now, the effect has economically prohibited the issuance of a CDO backed by ABS and CRE. The expected returns on such an issuance were not sufficient to attract equity investors.

Even now, the expected loss for a desired rating is determined by the loss severity of historical data that does not include ABS. As we pointed out in the ABS and CRE asset-quality sections, because ABS have no default record, expected losses are lower on ABS than corporate bonds. If we use historical corporate bond defaults to size any asset-backed transaction, the loss performance of that ABS will be superior to that of a corporate bond over time. The reason the rating agencies have modified their CDO requirements to accommodate ABS and CRE collateral is to close the gap between the corporate-bond and ABS default expectations. This market-driven arbitrage allows such transactions to be rated and issued.

The rating agencies have modified their approach to rating cash flow CDOs to accommodate ABS CDOs and CRE CDOs. The current approach will also be reviewed. A common theme has been to create more industry classifications for ABS. This has been a tacit recognition by the rating agencies that the rating performance of ABS has not been directly correlated to the industrial classifications used in the rating agencies' default studies.

When Moody's and Fitch rate a CDO backed by high-yield bonds or bank loans, they shadow rate all the underlying bonds they do not already rate.

S&P adopted a notching mechanism to arrive at its shadow ratings. For ABS CDOs and CRE CDOs, all the rating agencies use some form of notching, allowing securities not directly rated by them into the transaction.

The loss curves used by all three rating agencies are front-end, middle- and back-loaded, similar to the way they rate normal CDOs. The front-end loss curve is reasonable for corporates (e.g., event risk), but it is overly conservative for ABS, which go through a seasoning curve that causes the actual loss curve to peak in the middle years.

Moody's Approach to Rating ABS CDOs and CRE CDOs

Moody's uses the Binomial Expansion Model (BET) to rate ABS CDOs and CRE CDOs. This approach is the same as that currently used to rate cash flow CDOs. The BET compares the credit risk inherent in the underlying portfolio with the credit protection offered by the structure. This method essentially reduces, for modeling purposes, the actual pool of collateral assets (typically a pool of heterogeneous assets with correlated default behavior) to a homogeneous pool of uncorrelated assets via the diversity score. The diversity score represents the number of independent, identical assets that have the same loss distribution as the initial pool. The formula for the diversity score is rather imposing and is not explained here.

To calculate the diversity score, portfolio parameters must be input that include the rating profile, the par amount, the maturity profile and the default correlation assumptions. The formula uses the correlation coefficient between each of Moody's industry categories to reduce the number of bonds in the collateral pool to a number of uncorrelated units. Moody's has created 30 new industry classifications for use in CDOs backed by ABS or CRE. These are in addition to the 33 standard industry classifications. Moody's guidance to those structuring an ABS CDO or a CRE CDO is to look at ABS categories first when selecting the asset class and use only the standard industry categories if none of the structured securities categories fit. Furthermore, the current categories were tailored to individual transactions, although Moody's intends to standardize the categories and correlation factors.

Moody's has developed correlation coefficients within each group for use in the formula. For example, based on these correlation coefficients, 80 bonds may produce a diversity score of 45 or 70 depending on the degree of correlation. In addition, a set of rules has been developed to address an overlap in the collateral pool between the groups. Based on the individual recovery rates input, the Moody's diversity score model also provides an average recovery rate for use in the BET calculation.

In addition to these variables, the BET calculation requires the weighted-average probability of default of the original portfolio. This is derived from the Moody's default study using the weighted-average rating of the collateral portfolio. We have derived the rating factors listed in Exhibit 10 from the 1999 Moody's default study. These factors serve as a proxy for the weighted-average probability of default of a portfolio.

Exhibit 10: Derived Rating Factors

Rating	Factor
Aaa	1
Aa1	10
Aa2	20
Aa3	40
A1	70
A2	120
A3	180
Baa1	260
Baa2	360
Baa3	610
Ba1	940
Ba2	1,350
Ba3	1,780
B1	2,220
B2	2,720
B3	3,490
Caa1	4,770
Caa2	6,500
Caa3	8,070

Source: First Union Securities Inc.

Using a simple formula, a probability for each possible default path (from 0 to the total number of identical assets in the collateral pool) is calculated. The cash flow model is then used to test the structure of the transaction. Moody's currently has about 30 stress scenarios (six default curves and five LIBOR curves), each of which is used to uncover a possible weakness in a proposed transaction. After choosing one of the stress scenarios, the loss for each default path can be calculated. This loss is the present value of cash flows due to the noteholder of the tranche being tested discounted by the rated coupon. Each default path loss is then multiplied by its previously calculated probability. The expected loss of the stress scenario is determined by summing these products.

The expected loss (as a percentage of original par) is then compared with Moody's idealized cumulative expected loss rates. This is a table of yield change limits (percentage of the present value of losses) sorted by average life and rating. For a tranche to pass the test and achieve the desired rating, it must not exceed these limits. For example, a seven-year average-life Aaa CDO tranche must not exceed a 0.00286% idealized cumulative expected loss. An A2 rating would be allowed if the same tranche did not exceed an idealized cumulative expected loss of 0.39050%. These idealized cumulative expected loss rate tables are provided by Moody's and are derived from Moody's default study. As the study is updated every year based on the prior year's experience, the average 10-year cumulative default levels may change. In addition, the recovery assumptions used in the model may change based on current observations. The changes are usually small, but Moody's will occasionally update these variables if the default study levels diverge dramatically from the model assumptions. These calculations are done for each stress scenario and each tranche. Moody's also stresses prepayments on all prepayment-sensitive assets. The structure and cash flows are tinkered with until each test is passed. At that point, the transaction can be rated.

To accommodate ABS CDOs, Moody's has created loss-severity assumptions that vary by asset type, rating and the percentage each rated tranche is of the original transaction face value. This last requirement suggests Moody's believes loss severity increases as ABS are paid down. This determination is largely due to the decreased diversity of the collateral over time. There are six groups of loss severity assumptions — CRE, diversified ABS (commodity asset classes), residential real estate (e.g., manufactured housing, home equities), less-diversified ABS (e.g., franchise loans, aircraft), high-yield CDOs and emerging-market or low-diversity CDOs.

The other set of distinct requirements for this type of CDO define the correlation of tranches from the same issuer for the purpose of calculating the diversity score. Moody's specifies tranches of the same issue are 100% correlated. Moody's also indicates tranches of transactions issued by the same issuer within one year of each other are 100% correlated, within two years — 75% and so on.

S&P's Approach to Rating ABS CDOs and CRE CDOs

S&P continues to be criticized for keeping the details of its CDO rating model in what the market (and S&P) refers to as a black box. However, S&P has developed a version of the model in which default probabilities are visible, the loss distribution is viewable and the code that calculates the distribution is disclosed. Even so, as we write this article, S&P notes that some of the model described here will change. The CBO/CLO group at S&P rates ABS CDOs and CRE CDOs. Corporate defaults are used as a proxy for ABS. Although this approach is less than ideal, S&P is concerned with the short history of the ABS market. However, S&P recognizes ABS have been more stable than corporates over the past 10 years. To adopt its model to incorporate ABS and CRE, S&P has divided them into five classes and modeled correlation assumptions among them. S&P also placed limitations on some parameters such as a percentage limit for a particular class of ABS or CRE. The rating is based on the same cash flow analyses used to rate CDOs.

A cash flow model is constructed for each CDO with a goal of reflecting and modeling the transaction accurately and assuring the rating assigned is commensurate with the probability of default. S&P's default model produces an asset-specific default rate. The model also provides the expected level of default at each rating level and projects the expected level of gross defaults over the life of the asset pool. S&P uses its ratings as a measure of default probability. These probabilities have been derived from S&P's default study, which measures the average defaults of all the securities it rates. Based on the rating level desired on any given tranche and the weighted-average maturity of the assets, the tranche's default rate probability is obtained from the same default-rate table used for the asset-specific default rates.

Exhibit 11: Sample Default Patterns

Pattern/Year	1	2	3	4	5
1	15	30	30	15	10
2	20	20	20	20	20
3	40	20	20	10	10
4	25	25	25	26	—
5	10	15	30	30	15

Source: First Union Securities Inc.

Exhibit 12: Sample Recovery Assumptions

Corporate	Factor		ABS	Factor		Subordinated	Factor
Senior Unsecured	37		Senior			AA	35
Senior Secured	50		AAA	85		A	30
Subordinated	20		AA	75		BBB	25
			A	70		BB	15
						B	10

Source: First Union Securities Inc.

S&P typically assumes defaults start at the beginning of each of the first five years regardless of the reinvestment period. Five indicative default patterns are shown in Exhibit 11.

Recovery assumptions are different for ABS CDOs and CRE CDOs than for other types of CDOs. Recoveries vary by rating and degree of subordination. For transactions with floating-rate liabilities, S&P assumes certain interest rate curves. All hedges must be modeled into the transactions. S&P also stresses prepayment on all prepayment-sensitive assets. Combinations of swaps, caps and floors are common for hedging interest-rate volatility. Some transactions will use basis and timing swaps as well. Maintenance tests, such as interest coverage by tranche and par value, become part of the model.

Recovery Rates

Instead of using a dollar-based weighted-average recovery rate, S&P uses a risk-weighted recovery. This recovery rate is designed to take into account individual asset exposure and the probability of certain assets experiencing defaults. Recoveries on defaulted bonds are realized one year after the default. (See the samples in Exhibit 12.)

Interest Rates

S&P has provided FUSI with three LIBOR curves to be used in all default scenarios. These curves represent LIBOR increasing, LIBOR decreasing and LIBOR decreasing, then increasing.

Effectively, the recovery rate on lower-rated assets counts more than that of higher-rated assets.

Fitch's Approach to Rating ABS CDOs and CRE CDOs

Fitch's approach to rating ABS CDOs and CRE CDOs was significantly revised and modified in November 2000 and includes three major adjustments to its rating criteria for cash flow CDOs. These were the identification of eight major MBS/ABS sectors and 50 subsectors, the development of a scoring model to determine whether an ABS is sufficiently diversified so as not to require an adjustment to its baseline default, and the creation of separate recovery assumptions for MBS and ABS.

Fitch's default curve is a cumulative 10-year default probability taken from the company's observations and previously published studies. It serves as a baseline for measuring the default probabilities of the collateral pools to be securitized. The baseline curve is stressed by multiples to derive a range of default probabilities for each rating category. Fitch then calculates a weighted average rating for the collateral pool to be securitized and finds the Fitch Rating Factor associated with that rating. The Fitch Rating Factor is equal to 100 times the "AAA case stressed default rates" and is roughly 3 to 5 standard deviations away from the single B stress case, where the default rates by rating class are equal to the 10-year cumulative default rate. This rating factor and the rating desired for the tranche being stressed is then used to determine what default probability is used in cash flows. A minimum of two stress tests for each class of debt rated is required (front loaded and back loaded) where defaults are usually recognized over a 5-year period for investment grade classes, and longer for non-investment grade classes. Prepayment tests are also required for prepayment sensitive assets.

Additional considerations for the desired rating include the final maturity of the rated debt, the experience of the asset manager, and the relative concentrations (by issuer, industry group, and geographic location) within the proposed portfolio. Fitch also requires a weighted-average rating guideline for actively traded portfolios.

When a portfolio is well diversified across many ABS sectors, Fitch will begin with the same default-rate matrix as it would for a well-diversified corporate CDO. Fitch usually requires 10 different industries to rate a CDO. Fitch developed a scoring model to determine if a portfolio has enough diversity, which recognized the high degree of correlation among some of the ABS groups.

As mentioned earlier, Fitch created eight major category groups with minor categories. The major categories are CMBS, RMBS, REIT, consumer ABS, CDO, commercial ABS, corporate, and European ABS/MBS. The scores are weighted by the total of percentage allocations of the minor categories within the total limit allowed for each major category. The major category allocations are then totaled to produce a sector score. The higher the score, the more diverse the portfolio and the lower the default rate multiple. Default rate multiples range from 0.8 (diverse) to 1.5 (highly concentrated). For example, to seek a Fitch AAA rating on a tranche backed by a highly concentrated pool of BBB ABS, Fitch would require the use of a stressed default rate equal to 1.5 times the unadjusted stressed default rate of 14% or 21%.

This has been the most remarkable part of the changes made by Fitch. Although they have limited data, Fitch has stated that it believes ABS will have lower defaults than corporates over time hence the downward adjustment in the default rate because of the sector score. This implies that ABS deserve a higher rating in their own right.

The third major change was the creation of separate recovery assumptions for MBS and ABS. Fitch created a matrix that lists recoveries by rank in the capital structure of the CDO tranches being securitized. The matrix also allows less recovery when the stress case rating is one or two notches higher than the collateral rating. Senior secured, senior unsecured, and subordinate unsecured corporate bond recovery assumptions are 60%, 40%, and 20% respectively, regardless of whether the collateral is lower than the tranche rating. Fitch believes that subordinated structured product will experience greater losses than subordinated corporates due to their very nature. For example ABS senior investment grade tranches, ABS subordinated investment grade tranches, and ABS subordinated non-investment grade collateral recoveries would be 60%, 40%, and 10%, respectively.

A 10-year cash flow model is the end result. Additional adjustments are made for any mismatch in the average life of the deal, asset concentrations, and interest rate risk embedded in the transaction. If the structure survives without default, each tranche is rated in accordance with the desired rating-stressed default curve used for that tranche.

Chapter 8

Synthetic CDOs

Laurie S. Goodman, Ph.D.
Managing Director
UBS Warburg

ynthetic CDOs have become an ever increasing part of the marketplace. The first synthetic CDO was done in 1997, and was motivated by bank balance sheet considerations. Over the next few years, synthetic CDO transactions, similarly motivated, increased in size and importance. The debut of synthetic CDOs structured as hedging and arbitrage transactions appeared in 2000. We believe the growth potential of synthetic CDOs is enormous.

In this chapter we review the history and motivations for issuing synthetic CDOs. We then look at basic structures and various structural nuances. We also go over the unique challenges confronting the rating agencies in evaluating these products. We wrap up with the key differences between synthetic and non-synthetic transactions.

WHAT'S IN A NAME?

A synthetic CDO is so named because the CDO does not actually own the pool of assets on which it has the risk. Stated differently, a synthetic CDO absorbs the economic risks, but not the legal ownership, of its reference credit exposures.

This de-linking of ownership and the economic risk of the underlying assets provides substantial additional flexibility in bank balance sheet management. A synthetic CDO allows banks to reduce regulatory capital charges and reduce economic risk while retaining ownership of the attendant assets. The best way to appreciate the advantages of this structure is to trace the evolution of bank balance sheet management.

CLOS FOR BALANCE SHEET MANAGEMENT

CLOs were the first vehicles to explicitly address the balance sheet needs of commercial banks. In a CLO, a bank sells a pool of loans to a special purpose vehicle (SPV), and takes back the first loss piece. There is a huge capital advantage to the bank using a CLO structure. If the bank held those loans directly in portfolio, it must then also hold risk-based capital equal to 8% of the loans. (Loans are a 100% risk weight item, capital charges of 8% are levied on these items.)

141

Exhibit 1: Structure of a CLO

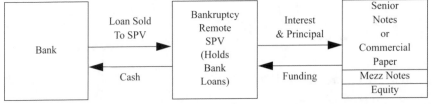

We have set out a typical CLO structure in Exhibit 1. Note that the loans have been transferred to the SPV, who funds these loans from the cash proceeds of the notes it has issued. The notes are credit-tranched. The senior notes (or commercial paper) are sold at a very tight spread. The mezzanine notes are sold in the marketplace to insurance companies, money managers, banks, and bank conduits. The equity is usually retained by the originating bank. Generally, the senior notes will be about 92% of the deal, the mezzanine notes 4%, with about 4% equity.

From the point of view of the originating bank, capital implications of this CLO structure are far more favorable than from holding the same loans outright. Banks are required to hold the lesser of (1) the capital charge on the unlevered amount, which would in this case be 8%, or (2) 100% of its liability. If 100% of a liability is the smaller number, as it generally will be in a CLO structure, we consider that institution subject to "low level recourse" requirements. In this case, the maximum liability of the originating bank is 4%. That is, a 100% capital charge on the 4% equity piece requires a 4% capital requirement. And that is precisely one half the 8% capital required if the bank alternatively held those same loans outright. This is shown in Exhibit 2, which is an exhibit we will refer to throughout this article.

BANK PROBLEMS USING CLO STRUCTURES

From the bank's point of view, CLO structures go a long way toward more efficient capital utilization. However, two problems still remain. First, there is a funding issue; and second, there is a confidentiality issue.

To address the first aspect, most banks are low cost funders. And it doesn't pay to transfer AAA risk from a low cost funder to a higher cost funder, as that higher cost funder cannot profitably fund higher rated assets. Exhibit 3 shows us why. Assume that a high cost funder borrows at LIBOR + 30, while a low cost funder can achieve a funding cost of LIBOR − 5. Further assume a high quality asset (loan) paying LIBOR + 35, with the cost of laying off the credit risk on this asset at 20 basis points. So after netting out credit risk, the asset yields LIBOR + 15. The high cost funder could only finance this asset at a deficit of 15 basis points, while the low cost funder carries the same asset at a surplus of 20 basis points.

Exhibit 2: Comparison of Capital Charges

Type of Security	Equity Retained	Capital Charge Methodology	Capital Charge Incurred
Hold Loans on Balance Sheet	n.a.	100% risk weight, 8% risk-based capital (RBC) requirement	8%
CLO	4%	Low level recourse requirement: lesser of the capital charge on the unlevered amount or 100% of bank liability.	100% of 4% equity retained=4%
Fully Funded Synthetic CLO	1%	Low level recourse requirement on equity. 20% risk weight on credit default swap if swap is with OECD institution. 0% risk weight if swap is with SPV and fully collateralized with 0% RBC securities (cash or cash substitutes or Treasuries).	If credit default swap is with an OECD institution: 100% of 1% equity + (20%×8%) on swap = 2.6%

If credit default swap is collateralized with 0% RBC securities: 100% of 1% equity + 0% on swap = 1% |
| Partially Funded Synthetic CLO | 1% (10% junior credit default swap, 90% senior default swap, always with OECD institution) | For U.S. banks, the super senior piece always receives a 20% risk weight regardless of whether it is retained or laid off. Treatment on equity and junior credit default swap is the same as above. | If junior credit default swap is with OECD institution: 100% of 1% equity + (20%×8% on swaps) = 2.6%

If junior credit default swap is collateralized with 0% RBC securities: 100% of 1% equity +(0%×10% junior swap)+(20%×8%×90% on super senior swap) = 2.44% |

Exhibit 3: Transferring AAA Risk from Low Cost Funder to High Cost Funder

	Low Cost Funder	High Cost Funder
Yield on high quality asset	LIBOR +35	LIBOR +35
Less funding cost	LIBOR −5	LIBOR +30
Less cost of laying off the credit risk	20 bps	20 bps
Net excess return	20 bps	−15 bps

That difference in funding costs is important, because CLO financing is relatively expensive. The AAA tranches sell for LIBOR + 35 – 45. Thus, efficiently managing regulatory capital can cause a bank to accept an inefficient means of financing. (But all is not gloom and doom. Realize that the CLO funding is *term funding*, which is more advantageous than funding which must be *rolled* over. It both guarantees availability and avoids the risk that credit spreads may widen.)

The second disadvantage of the CLO structure is one of confidentiality. If a loan is transferred into a special purpose vehicle for use as collateral for a CLO, borrower notification is always required, plus borrower consent often required. Banks believe it looks kind of shabby to sell customer loans. It's akin to selling your own kid's toys at a garage sale before they've outgrown them. Better that they don't know. So customer relationships understandably put an impediment on a bank's willingness to sell or transfer customer loan assets into outside pools. These disadvantages are shown in Exhibit 4.

A related disadvantage to the CLO structure is that terms and conditions of loan collateral cannot be modified within the structure. In order to modify any terms and conditions, that specified loan must be pulled out of the pool and another substituted. The substitution process required adds a substantial hassle factor.

CREDIT DEFAULT SWAPS

The basis for synthetic securitizations are *credit default swaps*. These allow institutions to transfer the economic risk, but not legal ownership, of the underlying assets. This, in turn, permits those institutions to shed the economic risk of assets without having to notify borrowers or seek their consent. It also enables the securitization of the associated credit risk with a wider range of bank assets, including derivatives and receivables. Finally, it gives greater flexibility in modifying the terms and conditions of loans.

Credit default swaps are really quite simple—they are conceptually similar to insurance policies. The protection buyer is purchasing protection against default risk on a reference pool of assets. That reference pool can consist of loans, bonds or derivatives or receivables. In a credit default swap, the protection buyer pays a periodic fee in return for a contingent payment by the protection seller in the event of a "credit event" with respect to the reference entity. The fee or insurance premium paid by the protection buyer is typically expressed in basis points per annum, and is paid on the notional amount on the swap. The protection seller only makes a payment if that "credit event" occurs. This is illustrated in Exhibit 5.

CREDIT EVENTS

In July of 1999, ISDA (International Swap Dealers Association) published revised credit swap documentation, which standardized the definition of a "credit event." Credit events can include bankruptcy, failure to make interest or premium payments when due, repudiation, restructuring, or the cross default/cross acceleration of an obligation.

Exhibit 4: Comparison of Bank Balance Sheet Management Techniques

Option	Achieve Capital Relief?	Achieve Confidentiality?	Wide range of assets allowed?	Achieve favorable funding?
Leave Assets On Balance sheet	No	Yes	Yes	Yes
CLO	Yes	No	No	No
Fully Funded CDO	Yes	Yes	Yes	No
Partially Funded CDO	Yes	Yes	Yes	Yes

Exhibit 5: Credit Default Swap

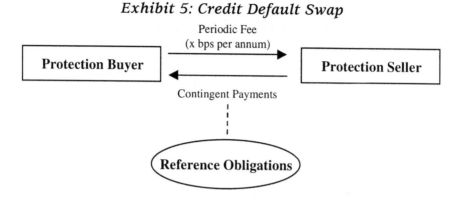

In the wake of Conseco's restructuring (which triggered payouts on credit default swaps), the dealer community has split widely over whether restructuring should be a "credit event." ISDA is considering eliminating restructuring as a "credit event," but no final decision has yet resulted as of this writing. Meanwhile, certain dealers continue to include it as a standard part of documentation, while a number of others eliminate it. Obviously, the protection seller (the investor, through the SPV) would prefer not to have restructuring as a "credit event," while the issuer has a preference to include it. Investors should be aware of this issue and ask about it.

The credit default swaps embedded in synthetic CDOs are based on a broad basket of credits. That wide range is necessary to achieve the required diversity scores from rating agencies. The basket of exposures can change over time, and one of the advantages of this structure is that it can easily accommodate changes in the reference collateral. If a "credit event" occurs, the payoff under the credit default swap is typically the difference between par and market value on that credit exposure.

FULLY FUNDED SYNTHETIC CDOS

In a fully funded synthetic CDO, notes equal to approximately 100% of the reference pool of assets are issued by a special purpose vehicle (SPV). The notes are generally tranched by credit quality. The first fully funded synthetic CDO was Glacier Finance Ltd., done by Swiss Bank in August of 1997.

The proceeds of these notes are generally invested in a portfolio of high quality securities, which is used as collateral. These high quality assets consist of government securities, repurchase agreements on government securities, or high quality (AAA) asset-backed securities. Meanwhile, the originating bank enters into a credit default swap either directly or indirectly with the SPV. Essentially, the originating bank buys default protection in return for a premium that subsidizes the coupon to compensate the investor for the default risk on the reference credits. The mechanics of this are illustrated in Exhibit 6.

Exhibit 6: Fully Funded Synthetic CDO
Swap Directly Between Originating Bank and SPV

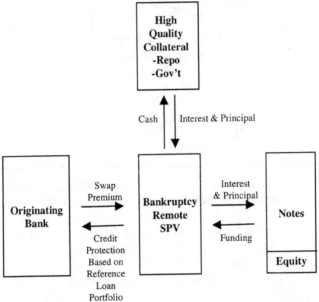

Intuitively, the investor is receiving an interest payment equal to the yield on the high quality securities plus the credit default swap premium. The investor is, in turn, providing the credit protection to the bank portfolio, which allows the bank to reduce the regulatory capital it is required to maintain.

In synthetic CDOs, just as in the CLO structure, the originating bank retains a first loss (equity) position. That's really the equivalent of an insurance deductible. That is, the originating institution generally absorbs the first 1%-1.5% of losses. This is generally achieved by having the bottom tranche of securities be equity (retained by the originating institution).

Using an example can make this clearer. Assume that the obligations of the SPV are comprised 95% of securities with an AAA rating, 2% of securities with a BBB rating, 2.0% of securities with a BB rating, and 1% as equity. Moreover, assume 2% of the notional amount of loans experiences a "credit event," and that payout on each credit event is 50%. The trustee would liquidate 1% of the high quality securities in the collateral account to pay off the originating bank. Interest payments to the equity holders would cease, and they would not receive any principal. If this were all the losses that arose in the course of the transaction, the rated noteholders would received all monies (both principal and interest) due them. If an additional 1% of loans in the portfolio experienced a credit event, also compensated at 50%, then an additional 0.5% of the high quality securities in the collateral account would be liquidated, so the BB security would then take a hit.

Exhibit 7: Fully Funded Synthetic CDO
Swap with OECD Bank as Intermediary

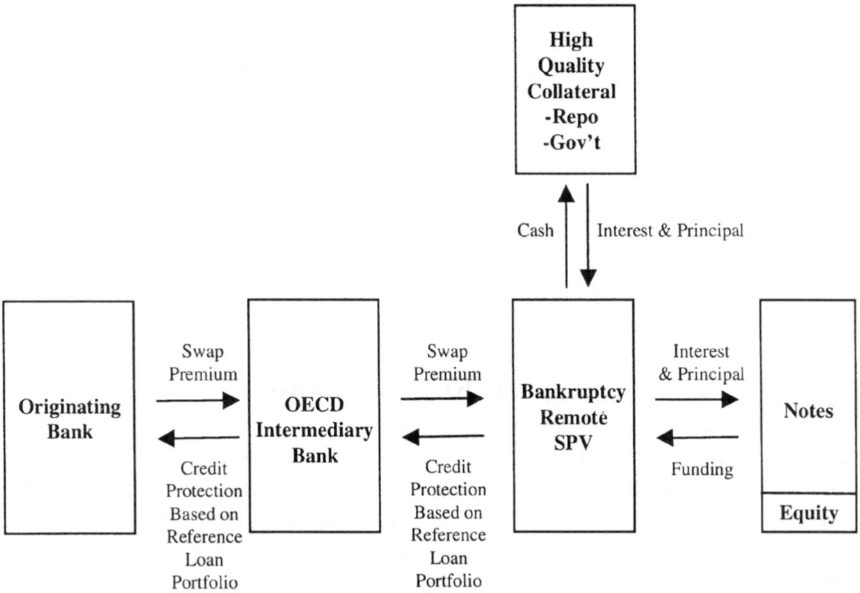

SWAP ARRANGEMENTS

The originating bank is usually the protection buyer, and the SPV is usually the protection seller. The credit default swap can be done directly with the SPV. Alternatively, the credit default swap can done indirectly with the SPV, by introducing another OECD bank which acts as the counterparty on both sides. The originating bank (protection buyer) enters into a credit default swap with another OECD bank (protection seller). This OECD bank (the protection seller) offsets the risk on that first swap by entering into another swap with the SPV, with the OECD bank being the protection buyer and the SPV selling the protection. These back-to-back swaps have the economic effect of mitigating the risk for the OECD bank, and they leave the originating bank as the protection buyer and the SPV as the protection seller. This is illustrated in Exhibit 7.

While these structures are conceptually similar, there are subtle differences. If the swap is done directly with the SPV, then capital treatment for the originating bank will depend entirely on the risk weight of the investments of the SPV. That is, if the SPV invests the assets solely in cash, cash substitutes or Treasury securities, the risk-based capital charge associated with the swap is 0%. If the SPV invests in AAA assets with a current risk weight of 100%, risk-based capital charges then become a prohibitive 100%.

Introducing the intermediary bank changes the risk-based capital treatment. If the risk transference between the originating bank and the SPV is done indirectly, via introducing another OECD bank as an intermediary, the risk-based capital charge on the swap is 20%. Essentially, since the credit risk of the underlying asset has truly been transferred to the protection seller, the risk weighting of the underlying assets (the loans) is replaced with the risk weighting of the protection seller. Under BIS guidelines, the risk weighting of another OECD bank is defined as 20%.

Thus, when setting up the synthetic CDO, the originating bank must decide whether it is more favorable to (1) limit the collateral account to 0% risk weight assets, which will constrain the choice of high quality assets that can be used; or (2) introduce an OECD bank as intermediary and incur capital charges on a 20% risk weighted asset.

Capital Requirements

The equity that is retained by the originating bank will always carry a 100% risk weight. Assume this equity portion is 1%, as is shown in Exhibit 2. Additional capital requirements depend on whether there is an intermediary bank. Absent an intermediary bank, and if the SPV invests entirely in 0% risk weighted assets—then the capital charge on the swap is 0%, as mentioned above. Thus, the total capital charge on the CDO would just be the retained equity of, say, 1%. If there is an intermediary OECD bank, the risk-based capital requirement on the swap is 20% of 8% (equaling 1.6%) of the notional amount of the credit default swap. Thus, if a bank entered into a fully funded synthetic CDO with a 1% first loss position, the capital requirement is 100% of the first loss piece, plus the risk based capital requirement on the credit default swap. This would mean a capital charge of 2.6%.

Advantages and Disadvantages

Now let's focus on the advantages of the synthetic fully funded CDO, as shown in Exhibit 4. First, the structure is confidential with respect to the bank's customers. None need be notified that their loan is being used within this structure, as the loan clearly stays with the bank. The names in the reference pool must be provided to the protection seller, but need not be publicly disclosed. For European banks, this point is particularly important, as selling a loan into an SPV is looked at by many as compromising a customer relationship. This explains the prevalence of the synthetic CLO structure there. Second, the bank has the flexibility to use the contract as a hedge for any senior obligation of the reference entity (including not only loans, but also bonds, derivatives, receivables, etc.) Third, the capital treatment is favorable.

However the disadvantage of a fully funded synthetic CDO is that the loans must be funded by a high cost funder (which is the marginal buyer in the capital markets) rather than a low cost funder (the bank itself). Moreover, in a fully funded structure, the amount of notes issued is approximately the same as the amount of loans backing the credit default swap, hence the nomenclature. That means that there's quite a bit of funding required, and hence a high cost associated with the reduction in required regulatory capital. This is again summarized in Exhibit 3.

PARTIALLY FUNDED SYNTHETIC CDOS

The building blocks are the same in a partially funded structure, but the notes issued only amount to 5%-15% of the notional amount of the reference portfolio. Partially funded synthetic CDOs deliver the favorable capital treatment while achieving *more favorable funding* than do fully funded CDOs. As a result, partially funded CDOs are far more common than fully funded structures.

The first partially synthetic CDO was actually the BISTRO transaction, pioneered by J.P. Morgan in December of 1997. (BISTRO stands for Broad Index Secured Trust Offering).

The structure behind partially funded synthetic CDO transactions is very similar to that on fully funded CDOs. The originating bank buys protection on a portfolio of corporate credit exposures via a credit default swap, either directly or indirectly, from an SPV. This is shown in Exhibit 8a. Thus, the originating bank is the protection buyer, the SPV the protection seller. As in fully funded transactions, there may or may not be an intermediary OECD bank which sells the credit protection to the originating bank and buys it back from the SPV. In the BISTRO transactions there is generally an intermediary bank, while in most other partially funded transactions, the credit default swap is directly between the bank and the SPV. The partially funded structure in which there is an OECD intermediary is shown in Exhibit 8b. The credit protection is usually subject to a "threshold" level of losses (equivalent of a deductible) that must be experienced on the reference portfolio before any payment is due to the origination bank under the portfolio credit swap. This accomplished by having the originating bank hold the equity issued by the SPV.

The SPV is collateralized with government securities, repurchase agreements on government securities or other high quality collateral, and funds these through issuance of notes. Those notes are credit tranched, and sold into the capital market.

However, in a critical departure from traditional fully funded securitization, the SPV issues a substantially smaller amount of notes, and holds substantially less collateral, than the notional amount of the reference portfolio. This is clearly shown in Exhibits 8a and 8b. Typically, the note issuance will amount to only 5%-15% of the notional amount of the reference portfolio. Thus, only the first 5%-15% of losses in a particular portfolio are funded by the vehicle, which leaves the most senior risk position unfunded.

Exhibit 8: Partially Funded Synthetic CDO
a. Swap Directly Between Originating Bank and SPV

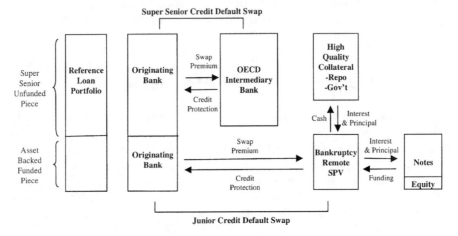

b. Partially Funded Synthetic Swap

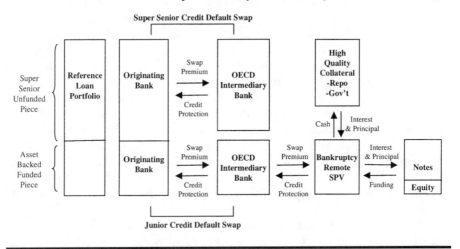

Realize that the unfunded portion — known as the "super senior piece" — is a very high quality piece of paper. Given the quality of the underlying reference portfolio, there's only a remote probability that a loss might exceed the 5-15% of the exposure that has been funded. The unfunded (super senior) piece is, in essence, better than an AAA credit risk. Another way to look at this is to realize that some of the credit support below the super senior piece is often still rated AAA. (The senior tranche issued by the SPV, which absorbs losses before they hit the super senior piece, is often rated AAA.) In bank balance sheet transactions, the risk on the super senior piece can be laid off via a second credit default swap, often referred to as the "super senior credit default swap," again shown in Exhibits 8a and 8b. And the swap on the funded portion of the transaction is often referred to as the "junior credit default swap."

CAPITAL TREATMENT

Investors should realize that in a partially funded structure, the super senior piece is often afforded the same capital treatment whether or not the risk is laid off on another OECD bank. If the risk is laid off via a credit default swap on another OECD bank, the bank will be afforded a 20% risk weight. If the risk is not laid off, but is retained by the originating bank, the bank may still qualify for a 20% risk weight. That is, on November 15. 1999, the Federal Reserve issued a set of capital interpretations on synthetic CLOs, which apply to U.S banks.[1] These guidelines allow the retained super senior piece to achieve a 20% risk weight, as long as a number of conditions are met including the presence of a senior class of notes that receives the highest possible rating (i.e., AAA) from a nationally recognized credit rating agency. Prior to this interpretation, if the risk on the super senior piece was not laid off there was no capital relief, and the risk weight was 100%. For European banks, the treatment will vary jurisdiction by jurisdiction.

The regulatory capital charge on the equity and on the junior credit default swap follows the same rules as on the fully funded synthetic, and are summarized in Exhibit 2. If the junior swap is done directly with the SPV, and the SPV is collateralized with 0% risk weight assets, then the assets backing the junior swap have a 0% risk weight. The capital charge on this would be 100% of the first loss piece (the equity portion), plus the capital charge on the super senior credit default swap. Assume, again a 1% first loss piece, and assume that the junior credit swap is for 10% of the transaction amount. Thus, the super senior portion is 90% of the notional amount. The credit charge on this portion is ([the 20% risk weight] × [the 8% capital charge] × [90% of the notional amount]) or 1.44%. Thus, the total capital charge is 2.44% (1% on equity + 1.44% on the super senior swap).

If an OECD bank serves as the protection seller to the originating bank on the junior default swap, the 20% capital charge would apply to 100% of the notional loan amount. Thus, the capital charge would be [20% of 8%] or 1.6%. The total capital charge on the transaction would be [the capital charge on the swaps] + [the capital charge on the equity], or 2.6%.

This partially funded structure has several advantages. It allows banks to reduce the risk on a large number of on-balance sheet assets. Confidentiality issues are also preserved, as is a funding advantage (since only 5%-15% of the loans are funded). Finally, favorable regulatory capital treatment is achieved, as shown in Exhibit 4.

---

[1] The document is entitled "Capital Interpretations, Synthetic Collateralized Loan Obligations" November 15, 1999 and can be found on the Federal Reserve Website.

HEDGING AND ARBITRAGE TRANSACTIONS

While the overwhelming majority of synthetic CDOs has been driven by regulatory capital treatment for banks, a few came from the desire to hedge on- or off-balance sheet trading exposures. While those driven by a desire to hedge dealer exposure have thus far been very limited, we believe that this is potentially a very important growth area for the CDO market. It is also a potentially important risk management tool for dealers. For dealers, hedging credit risk is more difficult than ever, as credit spreads have been more volatile than ever historically. Moreover, default rates on high-yield securities are higher than at any point since 1991. Partially mitigating the credit risk on an inventory of trading positions (either bonds or positions in the swap book such as credit default swaps or total rate of return swaps) is very valuable for a dealer. Moreover, it is not unreasonable to think that if this method became a trusted credit risk management tool, dealers would be willing to hold larger inventories, as they would be able to lay off more of the risk than is currently the case.

While only a few hedging transactions have been done to date, many institutions are looking at these types of transactions, and quite a few are currently in the pipeline. These hedging transactions, like the bank balance sheet deals, allow an institution to de-link ownership from the economic risk, and transfer economic risk on an item that is otherwise difficult to hedge.

In *arbitrage transactions*, a portfolio of bonds is purchased. The intent is that portfolio default risk will be mitigated by the credit default swap, as the bond portfolio then becomes the reference portfolio for the CDO. The arbitrage is created because the issuer believes that spreads on the underlying assets are wider than warranted by the cost of laying off the default risk. Structured securities (ABS, CMBS, CBOs) have been used on the majority of the arbitrage structures to date.

Structural Issues — Hedging and Arbitrage Driven Transactions

Hedging and arbitrage-driven transactions are structured identically to the bank balance sheet restructuring CDOs we covered earlier in this chapter. The hedging or arbitrage-driven transactions may be fully or partly funded, with the primary determinant being the type of underlying collateral comprising the reference pool. For bond collateral, partial funding is the norm. For off-balance sheet collateral, full funding is required at this point, as rating agencies have little experience with the loss experience.

The position to be hedged, or the arbitrage portfolio that has been purchased, becomes the reference portfolio for the credit default swap. In this type of structure the hedging institution is buying protection against "credit events," which is purchased from a swap counterparty. The swap counterparty, in turn, lays off the risk of the credit default swap onto the SPV. The SPV then becomes a protection seller, with the originating institution the ultimate protection buyer.

Just as in the bank balance sheet deals, the SPV issues notes, with the proceeds invested in a portfolio of high quality securities. In the aggregate, the investors receive [coupon equal to the premium on the credit default swap] + [the yield on the risk free assets].

HYBRID TRANSACTIONS

A number of traditional CDOs also had a synthetic component, at least initially, as the needed assets were either unavailable during the ramp-up period, or the assets available did not allow for appropriate diversification. For example, assume a money manager is ramping up a high-yield deal, but most of the recent issues have been telecom, so a sufficiently diversified portfolio cannot be easily purchased. The non-telecom exposure could be provided via a credit default swap. This swap could be unwound as other bonds became available. Similarly, during a short ramp-up period, there may not be enough diversification in emerging market bonds, and a money manager may want to add exposure to a given area (say Asia) via a credit default swap.

RATING CONSIDERATIONS

The rating agencies face a number of unique difficulties in rating these transactions. While each uses a slightly different approach, they all tend to rely on historical default and loss information. There is a considerable amount of such information on bonds and loans. However, in the credit default swap inherent in a synthetic CDO, a "credit event" need not correspond with what would have been an interruption in payment. In fact, it is not only the inclusion of restructuring into credit events that makes the rating agencies nervous, but also the acceleration of payments due to cross default/cross acceleration clauses. The definition of a "credit event" means that much of the historical work on defaults must be used very cautiously. This is a topic that has received considerable attention in both the dealer and the rating agency communities. However, it has received relatively little attention in the investor community.

The second conundrum for the rating agencies is the degree of trading that can be done in the reference portfolio. One of the largest changes in bank balance sheet synthetic CDOs through time has been the amount of trading permitted. The right of substitution was very limited in many early transactions. While it varies from deal to deal, substitutions in and out of the reference portfolio can now be made fairly freely, subject to quality considerations.

This substitution is very important in hedging and arbitrage transactions. In hedging dealer inventories, the exposures will change over time, thus so, too, must the reference portfolio. Similarly, for arbitrage transactions, the more trading that is permitted, the more flexibility the portfolio manager has. From the rating agencies' point of view, a conservative methodology is called for. Unlike market value deals, where the market enforces the discipline, in a cash flow deal with liberal substitution, the rating agency must assume the worst in their rating. This is particularly true where the equity "first loss" piece is small in relation to the total transaction.

The third issue for the rating agencies is the use of unusual asset classes as the reference portfolio. For example, there is very little historical experience on the default history of swaps, as the transactions are private. As with all new asset classes, the rating agencies tend to be very conservative.

Having said this, it is important to realize that synthetic CDOs are a new product. Furthermore, the rating process for these products is being refined, as experience accumulates and deals keep sporting new variations. And, again, with new products, the rating agencies are apt to be initially conservative, which works to the advantage of investors.

SUMMARY — STRUCTURAL DIFFERENCES

There are a number of structural differences between a synthetic CDO and a CDO backed directly by bond or loan collateral. These differences all stem from the fact that ownership and economic risk of the securities or exposures have been de-linked.

- The term of the synthetic instrument is well defined. The investor is not dependent on the cash flows of an underlying bond or loan instrument. The maturity of the instrument is governed solely by the maturity of the underlying credit default swaps.
- On the synthetic CDO, there is no interest rate risk, either at initial investment or at liquidation. This is because the credit default swap addresses only the credit risk on the instrument. If there is no "credit event," but the security is worth considerably less at liquidation, then that is not the problem of the rated noteholder.
- The synthetic CDO cannot benefit (or lose) on any discretionary trading done in the portfolio. The results of this discretionary trading would be reflected in higher (lower) market values when the security is eventually sold, but the synthetic is not dependent on changes in market values.

CONCLUSION

Synthetic CDOs have grown tremendously in a short period of time. Bank balance sheet deals have increasingly been effected in synthetic form rather than in CLO form. The debut of synthetic hedging and arbitrage deals was in 2000. While relatively few of those have been done to date, we believe they represent a huge growth area for the CDO business.

Rating synthetic deals presents some unique challenges to the rating agencies, and methodologies will be refined over time. Meanwhile, in early deals in newer asset categories, the rating agencies tend to err on the conservative side, which gives investors an opportunity to invest at generally favorable conditions. However, investors must understand the unique characteristics of these instruments in order to profit from this.

Chapter 9

Cash and Synthetic European Bank CLOs

Alexander Batchvarov, PhD, CFA
Managing Director
International ABS/MBS Research
Merrill Lynch

Ganesh Rajendra
Vice President
International ABS/MBS Research
Merrill Lynch

William Ross, CFA
Assistant Vice President
International ABS/MBS Research
Merrill Lynch

Xavier De Pauw
Assistant Vice President
International ABS/MBS Research
Merrill Lynch

I n this chapter we focus on the market for balance sheet, cash flow and synthetic CLOs issued by commercial banks — the CDO sector that dominates the European market. Such securities can be broadly differentiated from other collateralized debt obligations given their collateral, structure, and issuer motivation. We discuss the recent structural innovations and how they should be analyzed and draw conclusions regarding relative value and investment.

The market for collateralized debt obligations or CDOs experienced explosive growth between 1997 and 1999. Though not dissimilar in structure, the various types of CDOs can be broadly distinguished by four main aspects — collateral, issuer motivation, debt repayment profiles, and method of risk transfer. (See Exhibit 1 for a roadmap through the CDO universe.)

Exhibit 1: A Road Map Through the CDO Universe

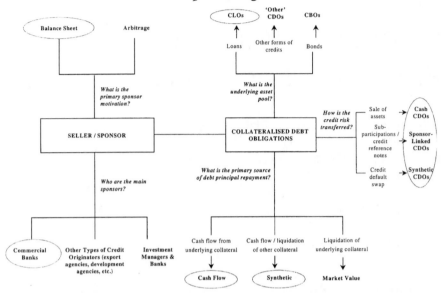

Collateral Make-Up Collateralized loan obligations (CLOs) and collateralized bond obligations (CBOs) are referred to as such given their collateral composition. Transactions backed by a hybrid of debt and loans (or
even other forms of credits/promissory notes etc.) are not uncommon.

Issuer Motivation The motive behind the transaction is commonly differentiated by whether the deal is "arbitrage" driven or "balance sheet"
driven. Managers of arbitrage driven deals exploit spread anomalies
between their assets and liabilities. By contrast, balance sheet transactions are done primarily to improve the economics of a bank's balance
sheet by transferring credit risk from their loan book and gaining commensurate regulatory capital relief, and by accessing alternative off-balance sheet funding sources.

Debt Service Profiles CDOs can be broadly categorized as either cash flow,
synthetic or market value structures. Cash flow CDOs rely on the amortization of the underlying assets for both interest and principal debt service. In this respect they are similar to other traditional financial
receivable backed ABS. While debt interest service in market value
driven structures is also drawn from underlying obligor repayments, debt
principal repayment is met ultimately by liquidating the portfolio in the
open market — thus the term "market value" structures. The asset manager in market value structures takes a hands-on role in maximizing their
arbitrage yield which, in practice, amounts to actively trading the portfo-

lio. Synthetic structures rely on a separate, high credit quality collateral portfolio to generate cash flow for debt service purposes, with the sponsor bank normally covering any interest deficiency between these assets and the issued liabilities or notes.

Methods of Credit Risk Transfer In cash flow CDOs, the sale or equivalent transfer of the assets ensures that all risks associated with the assets is passed on to investors. With sponsor-linked CDOs, the subparticipation of or credit reference to the underlying assets ensures risk transfer. Synthetic CDOs rely on credit default swaps (or equivalent) to realize risk transfer.

To be sure, there is no clear delineation of one CDO grouping from another. Issuer motivations, asset types, and even the principal repayment mechanism may overlap among the categories we have loosely defined above. Yet, for the most part, CDOs can be classed as either arbitrage driven (market value or cash flow based structures), or balance sheet driven (cash flow or synthetic based structures). Collateral in the former would typically comprise debt securities given their liquidity and tradability. By contrast, collateral in balance sheet driven, cash flow or synthetic based CDOs is usually loans and credit facilities, directly originated and/or purchased whole or in part (through syndication, for example) by the issuing financial institution. The key differences between bank CLOs and high-yield CBOs/CLOs are summarized in Exhibit 2.

In this chapter we focus on the market for balance sheet driven, cash flow or synthetic based collateralized loan obligations sponsored by commercial banks — a sector that dominates the European CDO marketplace. Collateral underlying such bank CLOs normally comprises commercial and industrial loans originated in the normal course of the bank's business. We limit our discussion to transactions financed in the term market as opposed to commercial paper funded programs or non-funded transactions.

Exhibit 2: Bank CLOs versus High Yield CBOs/CLOs

	Bank CLOs	High Yield CBOs / CLOs	
Sponsor	Commercial Banks	Investment Managers mainly	
Collateral	Commercial and Industrial (C&I) Loans	High Yield Bonds, Leveraged Loans	
Structure	Cash Flow or Synthetic	Cash Flow	Market Value
Seller Motivation			
Manage Credit Risk	Yes	Limited	No
Gain Regulatory Capital Relief	Yes	No	No
Free Up Credit / Lending Lines	Yes	No	No
Achieve Off Balance Sheet Treatment	Limited*	No	No
Maximise Asset-Liability Spread / Returns	No	Yes	Yes
Portfolio Trading Flexibility	No	Limited	Yes
	Balance Sheet Driven	Arbitrage Driven	

* Not achievable for synthetic structures.

Source: Merrill Lynch

Overview of the Global Bank CLO Market

The global bank balance sheet term CLO market accounted for nearly a quarter of total CDO issuance (including CP funded issues) in 1999. This represents the second largest component of the global CDO market, behind the high-yield debt backed CDO sector, which accounted for 48% of the CDO market in 1999.

The market for bank CLOs took off in late 1996 as the major lending institutions came to endorse securitization of their corporate loan portfolios as a viable funding and balance sheet management tool. Following the burst in supply of bank CLOs into the fixed income markets over the next two years, growth in new issuance in this sector proved less dramatic over 1998 and 1999. However, the number of transactions increased perceptibly. We found 22 and 26 transactions in 1998 and 1999, respectively, following just 12 in 1997. Cumulative bank CLOs outstanding at the end of 1999 amounted to over $90 billion. The above statistics include dollar-denominated CLOs issued by Japanese banks internationally, but do not include the yen-denominated CLOs issued by Japanese banks based on their domestic loan portfolios and funded privately or through commercial paper programs.

The recent slowdown in issuance volumes compared to the early years can be explained by:

- Lower levels of issuance by Japanese banks, which were the main CLO sponsors in previous years using their U.S. loan portfolios. Many Japanese banks exited the U.S. commercial lending business by liquidating existing portfolios or ceasing new business.
- The diversion of some issuance since the credit crisis of autumn 1998 into the conduit or credit derrivative markets as a result of weaker demand in the public markets.
- The decrease of average transaction sizes. While large deals were characteristic of 1997 issuance (averaging $2.5 billion), average transaction size in 1998 was $1.4 billion and $1 billion in 1999.

Taken in perspective, however, the bank CLO market continues to represent one of the major segments of the global asset backed markets. Transaction sizes typically dwarf that of the traditional consumer ABS sector. Sponsors of the majority of bank CLOs are well established, recognizable global lending institutions. And bank CLOs normally command a wide distribution using either an Euro/144A or Global format. These characteristics continue to underpin this sector's presence in the global fixed income credit markets.

European CLOs Standing in the Global Market

Banks of European origin have issued a significant share of the global CLO volume since 1996 (see Exhibit 3). Yet the majority of bank CLOs outstanding are backed by U.S. collateral. Indeed, there have been as many European banks securitizing their U.S. portfolios (e.g., Barclays, Deutsche Bank, to name but a few) as there have been European collateral CLOs. To date, Citibank and Sumitomo Bank are the only non-European banks to securitize their European loan portfolios.

Though perhaps not just yet the largest segment of the global CLO market, European collateral CLOs have taken the most initiative in terms of new structures and assets types in their securitization transactions.

EUROPEAN BANK CLO MARKET OVERVIEW

Issuance volume of European bank CLOs has slowed compared to the heady days of 1996 and 1997. Yet market activity in terms of the number of transactions has increased perceptibly. The typical issuer profile that drives new supply remains unchanged — a major European bank seeking primarily to manage its credit exposure and improve capital efficiency. CLO structures have evolved along with the market. Pure sponsor-linked structures have given way to synthetic CLOs, structures that better align investor needs with issuer objectives. The proliferation of synthetic CLOs has not yet, however, crowded out the issuance of the more conventional true sale cash flow deals.

The first European bank corporate loan securitizations — and indeed one of the very first CLOs of significance — was the Rose Funding transaction in late 1996, backed against a portfolio of mainly UK commercial loans originated by the National Westminster Bank. Issuance of European CLOs proved sporadic over the next year or so, well surpassed by the influx of Japanese and, to a lesser extent, US CLO issuers. Only in 1999 did we see the resurgence of European CLO product in the fixed income markets.

Exhibit 3: Global Bank CLOs Outstanding by Sponsor Nationality (as of end September 2000)

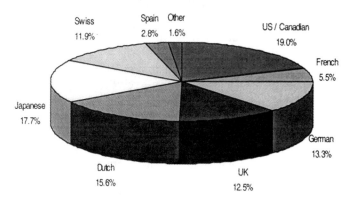

Source: Merrill Lynch

Exhibit 4: Supply Technicals

Volume	(Bn)	Number of Deals
1997	$17.57	4
1998	$15.92	7
1999	$13.22	13
3Q2000	$5.83	13

Source: Merrill Lynch

Issuance volumes have not matched the increase in number of transactions (see Exhibit 4), with the average size of CLO deals significantly trimmer compared to what was seen at the time of the market's inception. We estimate there is nearly $50 billion in public European CLOs outstanding in the markets currently. Bank CLOs accounted for just under 20% of total asset-backed issuance in Europe over 1999.

Some 98% of European bank CLOs are floating-rate instruments with average lives of five years or less, catering to the LIBOR-based investor community accustomed to bank paper. European CLOs have been structured as soft bullets, securities with a controlled amortization window or passthroughs. The bulk of European CLOs outstanding are dollar denominated paper, reflecting the trend where many of the large ($1 billion or more) deals tapped the dollar investor base in order to accommodate the size of the issue.

Unlike the broader asset backed market, the major part of European CLOs issued since 1996 are rated in the double-A category. Much of this reflects the types of structures used in the early years, namely that of sponsor-linked notes, where the rating of the senior notes are capped at that of the issuing bank. Examples of sponsor-linked notes are the NatWest ROSE and SBC Glacier transactions. By contrast, European bank CLOs priced more recently have been structured with triple-A tranches.

Issuer Profile

The bulk of European CLOs have been issued by the larger, more prominent and well capitalized lending institutions in Europe. (See Exhibit 5.) Such issuing banks are typically rated in the high single-A to triple-A category. Hitherto, the market has been dominated by "repeat issuers," i.e., banks that have tapped the CLO markets more than once. We have calculated that over 90% of CLO issued have been by repeat issuing institutions. Only in year 2000 did we see a number of debut issues from the likes of Banco Bilbao Vizcaya and Banca Commerciale Italiana.

Borrower Motivation

The benefits of securitizing a corporate loan book are manifold. Off balance sheet transfer — should this be achieved — reduces asset leverage. The release of regulatory capital held against risky assets improves liquidity and return on equity/capital. Banks' lending capacity improves. The typically higher cost of securitization for highly rated banks is offset by the benefits of a stable, diversified funding channel that is often complimentary to traditional funding sources. Securitization also allows banks to improve on their asset-liability management. (See Exhibit 6.)

For European banks — and arguably unlike their U.S. counterparts — the key motivation behind CLO issuance is in the management of credit exposure and the release of regulatory capital. Transferring assets off balance sheet is often not the primary motive if only because achieving a "true sale" of assets in many European jurisdictions remains a cumbersome exercise.

We illustrate the benefits of equity release under a securitization in Exhibit 7. In a bank funded structure, retaining the credit risk inherent in assets requires an 8% cushion of regulatory capital (funded by equity and Tier 2 capital). In transferring the loan credit risk to the capital markets through securitization, the bank is charged only for its first loss position on a dollar-for-dollar basis. The reduced capital requirements — and subsequent equity release — improves the banks' return on equity (all other factors constant), though nominal profit may be reduced given a typically higher securitization funding cost. In the example below, we have not paid any credit to the benefits from a more profitable use of released equity, nor have we counted the cost of equity under either funding structure.

Most bank CLOs to date have been securitizations of investment grade credits. With regulatory capital charges during the 1990s the same irrespective of credit risk, there clearly is economic incentive for a bank to retain higher yielding assets on its books in order to optimize its return on risk-adjusted capital and other similar performance measures.

Exhibit 5: The Largest European CLO Issuers (as of end September 2000)

Issuer	Number of Deals	Issuance Volumes
Rabobank	2	$12.5 bn
National Westminster Bank	3	$11.6 bn
Deutsche Bank	6	$10.1 bn
Credit Suisse*	4	$8.7 bn
Hypovereinsbank	2	$3.3 bn
United Bank of Switzerland	2	$2.2 bn

* Includes subsidiaries.

Source: Merrill Lynch

Exhibit 6: Primary Motivation of European CLO issuers

	Regulatory Capital Relief	Assets Off-Balance Sheet Treatment	Credit Separation from Sponsor Bank
De-linked CLOs			
True Sale	Yes	Yes	Yes
Synthetic	Yes	No	Yes
Sponsor-Linked CLOs	Yes	No	No

Source: Merrill Lynch

Exhibit 7: Illustration of the Benefits of Issuing CLOs

Assets	Bank Funded		ABS Funded
Portfolio (100) Yield: L + 50bp Losses: 6bps pa.	AA rated Senior Debt (92) L+18 bps	VS	AAA rated Senior Debt (91.5) L+24 bps
	Tier 2 (4) L+50 bps		A- rated Junior Tranche (7.5) L+60 bps
	Equity (4)		Retained First Loss Piece (0.5) L+100
			Equity (0.5)

	Bank Funded		ABS Funded	
Assume LIBOR = 6%	**Bank Funded**		**ABS Funded**	
	Funding Cost	= 5.95%	Funding Cost	= 6.24%
Net Income = 6.44%	Profit	= 0.49%	Profit	= 0.20%
	ROE	= 12.2%	ROE	= 40.0%
	Reg. Capital	= 8.0%	Reg. Capital	= 0.5%

Source: Merrill Lynch

Types of CLO Securitization Structures

Generally speaking, there are three types of CLO securitization structures depending on the mechanism of risk transfer as described earlier. (See Exhibit 1.) These are true sale cash flow CLOs, sponsor-linked CLOs, and synthetic CLOs.

The main constraint to structuring a "true sale" CLO in Europe remains the onerous process of "perfecting security interest." Aside from a number of regulatory hurdles, underlying loan contracts often have assignment clauses, which necessitate obligor notification or consent prior to sale. Moreover, many European banks prize their business relationships and maintaining obligor confidentiality remains very much in their interests. In a number of jurisdictions (e.g., Spain and the UK), however, the true sale CLO continues to be widely used.

It is therefore not surprising that the true sale format as used in the U.S. has not been the most favored securitization template among European CLOs. Instead, the European banks have set the pace in structural innovation with new securitization templates to allow banks to transfer credit risk to the capital markets, while taking into account both borrower and investor requirements.

In the formative stages of the European CLO market, borrowers circumvented the "true sale" hurdle by issuing sponsor-linked CLOs, based either on sub-participations or credit linked reference notes (CLNs). At the end of the 1990s however, such structures have given way to (or evolved into) credit derivative based, synthetic CLO structures.

Exhibit 8: A Typical "True Sale" CLO

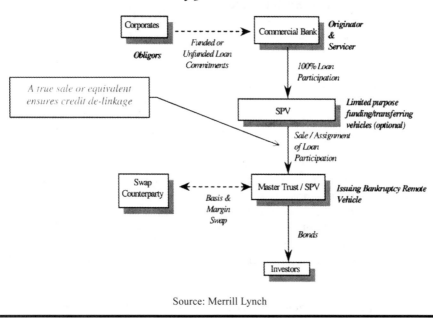

Source: Merrill Lynch

Below we explain in more detail the three main types of CLO structures as seen in the European market place — the "true sale" CLO, the sponsor-linked CLO, and the synthetic CLO.

"True Sale" CLOs

The traditional 'true sale' CLO is a structure that closely resembles that of a typical credit card ABS (see Exhibit 8). The underlying assets are sold to a trust or special purpose vehicle (and, where possible, together with the loan security); the CLO bonds are issued in order to finance the above purchase, and later repaid with the cash flow generated by the asset pool. As with other off-balance sheet ABS, a legal separation of assets from seller means that the credit quality of the pool of loans, together with any credit support, determines the credit strength (and rating) of the bonds. That is, the bonds are de-linked from the credit quality of the originator.

Certain non-U.S. jurisdictions rely on transfer mechanisms other than an outright sale to achieve what is effectively a "true sale." In the UK for example, the use of an "equitable assignment" is more common, allowing the originator to avoid notification requirements and potential stamp duty liabilities. The underlying loans may be retained by the bank on trust for investors, with any economic interests accruing to the loans transferred to investors via an equitable assignment. This "Declaration of Trust" format, cemented by an irrevocable power of attorney granted for the interests' of investors, suffices in so far as investors' legal recourse to the assets is deemed incontestable in the event of sponsor bankruptcy. This therefore is tantamount to a "true sale."

True sale structures have been used in European CLOs issued to-date by UK, German, Spanish, and Italian originators as detailed in Exhibit 9.

Sponsor-Linked CLOs

In a sponsor-linked CLO, investors do not have a legal or beneficial entitlement to the loans and, furthermore, rely on the ability of the originator/servicer to perform on their obligations under the transaction (see schematic on Exhibit 10). In the event of originator insolvency, investors would rank as general unsecured creditors to the bankruptcy estate. Sponsor-linked CLOs, therefore, have ratings that are capped at that of the originator. European sponsor-linked CLOs take two forms — credit linked (reference) notes and sub-participations. For illustrative purposes, selected transactions are listed on Exhibit 11.

Sponsor-linked CLOs, employed prior to the now more commonly used synthetic CLOs, did not normally require obligor disclosure thus allowing the originator to maintain confidentiality in their relationships with customers. Indeed, in a number of sponsor-linked CLOs there is no disclosure even at the portfolio level.

Credit Linked 'Reference' Notes Credit linked notes (CLNs) — in its narrower definition — gets their name from the use of non-vanilla derivatives of the same name in corporate loan securitizations. These are used to synthetically transfer default risk in the underlying loans to the issuing SPV (and ultimately the investors). CLNs are "referenced" to either an identified pool of loans or to each loan in an identified pool.

The mechanics of loan loss transfer within credit linked structures may vary, just as they do in other synthetically structured CLOs (see below). Upon a credit event in any underlying loan, the losses incurred that are transferred to investors may be based on:

- A fixed percentage of the underlying loan face value.
- Competitive market bids for the defaulted underlying loan.
- Crystallized recovery values.
- A combination of fixed percentage initially followed by further drawing or reimbursement depending on final recovery values.

The reference loans remain on balance sheet and investors underwriting credit risk in these loans rely on the performance of the originator in remitting funds to the SPV. The rating on the notes are capped at that of the sponsoring bank. CLNs normally allow the bank to gain regulatory capital relief commensurate with the loan portfolio risk transfer.

Exhibit 9: Selected European 'True Sale' CLOs

Offer Date	Issuer	Currency	Tranches	Amt (M)	Originating Bank	Obligor Domicile
Apr-98	Aurora Funding No. 1 plc	GBP	6	$2,330	Sumitomo Bank	UK
Jul-98	CORE 1998-1 Ltd	DEM/USD	8	$2,386	Deutsche Bank	German
Feb-99	CORE 1999-1 Ltd	EUR/USD	12	$2,732	Deutsche Bank	German
Mar-99	SPQR Funding plc	EUR	2	$281	Banca IMI/Industrial Bank of Japan	Italian/UK
May-99	Globe Limited	EUR	5	$905	Deutsche Bank	German
Jun-99	CORE 1999-2 Ltd	EUR/USD	12	$1,415	Deutsche Bank	German
Feb-00	BBVA-1 Fondo de Titulizacion de Activos	EUR	5	$1,115	Banco Bilbao Vizcaya Argentaria	Spanish
Mar-00	FTPYME ICO-TDA	EUR	2	$462	Banco Sabadell, Group Banco Popular, Unicaja	Spanish
Apr-00	Clover Funding No 1 Plc	GBP	5	$829	HSBC	UK
Jun-00	Ahorro y Titulizacion 3, FTPYME-ICO	EUR	5	$156	11 Spanish savings banks	Spain
Jun-00	BCL Municipios I	EUR	3	$1,137	Banco de Credito Local	Spain

Source: Merrill Lynch

Exhibit 10: A Typical "Sponsor-Linked" CLO

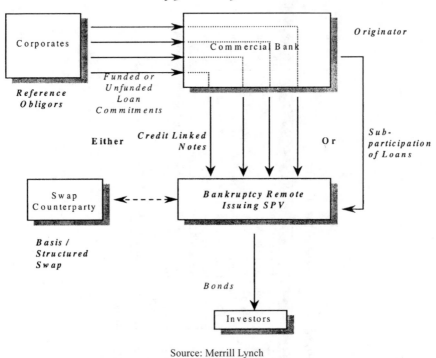

Source: Merrill Lynch

Transfer Through Sub-Participation Certain corporate loan securitizations involve the SPV purchasing participation rights (as opposed to purchasing loans outright) to an underlying loan portfolio of a bank. Sub-participation's are essentially unsecured claims against the originating bank, as investors have no beneficial nor legal interest in the underlying loans and are consequently reliant on the originating bank to pass-through payments received from the underlying obligors. As with CLNs, this means that the rating on the notes is linked to the creditworthiness of the bank. It is not uncommon in these structures for principal cash flows to be attributable to investors only after principal payments are made to the seller for the portion of underlying loans that was not sub-participated.

Synthetic CLOs

The mechanics of a typical synthetic CLO can be broken down as follows:

- The SPV issues bonds and uses the proceeds to purchase collateral for the notes. Some or all of such collateral would normally compose triple-A, liquid assets such as government or equivalent securities. The collateral is normally sold in the market or repurchased by the originating bank to pay down the notes.

Exhibit 11: Selected European "Sponsor-Linked" CLOs

Offer Date	Issuer	Currency	Tranches	Amount (M)	Originating Bank	Structure Type	Obligor Domicile
Oct-96	ROSE Funding No 1 Ltd	USD/GBP	11	$5,094	National Westminster Bank	Sub-Participation	UK/US
Sep-97	SBC Glacier Finance Series 1997-1 & 2	USD	10	$1,740	Swiss Bank Corp	Credit Linked Notes	Undisclosed
Oct-97	ROSE Funding No 2 Ltd	USD	11	$5,524	National Westminster Bank	Sub-Participation	UK/US
Oct-97	Triangle Funding Ltd 1997-1, 2 & 3	USD	14	$4,999	Credit Suisse First Boston*	Credit Linked Notes	US/UK/Australia
Dec-97	Atlantis Finance One Ltd. 1997-1**	USD	3	$5,304	Rabobank Nederland	Sub-Participation	Netherlands
Jun-98	York Funding Ltd. Series 1998-1	USD	6	$1,000	Credit Suisse First Boston*	Credit Linked Notes	Undisclosed
Sep-98	York Funding Ltd. Series 1998-2	USD	5	$279	Credit Suisse First Boston*	Credit Linked Notes	Undisclosed
Nov-98	Atlantis Finance Two Ltd. 1998-1**	USD	3	$7,200	Rabobank Nederland	Sub-Participation	US/pan-Europe

* Includes subsidiaries of CSFB. ** Issued as term notes but funded by single purpose CP conduits.

Source: Merrill Lynch

- The sponsor bank enters into a credit default swap (or equivalent, such as guarantees) with the SPV. This is the component of the structure that transfers credit risk on the pool of reference assets to the investors. The losses are allocated to investors by reducing the amount of collateral held by the SPV, which is then applied sequentially to the capital structure taking into account note seniority.

- Interest debt service is met by the collateral yield, credit swap premiums (or guarantee fees) due from the sponsor bank and repo payments (if any). Principal repayment is met from the liquidation or redemption of the separate collateral pool. Other forms of structural credit support ensure that the likelihood of cash flows due to investors is consistent with the assigned ratings.

In a synthetic CLO, investors essentially underwrite the credit risk in the sponsor bank's reference portfolio through conventional, credit tranched asset backed bonds. As the protection buyer, the bank pays regular credit protection premiums to investors (through the SPV) by way of credit default swap premiums or equivalent. Investor exposure to the reference portfolio is "synthetic" in that servicing of the issued notes is based on a separate pool of assets owned by the SPV and not directly reliant on the amortization of the reference portfolio.

The credit default swap mechanism allows the originating bank to hedge the credit exposure on a portfolio of reference assets, without having to sell the portfolio outright. Yet despite there being no transfer of underlying reference assets, the transaction can be structured to achieve de-linkage for the issued notes. Unlike cash based CLOs, the originating bank may not secure any funding in a synthetic CLO as the issue proceeds are used separately to collateralize the notes. CLO notes may be issued against partial or full amount of the reference portfolio, hence partially or fully funded CLOs. Examples of partially and fully funded CLOs are given in Exhibit 12.

Given their growing importance and presence in the European CLO market, we explain the mechanics of synthetic CLOs in more detail in a separate section.

Recent Developments in the European Bank CLO Market

A number of trends highlight the maturity and pace of innovation in the European marketplace for bank CLOs. The most pronounced of these trends, unquestionably, has been the explosive growth in synthetic CLOs issuance. Other trends include variations in the portfolio composition, SPV-less CLO structures, etc.

The Proliferation of Synthetic CLOs

The most pronounced of recent trends in the bank CLO market has been the proliferation of synthetic CLO structures. Eight out of the 13 European CLO transactions in both 1999 and 2000 year-to-date were synthetic CLOs. Pioneered by JP Morgan's BISTRO transaction in 1997, synthetic bank CLOs have since evolved to become a predominantly European product.

Exhibit 12: Selected European Synthetic CLOs

Offer Date	Issuer	Crncy	Tranches	Amt ($Mn)	Originating Bank	Structure Type	Senior Note Collateral	Obligor Domicile
Sep-98	Triangle Funding II LLC–1998-1&2	USD	11	$2,473	Credit Suisse First Boston	Fully Funded	USTs	US/Europe
Oct-98	Eisberg Finance Ltd	USD	6	$251	United Bank of Switzerland	10% Partially Funded	USTs	Undisclosed
Feb-99	Geldilux 1999-1 Ltd	EUR/USD	6	$2,536	HypoVereinsBank	Fully Funded	Pfandbriefe	German
Jun-99	Blue Stripe 1999-1	EUR/USD	11	$731	Deutsche Bank	15% Partially Funded	Pfandbriefe	US/UK
Jun-99	C*STAR 1999-1 Ltd	EUR	3	$293	Citibank	7% Partially Funded	BUNDs	Europe
Jul-99	Olan Enterprises plc	EUR	3	$189	Banque National De Paris	11% Partially Funded	OATs	US/Europe
Sep-99	Geldilux 1999-2 Ltd	EUR	6	$794	HypoVereinsBank	Fully Funded	Pfandbriefe	German
Nov-99	Scala 1 Ltd	EUR	4	$253	Banca Commerciale Italiana	6% Partially Funded	BUNDs	US/Europe
Nov-99	CAST 1999-1	EUR	12	$415	Deutsche Bank	14% Partially Funded	Pfandbriefe	German
Dec-99	BarCLO Finance 1999	USD	5	$200	Barclays Bank	10% Partially Funded	USTs	Undisclosed
May-00	Sundial Finance Ltd	EUR	4	$193.3	Rabobank	9% Partially Funded	OECD Govt	Undisclosed
Jun-00	OLAN Enterprises II Plc	EUR	5	$307	BNP Paribas	8% Partially Funded	Euroland Govt	Europe/US
Jun-00	Globe-R 2000-1	EUR	12	$270	Deutsche Bank	14% Partially Funded	Pfandbriefe	Europe
Jun-00	Cygnus Finance Plc	EUR	4	$329	Krediet Bank Cera	8% Partially Funded	OLOs	Europe
Jun-00	HAT (Helvetic Asset Trust) AG	CHF	2	$212	UBS	14% Partially Funded	Austrian Govt	Switzerland
Jun-00	CAST 2000-1	EUR	16	$319	Deutsche Bank	8% Partially Funded	Pfandbriefe	German
Jun-00	Blue Stripe 2000	USD	6	$450	Deutsche Bank	15% Partially Funded	Pfandbriefe	US/Europe
Jun-00	Natix Plc	EUR	3	$46	Natexis Banques Populaires	11% Partially Funded	OLOs	US/Europe

Source: Merrill Lynch

In Europe, synthetic structures are also being increasingly applied to asset types other than CLOs, notably real estate mortgages (residential and commercial) and corporate bond portfolios.

Decline of the Sponsor-Linked CLO
The decline in importance of sponsor-linked CLOs can be attributed to the advent of the synthetic CLO. Sponsor-linked CLOs, as defined either as the pure credit-linked note structures or sub-participated structures, have not been seen in the European marketplace since the middle of 1998.

Changes in Portfolio Composition
A number of recent transactions have departed from financing or hedging the more conventional portfolio types. As opposed to securitizing a discrete portfolio of (relatively few, but large) corporate loans, these newer deals have financed or hedged a portfolio of loans to small-to-medium sized (unrated) entities, in many instances with the sponsor's option to replenish the portfolio. Underlying loans in such transactions typically number in the thousands. Rating agencies would normally use an approach different to the standard CLO model in assigning ratings to such transactions, relying more on the fundamentals used in rating securities backed by liquid, diverse financial asset pools (such as credit card ABS).

Use of Variable Funding Notes
Variable funding notes (VFNs) have been structured into term CLO transactions essentially to finance underlying revolving credits. The growth in use of VFNs ties in with the difficulty in securitizing revolving credits through conventional asset backed bonds. Under VFNs, investors make commitments that can be drawn upon, repaid and/or redrawn, basically replicating the activity on revolving credit facilities in the underlying portfolio. Pricing of VFNs is a function of the commitment fee for the undrawn portion of the notes, coupled with a credit spread for the drawn part.

Issuing CLOs Without SPVs
A number of transactions, such as the Deutsche Bank's CAST and GLOBE deals, were structured without the conventional bankruptcy remote SPV. In fact, the first ever synthetic transaction without the use of an SPV involved the securitization of a German commercial mortgage portfolio (Deutsche Hypotheken Hannover).

With the exception of the senior tranches rated above the sponsor bank's rating, all other notes are structured as direct, unsecured obligations of the issuing bank. That is, investors have no preferential claims in bankruptcy, and thus these more junior notes are in effect CLNs. The senior notes take the form of secured obligations of the bank — yet these obligations are supported not by the bank directly, but rather are fully backed by a ring-fenced portfolio of Pfandbriefe collateral which, in the absence of an SPV, is deposited with a custodian in the name of the trustee. The isolation of the collateral from the bankruptcy estate of the sponsor bank allows the senior notes to attain ratings higher than that of the sponsor bank. These structures are not a constraint to achieving regulatory capital relief.

Sovereign Guaranteed CLOs

Sovereign guaranteed CLOs (benefiting from 0% risk weighting typically) have added a further dimension to the European bank CLO landscape recently. For now, the CLOs in question have been from Spanish banks.

In May 1999, the Ministry of Economy issued an order promoting government guaranteed securitization of loans originated to small and medium sized Spanish businesses (*pequenãs y medianas empresas* or PYMEs). Such loans are subsidized by the state funding agency *Instituto de Crédito Oficial* (ICO). There have been two conventional securitizations of such loans in 2000.

The guarantee by the Kingdom of Spain applies under certain conditions such as the requirement for the lending institutions to reinvest the issue proceeds in loans to other small businesses. The guarantees explicitly cover up to 15% of BBB securities, up to 50% of A-rated securities and 80% of AA-rated bonds. Transactions usually incorporate this by issuing guaranteed and unguaranteed tranches.

(Not) Retaining the First Loss Piece

First loss (equity) tranches usually attracts dollar-for-dollar regulatory capital charge. Selling the piece into the market, while expensive, increases significantly the equity release for the sponsor bank. Certain banks have expedited the placing of first loss pieces by enhancing the credit quality of the most junior tranches of the CLOs, discussed below.

Enhancing the First Loss Piece

One method of enhancing the quality of the most junior tranche of a CLO, applied so far only in Germany, is for the bank to grant the most junior noteholders limited sub-participation interest in the interest accruing to the underlying reference portfolio. This in effect protects the equity investors against losses allocated to the notes. We remind investors again that the cash flows generated by the reference pool are not normally used for debt service in a synthetic CLO.

These enhanced first loss notes, usually privately placed, have ratings capped at the level of the bank's own rating, reflecting the fact that assuming sub-participation interests equates to taking unsecured credit risk of the bank. Interest sub-participation in such transactions can be used only to the extent of covering the size of the first loss piece.

Call Options to Hedge the BIS Proposals

Recent European CLOs — and particularly synthetic transactions — have been structured with options that allow the originator to call the notes should the new BIS or other regulator proposals (when implemented) alter the economics of the transaction. In a number of deals these options are exercisable only after 2002, while in some others the option to redeem is available from the outset.

Issuers have built in such call options with good reason. These options will be in the money for bank issuers should the extent of capital relief attainable be adversely affected by the new regulatory capital regime. The economics could work in two ways. First, there could be a reduction in regulatory capital treatment of the underlying reference assets that have been hedged through the synthetic transaction. And second, there could potentially be an increase in risk weighting applicable to the assets collateralizing the notes (which is a direct determinant of the issuer's post-transaction capital charge for the reference assets hedged under the securitization).

SYNTHETIC CLOS EXPLAINED

A synthetic CLO is effectively a combination of a short position in a credit default swap (allowing the bank to transfer credit risk) and a long position in a portfolio of highly rated bonds (which generates the cash necessary to repay the synthetic bond). These structures can be fully or partially funded. Key features to consider include the flow of funds mechanism within the capital structure, and the determination and allocation of credit loss. Synthetic CLOs can be de-linked from the bank sponsor through a number of mechanisms, which assure the synthetic bonds' credit independence.

Why Issue Synthetic CLOs?

Synthetic CLOs allow banks to meet their primary objective of managing credit exposure while overcoming many of the limitations of true sale and CLN structures. Some view them as a refined version of pure CLN structures (limiting or eliminating the credit linkage to the sponsor bank), while others consider them a logical step in the development of credit derivatives structures (from single name credit default swaps through to portfolio credit default swaps to public partially funded credit default swap structures).

In particular, synthetic CLOs can be structured to eliminate or limit any investor exposure to the credit worthiness of the bank, allowing for credit ratings that exceed that of the sponsor. Synthetic CLO structures emerged, not surprisingly, during the credit bearish period in autumn 1998 when investors' were beginning to penalize CLOs with any credit linkage to the bank. Yet like CLNs, however, the bank remains the lender of record and can maintain its confidential business relationship with its client that comes with continued servicing of the loan. Non-disclosure of obligor identity is particularly useful in jurisdictions with stringent banking secrecy regulations.

One of the other key advantages of synthetic CLOs — and one that is arguably the primary driver behind growth of European bank synthetic CLOs — is that such structures allow for on balance sheet credit hedging of an asset pool that may otherwise be unsuitable for securitization, or funding off-balance sheet.

This would include unfunded assets (guarantees, derivative positions, etc), loans with restrictions on assignment or loans from jurisdictions with legal or other obstacles on transferability. Indeed, many synthetic CLOs are referenced to a portfolio of multi-jurisdictional loans. The main characteristics of cash and synthetic CLOs are compared in Exhibit 13.

As a matter of course there is much less transaction documentation involved in European synthetic CLO deals compared to the true sale variety — it is enough to mention the absence of an asset sale and transfer agreement. Synthetic CLOs allow banks to avoid the onerous process of combing through each underlying loan document and unravelling assignment clauses or other restrictions in order to sell the asset. As a result, transaction execution is that much simpler.

The Cost-Benefit Economics of Synthetic CLOs

The economics of issuing a synthetic CLO is basically a function of the cost of buying protection versus the benefit from regulatory equity release. Banks typically get full capital relief in synthetic transactions where the collateral comprises zero risk weighted securities, such as government bonds. Pfandbriefe normally attract a 10% risk weighting, unless the securities are issued by one of the bank's mortgage subsidiaries, in which case we understand the bank achieves full capital relief on a consolidated basis. The super senior swap, if underwritten by an OECD bank, carries a 20% risk weighting.

To be sure, borrowers would face lower all-in costs using a synthetic structure compared to a conventional structure, quite simply because the risk is underwritten using swaps as opposed to bonds (the cost of issuing bonds equals the risk free rate *plus* a credit spread). In our example in Exhibit 14, we have used 10 bps as the cost of swapping the super senior risk (this being the most often quoted figure) and, together with other assumptions, have arrived at a lower cost for a partially funded structure compared to a fully funded synthetic transaction. But really, the difference in cost between fully funded and partially funded structures would depend on the extent of leverage in the latter, the yield accruing to the collateral pool relative to the costs of the funded liabilities (that is, the interest deficiency in the capital structure) as well as the cost of the super senior swap.

Exhibit 13: Cash versus Synthetic Securitization

	Cash	Synthetic
Credit Line Capacity Management	Yes	Yes
Regulatory Capital Management	Yes	Yes
Economic Capital Management	Depends on First Loss Retention	Depends on First Loss Retention
Funding	Yes	No
Off Balance Sheet Treatment	Yes	No
Transfer of Ownership	Necessary	Not Necessary
Ease of Execution/Administration	Medium	High
Flexibility	Medium	High

Source: Merrill Lynch

Exhibit 14: Example of Regulatory Capital Relief

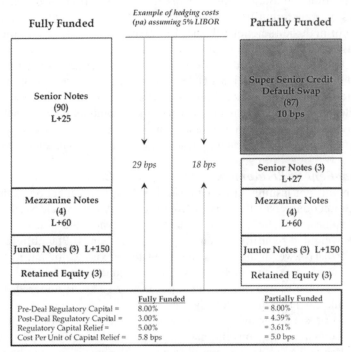

Assumes (1) dollar-for-dollar capital charge on retained equity, (2) 20% risk weight counterparty for super senior swap, and (3) assets that collateralize notes pay LIBOR minus 15 bps. Cost of equity ignored.

Source: Merrill Lynch

Partially and Fully Funded Structures

Synthetic CLOs can be either partially or fully funded structures — this a somewhat confusing terminology considering most sponsor banks do not actually realize any funding. A fully funded structure is where the risk in the entire portfolio of reference assets is hedged through the issuance of bonds. This structure is used less often — only three transactions in the European synthetic marketplace have been fully funded.

A partially funded structure (see schematic on Exhibit 15) is where CLO investors underwrite the riskiest (bottom layer) portion of the reference assets, with the top layer of the asset portfolio (so-called the "super senior" tranche) hedged through a credit default swap[1] contracted with a separate counterparty.

---

[1] Credit default swaps are derivative instruments used to hedge credit exposure on a reference asset, be it a single credit, a basket of credits or a portfolio of assets. In a plain vanilla credit default swap, the buyer of protection pays regular premiums (the swap quote) to the seller of protection in return for the seller agreeing to cover certain "credit events," as defined in the swap documentation. Payments to the protection buyer, contingent on the occurrence of losses following a "credit event," may be physically settled (being the norm for single name or basket swaps) or cash settled (being the norm for portfolio swaps).

Noteholders in a partially funded structure are effectively in the first loss position (subordinate to the "super senior" credit default swap). Of course, this first loss position is further credit tranched into notes of different seniority and ratings. Compared to fully funded synthetic or conventional CLOs, the most senior tranche of a partially funded synthetic CLO is much smaller in size.

In a partially funded structure, investors are typically long the first 6% - 15% of credit exposure in the reference portfolio. We understand that full regulatory capital relief on an asset pool may only be granted when the credit hedge covers the entire asset pool — this is primarily why a credit default swap is taken out for the (near riskless) senior most portion of a reference asset portfolio. The extent of capital release may vary between jurisdictions depending on the domestic interpretation of guidelines regarding capital treatment of credit derivatives.

Key Features of Synthetic CLOs
The Credit Risk Transfer Mechanism
Most synthetic CLOs use credit default swaps to effect credit risk transfer (see Exhibit 16). In the HypoVereins Bank's Geldilux transactions, however, the SPV issues limited recourse guarantees to the bank which protect against any credit loss in the reference portfolio. And in Deutsche's Blue Stripe deal, a 'financial contract' is drawn out allowing the bank to short the credit risk in its reference portfolio. There is little material variation in all cases, however. The sponsor bank makes regular premium payments to the counterparties underwriting the credit risk in its reference asset portfolio (i.e., the SPV and the super senior swap counterparty).

Exhibit 15: A Typical Partially Funded Synthetic CLO

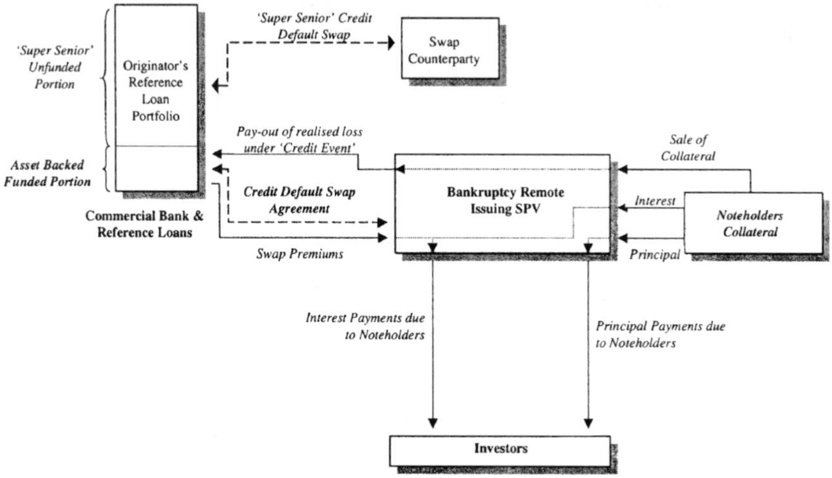

Source: Merrill Lynch

Exhibit 16: Credit Default Swap Cash Flows

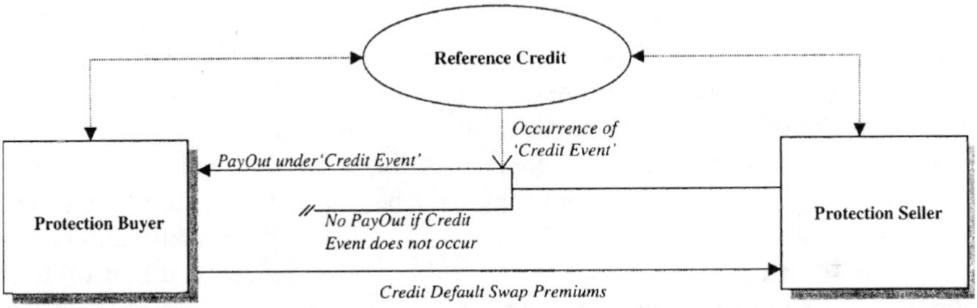

Source: Merrill Lynch

Credit Loss Allocation A key element in a synthetic CLO is the definition, determination and allocation of losses, against which the sponsor bank is seeking protection. Losses in this instance are contingent upon the occurrence of a 'credit event', as defined in the credit default swap documentation. Such 'credit events' would normally constitute some or all of the International Swaps and Derivative Association (ISDA) definitions of credit events, to include a failure to pay, bankruptcy, insolvency related reorganization of the underlying entity, repudiation or moratorium and obligation accelerations. Failure to pay and bankruptcy are the 'standard' credit events normally documented in a synthetic CLO. The restructuring of an underlying loan, repudiation, moratorium, obligation acceleration or a cross default with another obligation of the borrower may or may not constitute credit events in synthetic CLOs.

Losses in the reference portfolio are normally covered by reducing the collateral amounts held by the SPV. Depending on the particular deal structure, the SPV can:

- Sell the collateral to the extent required, remitting proceeds to the bank as a buyer of credit protection.
- Deliver the collateral in kind to the bank to cover any losses.
- Under a repo agreement, the bank repurchases the collateral less the value of any losses experienced in the portfolio.

The remaining collateral proceeds are sequentially allocated to redeem the notes at maturity in order of the notes' seniority, and hence the credit losses first affect the junior noteholders.

Under credit default swap or equivalent agreements, non-payment by an underlying borrower would normally have to exceed a minimum threshold before investors become liable. The amounts payable by the SPV for underlying reference credit losses in synthetic CLOs may be computed by the calculation agent in a number of ways:

- Cash settlement of the underlying defaulted loan. Such settlement can take place a defined number of days following default (ISDA definitions call for a 60-day period) based on market bids, or can be based on actual (realized) recovery values. If there are insufficient market bids for the defaulted assets, it is not uncommon for independent auditors or appraisers to value the asset for the purposes of loss determination.
- A fixed percentage of loan face value initially (i.e., a "digital" pay-out), following which any excess recoveries or losses within a specified time frame (12 months for example) may be allocated to investors. We understand that regulators do not usually give full capital relief for structures with digital pay-out provisions. (Digital pay-out structures are rare in synthetic CLOs, an example being Triangle Funding II.)

Realized losses usually include any costs associated with the recovery or sale of the defaulted reference claim, but may or may not include accrued interest. The timing of loss allocation may also vary. Losses may be allocated against the collateral at the time of default, upon the crystallization of recoveries or only when the notes are redeemed (i.e., at the termination of the deal).

Collateralization of the Notes and Credit Event Settlements
In a synthetic CLO, the issuing SPV either purchases the collateral on the market or from the sponsor bank. Purchases of collateral from the sponsor bank are normally transacted through a repo agreement where the originating bank is obligated to repurchase the collateral at some future date that would coincide with the bond redemption.

Assets used to collateralize synthetic CLOs are usually highly rated (typically triple-A), low risk weighted debt instruments, such as — but not limited to — government securities. A number of German bank synthetic CLOs have been collateralized by triple-A rated public sector Pfandbriefe. Where the Pfandbriefe is issued by the bank or one of its subsidiaries, the sponsor bank benefits ultimately from the issue proceeds and thus funding, in addition to risk transfer.

Flow of Funds
The mechanics of synthetic structure cash flow can be used to describe the generation and payment of interest and principal to investors.

Interest on the issued notes in synthetic CLOs is met from:

- Coupons due on the purchased collateral.
- The premium paid by the bank to the SPV for credit protection.
- Any net repo interest payable by the sponsor bank should the structure incorporate a repo agreement between the Issuer and the bank.

Synthetic CLO transactions are normally structured such that the premium payments, coupled with any repo interest, covers the residual negative carry (or interest deficiency) that would inevitably exist given lower coupons accruing to the collateral versus interest due under the capital structure.

Principal repayment on the issued notes is normally met from the sale of the collateral, either in the market or through a repurchase agreement with the bank. In the absence of a repo agreement, note redemption would be met by redemption and/or sale of the collateral into the market (examples of this include Scala 1, CitiStar 1 and the Blue Stripe transactions). As described earlier, the sale, redemption or repurchase of the collateral will be in effect net of any amounts needed to cover eligible losses accruing to the reference pool.

In a synthetic CLO referenced against a multi-currency asset pool, the sponsor bank usually assumes all foreign exchange risk (in cash structures, an adequately rated swap counterparty always assumes this risk). As an illustration, losses on foreign currency denominated reference assets can be based on the lower of market exchange rate or the rate determined at the outset (or replenishment date). Examples of such deals are Natix and Globe-2000.

Early Amortization and Acceleration Events

Broadly similar to cash flow based CLOs, early amortization events in synthetic CLOs would include economic triggers, such as accumulated reference portfolio loss or default thresholds. Should such triggers be breached, reference pool replenishments (or substitutions) are ceased and the notes begin to pay down. Note redemption in this instance usually mirrors the amortization of the reference pool. That is, the amount of collateral liquidated or repurchased to pay noteholders reflects the redemption profile of the reference pool, taking into account any losses. Under an early amortization event, therefore, synthetic CLO notes will in effect become pass throughs. This resembles what happens under similar events in conventional cash flow CLOs.

But unlike cash flow CLOs, certain "acceleration" events in synthetic CLOs — such as seller insolvency or material non-compliance of warranties — triggers the immediate redemption of the notes using available collateral.

De-Linking the Ratings of the Synthetic CLO from Sponsor Bank

Here we discuss how de-linkage of the synthetic CLO rating from the rating of the sponsor bank is achieved, looking specifically at the generation of cash flows necessary to service the notes and the features that mitigate risks associated with these cash flows.

Higher Reliance on the Purchased Collateral As a first step, de-linkage can be achieved for the notes provided the purchased collateral is itself de-linked from the creditworthiness of the sponsor. Government securities clearly are, and so are the Pfandbriefe, at least given the current approach to their credit analysis and ratings. Of course, a sound legal ownership or charge over the collateral is a necessary pre-requisite before de-linkage can be achieved.

Market risks to both the value and liquidity of the purchased collateral represent credit risks to the transaction and are usually mitigated through:

- Margin call provisions, where the sponsor bank would be required to post additional assets in order to maintain the required collateral value should this value fall below a certain threshold. Debt collateral backing synthetic CLOs is normally marked-to-market on a daily basis.
- A hedging agreement (essentially, put option) allowing the SPV to sell the collateral at purchase price plus any accrued interest at the redemption date. This option is underwritten either by the bank or by another adequately rated counterparty.

If the transaction's structure does not sufficiently hedge mark-to-market risk inherent in the collateral, there may be some measure of overcollateralization to further protect noteholders should the bank or counterparty fail to perform under its obligations as described above. The extent of overcollateralization would incorporate rating agencies' assessment of the potential decline in market value of the collateral during the time it takes the trustee to liquidate such collateral and de-lever the transaction sequentially.

Should the bank default and there is no ready market for the collateral (when, say, the collateral consists of non-government bonds), the transaction may allow an in-kind delivery of the collateral to investors in lieu of cash redemption.

It should be noted that synthetic CLOs can attain triple-A ratings even if the collateral is rated lower than triple-A (examples include KBC's Cygnus Finance where AA1/AA+/AA- rated Belgian OLOs are used). This is limited, however, to cases where the joint probability of collateral and bank default is deemed sufficiently remote to be consistent with a triple-A rating of the synthetic CLO. Further provisos would include a repurchase or similar agreement in place, and that the collateral bears no default correlation with the bank (government securities, for example).

Lesser Reliance on the Sponsor Bank The sponsor's bank credit comes into play in its ability to meet the residual interest payments (or, alternatively, the credit protection premium) under the capital structure.

Sponsor bank risk can be adequately mitigated by requiring the bank to fund its obligations one or more payment dates ahead of schedule. So if the bank defaults (a trigger event), payments already made allow for continued interest servicing of the notes while the trustee sells the collateral to repay noteholders. Interest deficiency in case of bank insolvency can also be adequately mitigated by insurance taken out with a suitably rated third party (HypoVereinsbank Geldilux deals being examples of this). Another method of hedging sponsor bank risk vis-à-vis credit protection premiums is by sufficiently overcollateralizing the notes such that interest coupons accruing to the issuing SPV's asset side matches payments due under its liabilities.

In a number of synthetic CLOs, investor exposure to the sponsor bank may extend to the bank being able to perform under a repurchase or hedging agreement. Additionally, certain transactions are structured such that payments made by the bank include a measure of "excess spread" which the notes are dependent on for the purposes of credit enhancement.

De-linking the notes in transactions where there is greater reliance on the bank is normally supported by adequate rating triggers built into the transaction. In particular:

- If the sponsor bank is downgraded, the risk to its obligations may be mitigated by, for example, the full pre-funding of such payments due to the SPV, or other similar measures (joint-and-several or performance guarantees, or a letter of credit, from adequately rated third parties) that would protect investors. Failing to do so would normally be captured by an early amortization trigger.
- A downgrade of the sponsor bank as repo/option provider is normally countered by finding an adequately rated replacement counterparty, or by cash collateralization of the obligations.

From a credit perspective, the bank's role in such synthetic transactions is, therefore, not dissimilar to the role of a swap counterparty in a more conventional ABS structure,[2] that is, its ratings need not be constrained by the ratings assigned to the notes provided adequate protection is in place. However, where the bank's role extends to being a hedging counterparty (or any other similar additional obligations), we would expect the bank to be rated in the highest short term rating category in order to support triple-A rated notes in the capital structure. The different features and their variations of synthetic CLOs are summarized in Exhibit 17.

FINDING VALUE IN EUROPEAN CLOS

The first step in bank CLO asset selection is to differentiate between linked and de-linked CLOs. We prefer de-linked structures. Through de-linked CLOs investors can gain exposure to the European corporate economy through bonds structured to be more credit resilient — yet typically cheaper — than plain vanilla bonds. We view diversification as an important consideration when comparing CLOs to other structured finance instruments. The synthetic structures add an additional layer of investment considerations for the European CLO investors. We view the lack of spread tiering within the synthetic CLO marketplace as an opportunity for investors to exploit synthetic CLOs with inherently stronger credit profiles, thus enhancing their risk-return exposures.

---

[2] See for example Standard & Poor's report titled "New Structured Finance Interest Rate And Currency Swap Criteria Broadens Allowable Counterparties," January 1999.

Exhibit 17: A Recap: Main Variations in Synthetic CLO Structures

Types of collateral	Possible sponsor bank roles	Types of protection against collateral risks	Types of protection against sponsor risks	Types of Credit Events	Types of loss settlement	Possible timing of loss allocation
• Government bonds • Public sector Pfandbriefe • Other triple-A credits • Bonds linked to sponsor	• Payer of credit protection premiums • Agreement to repurchase collateral at deal termination • Hedge counterparty (e.g. put option provider) against risk to value of collateral • Requirement to maintain collateral mark-to-market value • Other payment obligations, like the provision of 'synthetic' excess spread, etc.	• Repurchase agreement with sponsor/third party • Margin calls • Hedging agreement (e.g., put option) • Overcollateralization • Matching collateral and note maturities	• Credit protection premiums paid in advance • Overcollateralization • Full matching of collateral and note profiles • Interest deficiency insurance • Downgrade language	• Failure to pay * • Bankruptcy * • Restructuring of reference asset • Repudiation or moratorium • Obligation acceleration	• Cash settlement, based usually on market bids a defined number of days after default, recovery values following workout or independent valuation • Fixed percentage of loan face value **	• At loss settlement • At deal termination

* Credit Events that are standard in synthetic CLOs. ** Very uncommon type of loss settlement

Source: Merrill Lynch

The Question of Credit Linkage

As we already discussed, bank CLOs can be structured as linked or de-linked from the credit of the sponsor bank. A third variation, credit linkage that is contingent on specified events, the so-called contingent perfection structures, are unlikely to be seen on the European market. It should be noted that, each deal is different and even the de-linked structures may exhibit different levels of linkage to the sponsor bank. There are two key points to note.

First, sponsor-linked CLOs offer credit exposure to both the underlying portfolio and to the unsecured risk of the sponsor bank. While tranching of the capital structure allows investors to select their desired seniority vis-à-vis the allocation of portfolio credit loss, all investors in credit-linked CLOs with ratings equal to that of the bank are exposed to the creditworthiness of the bank, and thus any rating volatility that goes with it. The bulk of downgrades as of end of third quarter 2000 in the global CLO market have occurred in the credit-linked sector (examples include ROSE2 and York Funding).

The second point is that many sponsor-linked CLOs have high credit ratings only because of the high supporting ratings of the sponsor bank. Investors should understand how the ratings are achieved, noting that sponsor-linked CLO ratings are capped at those of the bank. This is particularly important in synthetic structures, where certain notes in the capital structure may be directly linked to the sponsor bank. Examples of such structures include the mezzanine/junior notes in SPV-less structures, or transactions where the notes are collateralized by bonds linked to the sponsor. A case in point: the mezzanine tranche (Class B) of the GeldiLux 1999-2 transaction was recently downgraded from Aa2/AA-/AA to Aa3/A+/AA- given a downgrade of the sponsor bank. The mezzanine and junior notes in this transaction are collateralized by cash deposits held at the bank and unsecured bonds issued by the bank under its MTN programme, thus underlining its credit linkage to the bank.

On a relative value basis, sponsor-linked CLOs should therefore trade at a reasonable discount to the de-linked market, though to us such tiering is not immediately observable in today's marketplace. This is particularly apparent among the subordinated CLO market, where sponsor-linked paper (from a number of synthetic deals, for instance) typically price similar to comparable de-linked CLOs.

We continue our analysis by focusing on the relative value of de-linked CLOs.

Comparison with Spread Products

European de-linked CLOs offers the credit investor an opportunity to gain a diversified exposure to the European corporate economy. Many CLOs also give investors exposure to a sector of the European corporate community that may otherwise be inaccessible — that is, credits originated to entities that rely wholly on bank financing (small-to-medium sized companies, etc.).

Exhibit 18: Euro Triple-A ABS and MBS Floaters
(as of November 2000)

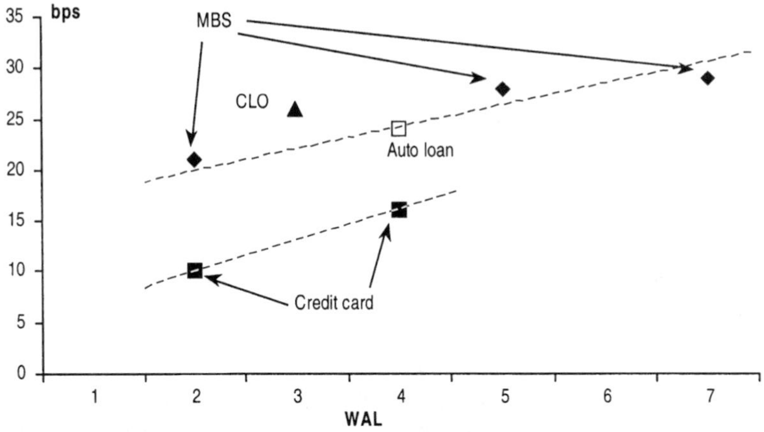

Source: Merrill Lynch

Credit enhancement and structural support in de-linked cash or synthetic CLOs underpin their ability to endure greater underlying credit deterioration compared to unsecured corporate or bank bonds. The degree of credit resilience will vary with bond seniority and ratings. Our point is that, given a rating, the CLO product is structured to be able to hold out against more credit stress compared to an unsecured bond and is therefore less at risk of being downgraded compared to an unsecured credit of the same rating (all other factors constant). We believe this strength of CLOs makes it an excellent defensive instrument for the credit investor, particularly in more credit volatile periods.

Yet CLOs normally trade wider compared to bank paper and corporates. Diversifying into CLOs can therefore add yield to a LIBOR based portfolio, without taking incremental credit risks. It should be noted, however, that spread performance of CLOs has historically been strongly correlated with other credit markets, creating less opportunities to diversify from a total returns perspective. For a spread comparison between CLOs and other ABS/MBS products see Exhibit 18.

Here are two examples of credit resilience of de-linked CLOs:

1. *Excelsior Master Trust* In 1999, collateral deterioration in this true de-linked CLO sponsored by the Japanese bank Sanwa but backed against US collateral was captured by an early amortization trigger. Benefiting from a relatively high payment rate, the bonds have since been paid down in full. There was no rating action taken on the bonds.

2. *Platinum Commercial Loan Master Trust* Following the take over of Long Term Credit Bank (LTCB) by Japan's Deposit Insurance Cor-

poration in late 1998, the LTCB sponsored de-linked CLO was unwound as the bank opted to withdraw from its international operations. The bonds were redeemed in full with no credit loss to investors, financed by the bank. There was no rating actions taken with regards to the notes.

Comparison with Other Structured Products

CLOs right across the credit spectrum usually trade on top of comparable consumer ABS or MBS in Europe. Investors switching into CLO products may not therefore pick up much in the way of yield.

Fundamentally, however, CLOs offer the traditional ABS investor an opportunity to diversify away from consumer based structured products such as MBS or credit card ABS (i.e., asset classes which dominate the structured finance market in Europe). Other key differences between CLOs and other ABS worth noting include:

- CLOs are typically issued by major banks that are usually highly rated (single-A to double-A categories). Investors should gain some comfort from the strength of servicing/underwriting functions as well as the lower potential for headline risk. This is generally true for credit card ABS and prime MBS, but not necessarily for sub-prime MBS and lease-backed ABS.
- CLOs are normally large transactions that benefit from a relatively liquid secondary market.
- More than half of European CLOs outstanding are structured as bullet securities, whereas the bulk of European ABS/MBS are securities with amortizing profiles (passthroughs).

Bank CLOs price and trade inside comparable high yield or leveraged loan CDOs (typically by more than 10 bps). To a large degree, this premium reflects the superior collateral credit quality of bank CLOs over other CDOs backed by higher yielding assets. Loans typically exhibit less credit volatility and benefit from higher recovery values compared to bonds. To that end, bank CLOs have experienced appreciably less adverse rating migration compared to CBOs. Moreover, bank CLOs are not actively managed loan portfolios and as such are not exposed to collateral manager risks, as are the arbitrage market value CBOs, for example.

Revisiting Synthetic Structures:
Synthetic Versus Cash Flow CLOs

Let's recap: In piecing together investors' exposure in synthetic structures, we note that the credit profile of a synthetic CLO is a function of:

- The reference assets (whose losses are allocated to noteholders).
- The collateral (liquidation or redemption of which pays-down the notes).
- The sponsor bank as credit protection buyer (payments from which cover residual interest servicing on the notes).

Exhibit 19 captures the credit considerations for synthetic structures compared to the more traditional cash based structures. The credit quality of the reference assets is, of course, an investment consideration in any structure. Beyond that, investor considerations for synthetic CLOs differ somewhat from analysis used in cash structures. Certain aspects of cash flow as well as servicer risks inherent in cash based structures are principally absent in synthetic structures. On the other hand, investors in synthetic CLOs may be potentially exposed to additional layers of risk associated with the collateral backing the notes and the sponsor bank's role in the transaction.

Below, we describe some of these key features that differentiate synthetic CLOs from cash based structures. These differences stem largely from the fact that investors in synthetic CLOs take synthetic exposure to the underlying reference pool, and cash exposure to the collateral backing the notes.

Some Differences Between Synthetic and Conventional CLOs
Below we have identified several key investment differences between a typical synthetic CLO and a conventional, true sale CLO.

Bullet Redemption, Liquid Collateral The availability of readily saleable collateral in synthetic CLOs allows for bullet redemption of the notes in most cases, which in itself is investor positive. A powerful feature here is that full note redemption — assuming a default neutral scenario — will be immediately realizable under certain acceleration trigger events (sponsor bankruptcy for instance). By contrast, in cash based transactions the length of an early amortization pay-out window will be determined by underlying pool payment rates.

Of course, full note redemption in this instance will depend on the value and saleability of the collateral in the open market and/or on the ability of the put or repo counterparty to meet its obligations.

Potential Exposure to Collateral Credit Risks The credit quality of the collateral determines the credit quality of the synthetic CLO notes.

From an investment perspective, the collateral presents less credit concerns when it is comprised of selected government securities. But a number of transactions are backed against non-government securities including most often Pfandbriefe.

The triple-A ratings on these non-zero risk weighted securities allow for the senior notes of synthetic CLOs to achieve similarly high ratings. Yet non-government collateral is likely to be more credit volatile than true "risk-free" paper. For example, it is far from certain whether Pfandbriefe ratings can withstand a significant deterioration of the respective bank's rating, or indeed a change in the legal or regulatory framework supporting these instruments.[3] A downgrade of the collateral may result in a downgrade of the notes.

---

[3] In its report titled "German Pfandbriefe, Moody's Analytical Approach" (June 1996), the rating agency stated that "the probability of default for Pfandbriefe can not be isolated from the creditworthiness of the issuing entity."

Exhibit 19: Key Risk Considerations in Bank CLOs — Conventional Versus Synthetic

Reference Pool Credit Quality	Originator / Servicer Considerations	Sponsor Bank Credit Risks	Risks Associated with Collateral	Structural Considerations	Market Considerations	
• Historical performance • Credit quality of obligors • Diversification • Type of reference assets • *Portfolio payment rate and profile* • *Margin on reference loans*	• Underwriting standards • *Competence in administrating collections and remitting payments* • Relationship with borrowers • Effectiveness of procedures in dealing with arrears • *Write-off policies* • *Potential for breach of duties and obligations (eligibility criteria, warranties, etc.)* • *Availability of back up servicer* • *Ability to call the notes, if applicable*	• *Ability to perform as swap counterparty (if applicable)*		• Credit enhancement as a cushion for potential losses *(including excess spread)* • Eligibility / substitution criteria • Priority of payments under different scenarios • Early amortisation triggers • *Protection against any risks of commingling, set-off, interest rate mismatch, forex, etc)* • Role of supporting parties (swap counterparty, etc.) and mitigants against associated risks • *Legal integrity (true sale)* • Retention of first loss	• Bond profile (pass through vs bullet, call options, etc) • Potential for headline and/or event risks • Secondary liquidity	CASH CLO
• Historical performance • Credit quality of obligors • Diversification • Type of reference assets	• Underwriting standards • Relationship with borrowers • Effectiveness of procedures in dealing with arrears	• *Ability to pay interest deficiency (credit protection premiums)* • Ability to perform other roles in transaction (for eg, a repo or hedge counterparty)	• *Credit quality, and scope for rating volatility* • *Reduction in market value* • *Liquidity or marketability* • *Potential linkage to the sponsor bank*	• Credit enhancement as a cushion for potential losses • Eligibility / substitution criteria • Priority of payments under different scenarios • Early amortisation and acceleration triggers • *Definition of Credit Events* • *Loss determination and timing of settlement, allocation* • *Protection against credit deterioration of bank* • *Protection against deterioration in value or saleability of collateral* • Role of supporting parties (like a hedge c/party, if different to sponsor) and mitigants against associated risks • *Legal integrity (perfection of security interest in collateral, use of SPV, etc)* • Retention of first loss	• Bond profile (pass through vs bullet, call options, etc) • Potential for headline and/or event risks • Secondary liquidity • *Extent of senior note leverage in partially funded structures* • *Reliance on trustee in being able to protect noteholder interests*	SYNTHETIC CLO

Text in italics denote considerations that are unique to the respective structure type.

Source: Merrill Lynch

Less Scope for Servicing and Structure Related Risks Adequate servicing of the asset pool (administering collections, remitting payments, etc.) in order to meet debt servicing under the capital structure is an important consideration in cash flow CLOs. The servicing aspect of a CLO is less of an issue in a synthetic structure:

- In case of the outright insolvency of the seller/servicer, there is no need to transfer the servicing function. Using the collateral pool, as described above, investors can be taken out of the transaction immediately. Hence, the risks inherent in cash based structures that a proficient substitute servicer cannot be found are of no relevance to synthetic CLOs.
- Any breach of servicer duties or warranties can be easily "reversed" as no sale/transfer of assets would have taken place. Having synthetic — as opposed to cash — exposure to the reference pool also means that any breach of structural criteria (such as eligibility conditions) can be quickly "reversed." A reversal in this instance amounts simply to cancelling the default protection covering those particular assets.
- As there is no cash flowing from the reference pool, risks associated with cash transfer, commingling or set-off inherent in true sale CLOs are not relevant for synthetic structures.

Synthetic CLOs also have less scope for other structural cash flow related risks such as basis or currency mismatches. In multi-currency denominated deals, for instance, foreign exchange risk can be assumed by the protection buyer. In cash structures, any collections denominated in currencies other than the issuing currency will need to be hedged, of course, exposing investors to counterparty risk.

Potential Exposure to Sponsor Bank Risk The exposure to the sponsor bank depends on the roles it performs in a synthetic CLO structure. Such exposure could include and be mitigated in the following ways:

- The risks to the payment obligations of the sponsor bank as credit protection buyer can be fully mitigated in synthetic CLOs, as noted earlier in the chapter, through — for example — an arrangement to deposit the payment well before the payment date.
- In addition to being the buyer of credit protection, the sponsor bank may also be a repo or hedging counterparty (vis-à-vis collateral mark-to-market risks) in the transaction. The risks associated with the sponsor bank being a repo or hedging counterparty based on its short-term rating can be mitigated through appropriate downgrade language. While not a constraint to rating the synthetic CLO notes, any deterioration in the bank's credit quality will require remedial action, failing which the collateral is liquidated and the notes paid down.

- Clearly, investors are directly exposed to the sponsor bank's credit in any synthetic structure where the collateral pool consists of bonds credit-linked to the bank. Where the collateral comprises highly rated non-government collateral that is "related" — though not technically "linked" — to the sponsor bank (to include, in our opinion, Pfandbriefe), the ability to pay down the notes under seller credit deterioration or insolvency may not be entirely assured either. Such collateral is likely to be sensitive to the performance and/or credit profile of the bank (a hedge provided by a suitably rated third party should mitigate this risk). In a number of synthetic CLOs, noteholders may ultimately have to take physical delivery of the collateral in lieu of redemption if a market sale or repurchase cannot be effected[4] (examples of such deals include Globe 2000 and Cast 2000).

In conclusion, many synthetic CLOs are structured in such a way that there is multiple reliance on the sponsor bank. That is, there may be many "layers" of bank risk in the transaction — for instance, credit dependence given the nature of the collateral, reliance on the bank as a hedging and/or repo counterparty, etc. The more such layers, the greater the ultimate linkage to the bank, in our view, even if such risks are mitigated at each level. True de-linked cash flow CLOs do not typically have exposure to the sponsor bank to the extent that many synthetic transactions may do.

Loss Determination and Settlement Synthetic CLOs have more complex settlement and valuation issues related to the credit events in comparison to the cash based structures, where loss crystallisation and impact on the deal's liabilities are relatively straightforward:

- On the one hand, credit events and pay-out amounts in synthetic CLOs are pre-defined, whereas in cash or 'true sale' based structures any form of underlying non-payment or default adversely affects investors. This feature of synthetic CLOs is clearly investor positive.
- But on the other hand, credit events that are too broadly defined may trigger premature and more severe loss for noteholders. In transactions where the credit events are not clearly described, investors would have to rely on a third party for the interpretation and validation of a covered event.

The credit events, therefore, need to be carefully examined. In our view, synthetic CLOs with broad credit event definitions and complex workout procedures prove a challenge to rating agency analysis — default probabilities and loss severity assumptions in such deals are far from being an exact science. Structures where the loss payout is fixed from the outset mitigate risk of loss volatility, but we realize that only very few deals are structured this way.

---

[4] In our analysis, we do not take into consideration the potential benefits of being delivered collateral in lieu of payment. Such benefits include the replacement of notes by lower risk weighted paper.

Greater Reliance on the Trustee There is a greater reliance on trustees in being able to protect the interests of noteholders in synthetic CLOs. Among other duties, the trustee in synthetic CLOs will be required to be vigilant vis-à-vis:

• Monitoring and selling the collateral as required.
• Verifying the determination and allocation of losses.

But there is one important exception — under a seller bankruptcy (as mentioned), the trustee's performance in a conventional structure becomes crucial. Continued deal servicing post seller insolvency, by contrast, is of no relevance in synthetic transactions.

Leveraging the Triple-A Tranche in a Partially Funded Structure In a partially funded structure, senior noteholders are in a more leveraged position compared to senior noteholders in a similar fully funded or cash flow CLO. Put differently, senior noteholders could face greater relative losses (as a percent of principal) compared to senior investors in fully funded or conventional structures should defaults reach a level where all subordination is wiped out. To be sure, the likelihood of such high defaults is extremely remote being as it is consistent with a triple-A ratings.

As for the subordinated tranches, noteholders in partially funded structures are no more aggressively long the underlying credit exposure from either a "first dollar of loss" or "expected loss" position compared to their counterparts in a conventional or fully funded structure.

Identifying the "Ideal" Synthetic CLO Structure

We urge investors to study each structure within the synthetic CLO universe. The collateral backing the notes, the role of sponsor bank and the aspects of credit events deserve diligent analysis, and these factors distinguish this structure from the more traditional cash flow CLOs. The high incidence of split ratings amongst synthetic CLOs would suggest to us that rating agencies differ in their analytical approaches, thus making investor analysis all the more important.

Based on the analysis above, we make several suggestions as to the "ideal" features of a synthetic CLO. This is in some respects a theoretical exercise, with the purpose of formulating a "benchmark" synthetic CLO. Investors should be able to compare all synthetic CLOs against this benchmark for analytical and pricing purposes.

Aside from the favorable features that should characterize any CLO (solid reference pool quality, strong servicer, adequate credit and structural protection, etc), our "ideal" synthetic CLO would comprise:

• Collateral that is made up of government or equivalent (zero risk weighted) bonds, with a secondary market that is sufficiently deep to readily absorb the sale of the collateral without adverse impact on its price. Essentially,

the collateral should be "risk-free" instruments that are wholly independent from the sponsor bank.
• Deals where sponsor bank participation or risk is limited and easily identi-
fiable and where such risk is fully mitigated by structural features of the
transaction (advance funding of protection payment obligation or guarantees by suitably rated third parties, for example).
• Narrowly defined and clearly determinable credit events like, for instance,
the failure to pay and bankruptcy. The occurrence of the credit event and
the determination of losses, including expected recoveries, can arguably be
more accurately projected the narrower the definition of credit events.
• Structures where losses are cash settled at the end of the workout process,
rather than settlement after a defined period following default. Recoveries
may be potentially greater under a workout or enforcement compared to
prices bid for a distressed asset soon after default. In this respect, the first
loss position should be retained by the servicer as an incentive to maximize
recoveries (this being no different to conventional CLOs). This first loss
could be in the form of issued (equity) tranches, a sufficiently generous
minimum threshold on portfolio losses before these losses are allocated to
investors, or even the obligation to sub-participate reference pool interest
to junior noteholders.
• Ideally, loss valuations should exclude accrued interest on the defaulted
reference claim. Losses should also preferably be allocated to the notes at
deal termination, allowing investors to benefit from full interest payments
until note maturity. By contrast, principal erosion in a conventional deal
would normally also result in an interruption to interest payments.

Spread Behavior in the Synthetic CLO Market

Synthetic bank CLOs typically price slightly wider to cash based, true sale CLOs.
(See Exhibit 20.) We are not at all surprised by this spread concession, and
attribute it to the complexity of synthetic structures. (The same reason largely why
generic asset backed structures are normally cheaper than plain vanilla corporates.) Lower secondary liquidity, a less receptive investor base for credit derivative based product, and the increased triple-A note leverage in partially funded
structures are likely also to play a part in this synthetic-true sale pricing disparity.

Exhibit 20: Average Primary Market Spreads in Mid-2000, Euro-Denominated Synthetic CLOs (De-Linked, Bullet Securities)

Rating Category	3 Year	5 Year	7 Year
Triple-A	26 bps	28 bps	32 bps
Single-A	60 bps	65 bps	70 bps
Triple-B	—	130 bps	135 bps
Double-B	300 bps	340 bps	—

Source: Merrill Lynch

Not all synthetic CLOs are the same. We believe synthetic CLOs that closely match our "benchmark" structure as described above will have a superior credit and investment profile compared to other synthetic CLO structures and arguably to many cash flow CLOs as well. Yet, to the extent observable, there is little spread tiering *within* the European synthetic bank CLO universe to reflect differences in the credit profiles of the different structures. What little spread tiering there is in the CLO market usually relates to the quality of the sponsor bank as a stand-alone entity. This lack of spread tiering should therefore provide opportunities for investors to selectively exploit. An even more obvious risk-return relative value play is in the subordinated sector, where pricing of de-linked and sponsor-linked synthetic CLOs appears to show little tiering to reflect the extra layer of bank risk in the latter.

One last point we would make on investing in synthetic CLOs is the potential for issuers to exercise regulatory call options built into many such transactions. As we pointed out earlier in this chapter, these options typically relate to proposed changes under the new BIS Accord and are normally exercisable after 2002. Given that funding the option (or refinancing the deal) will not be a deterrent to calling a synthetic CLO transaction, we would expect issuers to call their transactions at the earliest opportunity should the new regulatory capital regime adversely impact on the economic benefits of keeping the synthetic securitization in place.

These call options may therefore limit the opportunities for synthetic CLO investors to benefit from any spread rally post BIS. On the other hand, we note that callable synthetic CLO paper usually price to scheduled expected maturity rather than the call date, which in turn makes certain transactions look cheap relative to their call tenor. But identifying precisely which deals would be called is a difficult exercise currently given the ambiguity of what the final BIS proposals may look like.

OUTLINE OF CLO RATING APPROACH

Analyzing portfolio risk is a common denominator in the rating approach to bank CLOs, irrespective of structure type. Credit enhancement is sized taking into account simulations of loss expectations in the pool and is commensurate with the desired rating on the notes. We outline the key considerations in rating conventional cash based structures and synthetic CLO structures.

Analyzing Portfolio Risk

Rating agency analyses of portfolio credit risk as used for a standard CLO normally relies on an asset specific credit analysis, rather than on an actuarial approach as used for many other financial receivable structures (credit cards and auto loans, say). The exception is for transactions financing or hedging pools with short average lives and characterized by a high number of loans to small and medium sized (typically unrated) entities. Here, rating agencies would rely on an actuarial approach, i.e., a detailed study of the historical experience of the sponsor bank's loan book. (Deutsche Bank's series of CORE and CAST deals are examples of such transactions. The number of loans underlying/referenced in each transaction number between 2,000-5,000, with single obligor concentrations of 1-2%.)

Below, we review the broad outline of the rating approach for a standard CLO. The thrust of the credit analyses undertaken by each rating agency is based on broadly similar underlying themes, i.e., default and loss assumptions for each loan in the underlying pool.

Default Probabilities

Default probability assumptions are determined primarily by using the ratings of the underlying obligors. (See Exhibit 21.) Where public or shadow ratings are unavailable, the internal credit scoring of the bank is mapped to generic rating categories by statistically regressing historical performance data related to each internal rating category of the bank, and correlating the results with rating scales of the agencies. The mapping process is typically complimented with a comprehensive due diligence on the banks' underwriting and loan monitoring procedures.

The actual or mapped rating level for each loan is then paired with a default probability for a similarly rated corporate credit. Such probabilities are based on empirical studies of historical corporate bond defaults. In adjusting the cumulative period over which the corporate default probability relates to, rating agencies would take into account the maturity specifics of the underlying loans and issued notes. Rating agencies tend to apply a degree of conservatism to the analysis vis-à-vis the mapping process and default probability assumptions.

The weighted average rating for the aggregate portfolio is calculable using loan specific default probabilities (a scale of "rating factors" is typically employed).

Loss Severity

Loss severity for the underlying assets is projected by making assumptions about recovery values, based on the historical experience of the bank or from rating agency collated data. Rating agencies also make assumptions about the timing of recovery values.

Exhibit 21: Average 10 Year Cumulative Default Rates (%) — S&P/Moody's

Rating Category	S&P	Moody's
AAA/Aaa	0.67	1.09
AA/Aa	0.90	3.10
A/A2	1.48	3.61
BBB/Baa	3.63	7.92
BB/Ba	14.42	19.05

Source: *Historical Default Rates of Corporate Bond Issuers 1920-1999*, January 2000, Moody's Investor Service. *Ratings Performance 1999*, Stability & Transition, February 2000, Standard & Poor's.

Exhibit 22: Recovery Rate Assumptions (%)

Loan/Debt Type	Moody's	S&P	FitchIBCA*	DCR*
Senior Secured Loans	70	50-60	60	60
Senior Unsecured Loans	—	25-50	—	—
Senior Secured Bonds	52	40-55	—	50
Senior Unsecured Bonds	49	25-44	40	40
Subordinated Bonds	33	15-28	20	30

* Data prior to merger.
  Source: "Historical Default Rates of Corporate Bond Issuers 1920-1999," Moody's Investor Service, 2000. "Global CBO/CLO Criteria," Standard & Poor's. "Rating Criteria for Cash Flow Debt Obligations," Fitch IBCA, 1999. "DCR Criteria for Rating Cash Flow and Market Value CBOs/CLOs," Duff & Phelps, 1997.

Recoveries are not a function of the asset rating, but depend largely on the seniority and security of the obligations. Exhibit 22 shows the "generic" recovery assumptions used by rating agencies in their standard CLO models. Recovery assumptions for European CLOs may, of course, differ from this given their different insolvency regimes. To that end, rating agencies have recently conducted studies on expected recoveries in the European loan/debt marketplace.

As with default probabilities, some amount of conservatism is normally applied when computing recovery rates and loss severity. For instance, credit may not be given to loans with security, particularly in revolving structures where the underlying loans can be substituted. In specific circumstances, recoveries may be given no credit in the rating process (i.e., rating agencies assume a 100% loss severity).

Expected Loss = Default Probability × Loss Severity

Loss expectations are simulated for the underlying portfolio by taking into account assumed defaults and recovery rates. In running such simulations, rating agencies always incorporate interdependent default probabilities arising from correlated risk in the pool. Such correlations relate to loans originated from the same or related industries and geographical regions.

The issue of diversification is a key consideration in assessing the credit quality of an underlying portfolio. Rating agencies normally have base case definitions for a diversified pool that will include guidelines on obligor and industry concentration limits. Moody's well known diversity scores measure the risk of correlated defaults.

Sizing Credit Enhancement

Rating agencies size credit enhancement by stressing base case loss scenarios, with the extent of stresses commensurate with the desired credit ratings on the notes. (See Exhibit 23.) The higher the ratings, the more generous the loss cushion allowing the notes to withstand greater prolonged reductions in cash flow.

Exhibit 23: 'AAA' Stresses for 10 Year Default Rates for a Weighted Average Collateral Credit Rating of 'BB' (%)

Rating	DCR*	FitchIBCA*
AAA	38.6	43.5
AA+	35.3	33.5
AA	34.1	32.5
AA-	33.0	31.5
A+	29.5	28.1
A	28.5	27.0
A-	27.5	25.9
BBB+	25.5	22.4
BBB	24.5	21.5
BBB-	23.5	20.6
BB+	21.5	19.6
BB	20.9	18.7
BB-	20.3	17.7

* Data prior to merger.

Source: "Rating Criteria for Cash Flow Debt Obligations," Fitch, 1999. "DCR Criteria for Rating Cash Flow and Market Value CBOs/CLOs," Duff & Phelps, 1997.

Sizing credit enhancement will also factor in cash flows stresses on the liabilities side, such as interest paid to noteholders (unless a cap or equivalent is put in place) as well as any swap or other obligations of the SPV that are senior to debt service in the cash flow waterfall.

Final credit enhancement levels will typically take into account any further structural protection available to noteholders as well as other more qualitative factors.

Structural and Legal Considerations

Cash Based Structures

Underlying portfolio analysis aside, assigning ratings to cash based CLOs requires rating agencies to gain a sufficient degree of comfort with a number of qualitative aspects of the transaction. These encompass:

- Ensuring that the legal structure is clearly defined and that investors' interests are represented properly. Particular emphasis is placed on the legal integrity of the transaction, to include the transfer of assets and perfection, enforceability issues, bankruptcy remoteness of the SPV, integrity of servicing and other agreements, etc.
- Taking into account the adequacy of structural protection available to noteholders (early amortization triggers, reference pool guidelines, eligibility or substitution criteria to prevent credit quality migration over the life of the deal, spread trapping mechanisms, turbo features, etc.).
- Addressing structural risks. Set-off, commingling, liquidity and third party risks, to name a few.

• Assessing the competency of the sponsor bank within the context of the transaction. This would include the bank's underwriting and loan monitoring ability as well as other aspects of servicing.

Synthetic Structures

Similar to the approach taken with more conventional funded CLOs, the synthetic credit exposure to the underlying reference loans is determined by the credit analysis of the reference portfolio, actuarial or otherwise. Initial levels of credit enhancement are derived by stressing expected pool defaults to a degree consistent with the desired rating, taking into account the adequacy of put triggers protecting against any worsening of pool credit quality.

Adjustments to the rating process relate to the other two components of the synthetic structure — the collateral backing the notes and the role of the sponsor bank. Rating synthetic CLOs would further take into consideration:

• Perfection of security interest in the separate collateral pool or, if the collateral is held by the bank as custodian, the validity and enforceability of a pledge or charge over the collateral in favour of investors' interests. This degree of isolation is particularly important in CLOs issued without SPVs where reliance must be placed on some form of security arrangement.
• Sufficiency of structural mechanisms to hedge against any deterioration in the collateral value over the term of the deal. A further consideration will be the level of overcollateralization provided by the collateral over the notes, reflecting the rating agencies' assessment as to the severity of market value decline in the time it takes to liquidate the portfolio.
• Integrity of swap/repo documentation. For instance, the credit default swap documentation should accurately define credit events and determination of loss severity.
• "Loading up" the assumed default rates for each rated category to reflect the full scope of credit events. An offsetting factor here may be higher recoveries under a range of broader credit events.
• Assumption of recoveries consistent with the definitions of credit events and cash settlement features.
• Sponsor bank's stand alone rating and the extent of any structural support to protect against exposure to the bank.

Chapter 10

Analyzing Mezzanine Tranches of CBOs

Laurie S. Goodman, Ph.D.
Managing Director
UBS Warburg

Jeffrey Ho
Senior Vice President
Mortgage Strategy Group
UBS Warburg

F ixed-income investors are often rewarded, through higher yields, for taking advantage of new asset types. For example, in 1993 spreads on AAA commercial mortgage-backed securities (CMBS) were 70 basis points wider than on agency current coupon passthroughs, by February 2000 they were 30 bp tighter. Similarly, short AAA home equities initially traded 50 bp wider than CMOs, two years later they were trading 20 bp tighter. Collateralized bond obligations (CBOs) are one new, and rapidly growing, type of fixed income product. The first year of significant CBO issuance was 1996. Since then, the growth of CBO issuance has been dramatic; in 1996 Moody's rated $20 billion in CBOs, in 1999 it rated $92 billion. (We use the term CBOs throughout the course of this chapter to refer both to collateralized bond obligations and to collateralized loan obligations.)

In dealing with CBOs, as with any asset, investors need to evaluate whether or not they will be rewarded sufficiently for the risks entailed. Part of that process entails developing a comfort level about investing in CBO paper, via relative value comparison to other products. However, the risk-return profile of CBOs is very different from that on a typical corporate bond. Moreover, the collateral behind the CBO is often different from a corporate bond of the same rating. In this chapter, we focus on the methodology to determine value in the mezzanine tranches. We discuss the risk-return profile on the mezzanine tranches of CBOs, and focus on comparing the mezzanine tranche to corporate alternatives.

This topic is particularly important, as the mezzanine tranches of CBOs appeal to many different types of investors. The fixed-rate cash flows of the mezzanine tranches are an ideal fit for insurance companies, which seek to manage portfolio assets against their long-term, fixed-rate liabilities. The floating-rate coupons of CBO tranches fit quite well into LIBOR-plus portfolios. In all cases, investors need to be able to make relative value comparisons.

METHODOLOGY

We begin our demonstration by looking at risk-return profiles of a BBB rated CBO mezzanine tranche versus a BBB rated corporate bond. Comparing yields on representative bonds as a function of defaults readily shows the difference in the yield profiles between the two types of securities. We then tested to determine the better yielding bond at the same level of risk, by calculating breakeven default rates necessary to produce the same yield on the two securities. These default rates are then evaluated relative to historical experience.

Our analysis shows that given the spread configuration typical of December 1999 deals, BBB rated CBOs yield considerably more than do typical corporate bonds, even at the highest default levels the underlying collateral ever experienced over the past three decades. This indicates that there is definitely relative value within CBOs. *While this conclusion of relative investment value is dependent on the present spread configuration, our methodology is more general.*

INTRODUCING THE SECURITIES

There is no standard, generic, or "plain vanilla" CBO deal. Each has slightly different collateral, and a slightly different structure. The representative CBO we used for this comparison is a cash flow structure deal. For pricing purposes, we assumed that the deal is backed by collateral consisting of 80% bank loans and 20% high yield bonds. Funding has been divided into three classes:

1. 74% AAA rated senior floating rate notes
2. 16% BBB+ rated subordinated floating rate notes
3. a 10% unrated equity tranche

Our test case CBO deal has a 7.25-year expected maturity and a 12-year legal maturity. In this chapter, we focus on the BBB+ tranche, which is commonly called the "mezzanine" tranche, and compare it to 10-year BBB corporate securities.

We assumed a coupon on our representative Baa1/BBB+ rated CBO of LIBOR + 225. The bond was also issued at a slight discount, which produced a yield of roughly LIBOR + 230. To compare yield on the CBO to yield on an equivalently rated, fixed-rate corporate bond, we used the swap curve to convert the floating-rate LIBOR-based yield into a fixed-rate security. With 10-year swap yields at 6.78%, the equivalent fixed-rate yield on the CBO is 9.08% (6.78% + 2.30%).

As a proxy for a fixed-rate BBB security, we used the Merrill Lynch BBB rated corporate index (C0A4). We assumed that our representative corporate bond has the same coupon as the index's weighted average coupon — 7.356%, and same yield as the index — 7.76%. This corresponds to a spread of 180 basis points over the 10-year Treasury note. (The then-prevailing 10-year Treasury note was 5.96%, which equates to the 10-year swap yield of 6.78%, less the 82 basis points swap spread.) Assuming a 10.0-year average life, then the dollar price of the representative corporate bond is $97.32.

COMPARING DEFAULTS

It is a challenge to compare defaults on CBO collateral to those on a BBB corporate bond, as the underlying assets are so different. The CBO consists of both high yield and bank loan collateral, while our straw dog is a portfolio of BBB corporate bonds. We set up two alternative scenarios, which represent the upper and lower default bounds. We first assumed that the BBB corporate never defaults, while the collateral for the BBB CBO defaulted at rates assumed at the bottom of Exhibits 1 and 2. In our second iteration, we assumed that the two securities defaulted at the same rate. Both of these are obviously wrong. We know that BBB corporate bonds do default (although at a much lower rate than high-yield bonds, and they are usually downgraded first). Still, our assumptions provide bounds, albeit very wide bounds, for our analysis.

Exhibit 1: BBB CBO versus BBB Corporate with Base Case Recoveries

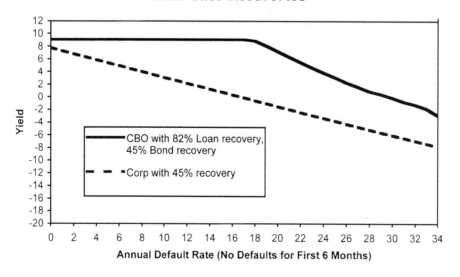

Exhibit 2: BBB CBO versus BBB Corporate with Stressed Recoveries

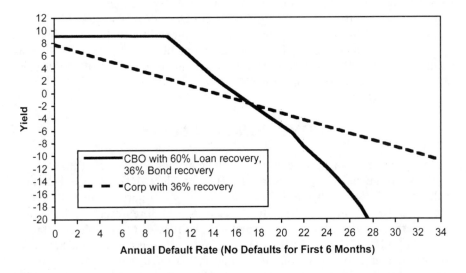

Exhibits 1 and 2 compare the yield profile on our representative BBB rated CBO tranche to that on a BBB rated corporate bond. We assume zero defaults for the first six months, then the annual default rate depicted on the horizontal axis of the two exhibits for the remainder of the term. Note that recovery rates on bank loans have typically been much higher than on unsecured bonds because of the built-in, risk-mitigating features of many bank credit facilities. For instance, bank lenders often require collateral before a loan is extended, which makes most bank loans senior to unsecured bonds, and therefore, likely to have a higher recovery. Accordingly, we used a lower recovery rate for both the high-yield bonds and the BBB corporate issue.

In Exhibit 1 we assumed 82% recovery on the loans, and 45% recovery on the unsecured corporate debt. In the exhibit, the yield profile on the CBOs is denoted by a solid line, The yield profile on the BBB rated corporate bond is presented as a dotted line. These levels correspond to historical evidence of recovery rates, sourced from Moody's and internally generated PaineWebber data. In Exhibit 2 we assumed 60% recovery on the loans and 36% recovery on the high-yield bonds. This is in line with the rating agencies' stress scenarios for recoveries.

Exhibits 1 and 2 demonstrate that the yield profile on the CBO is much more leveraged than that for the corporate bond. By this we mean that the CBO maintains its spread for a much longer period of time, but then deteriorates far more quickly.

RISK-REWARD PROFILES

Look at risk-return profiles using the historical recovery rates in Exhibit 1. If we assume that the BBB corporate bond never defaults, and that all the collateral backing the CBO defaults at the annual rates shown on the horizontal axis of Figure 1, then the "breakeven default rate" is 19.4%. That is, at a 19.4% default rate on the CBO collateral, the post-default CBO yields the same 7.76% as does the zero-default corporate bond. (To replicate: find the point on the CBO curve in Exhibit 1 where the yield is 7.76%, and observe the corresponding default rate.) In fact, as will be shown in the next section, this 19.4% default figure is nearly double the highest level of high-yield default rates ever experienced over the last three decades. If we assume that annual default rates on the CBO and the BBB corporate bond are the same, then the CBO outperforms the corporate bond in all default scenarios. The exhibit shows results as high as a 34% annual default rate, which is the highest we tested.

We repeated the same analysis in Exhibit 2, using a rating agency stress scenario for recoveries. Assuming zero defaults for the BBB rated corporate bond, the collateral on the CBO can default at close to 11% and the CBO will still outperform on a yield basis. This is higher than the highest default rates experienced by high yield bonds in the early 1990s. Assuming the BBB corporate defaults at the same rate as does the high-yield bonds, then the breakeven default rate is even higher — at 17%. We now show that this number is well outside the range of historical experience. [1]

HISTORICAL DEFAULT RATES

Exhibit 3 shows Moody's compilation of historical default rates for the high-yield market since 1971. These are trailing 12-month default rates, and are expressed as the percentage of defaults per annum. The statistics are tallied both by the number of issuers and by outstanding balance. The latter understandably tilts the average towards the results of larger issuers, while the former gives equal weighting to all issuers.

Note that default rates historically have been quite low. In fact, as measured by percent of balance, the average default rate over the 1971-1999 period has been just 3.24% (with a standard deviation of 2.49%). As a percent of the total number of issuers, the historical default rate was 3.37% (standard deviation of 2.22%).

---

[1] Clearly, these results are dependent on our assumptions. We have assumed equal annual default rates after the first 6 months. Changing the default timing will make a difference. In particular, defaults early in the life of the CBO/CLO have a larger negative impact. Changing the recovery assumptions will also have an impact. In addition, we have assumed a stable interest rate environment. Changing this assumption will alter reinvestment rates and could trigger call provisions on the corporate bond, the collateral underlying the CBO, or the CBO structure.

Exhibit 3: Historical Annual Default Rates

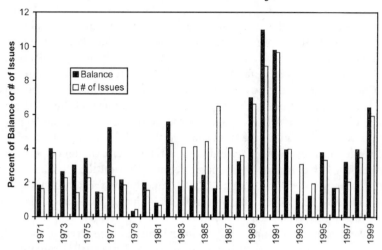

Exhibit 4: The Distribution of Annual Defaults

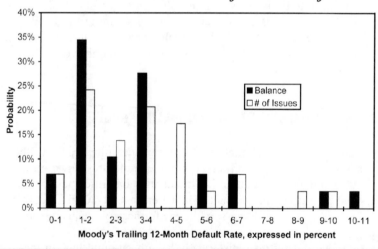

However, it's readily observable from Exhibit 3 that the "average" is heavily skewed by several very high default years during 1989-1991. Peak bond defaults typically occur 2-3 years after issuance. During the leveraged buy-out mania of 1987-1989, quite a few marginal deals were brought to market. Fall-out from that was reflected in the high default rates during the 1989-1991 period.

This skewness is also easily seen by looking at the frequency distribution of defaults, which is shown in Exhibit 4. The data in Exhibit 3 are regrouped into buckets to show the distribution more easily. Measured by outstanding loan balance, in fewer than 15% of the years were defaults greater than 4%.

BOTTOM LINE

Even though "average" numbers are skewed by the high default years of 1989-1991, we can still use these actual results to compare performance of our representative BBB+ CBO to a traditional BBB bond. We did so by interpolating data from Exhibit 1. (We looked up the yield for each of the two securities that corresponded to the average default rate of 3.24%.) It is clear that the CBO delivers its promised yield of 9.08%, while the BBB index is impacted by any defaults that occur. Assuming the BBB corporate bond never defaults, its base case yield is 7.76% — which the CBO outperforms by 132 basis points. Assuming the bonds both default at the 3.24% annual average for high-yield bonds — then the yield on the CBO is 9.08% versus the 6.25% for the BBB corporate bond — which is a 283 basis point difference. Using this market pricing, the CBO is expected to outperform by 132-283 basis points, and is hence, the more attractive opportunity.

The case for CBOs as of this writing is even stronger than indicated above. Even gilding the lily of the BBB corporate by assuming it never defaults, the CBO can still sustain default rates higher than ever been experienced over the last three decades — and still outperform.

STRESS TESTING

In performing any analyses, results are only as robust as the assumptions upon which they stand. The two we have made are that (1) recovery rates are higher on bank loans than on bonds; and (2) the BBB corporate bond either doesn't default at all, or defaults at the same rate as high-yield bonds. While we believe that our first assumption is fair, and our second provides fair bounds, it is certainly prudent to stress our assumptions.

Historically, recovery rates have been far higher on bank loans than on bonds. Nonetheless, we can test our comparison by assuming identical recovery rates and look at the results. Exhibit 5 shows the results of a single 36% recovery rate on both the loans and the bonds. Remember, this is the stress scenario. As can be seen, the breakeven default rate (the default rate at which the two securities yield the same) is 7%, assuming no defaults on the BBB corporate. That breakeven default rate is 10% if we assume equal defaults on the BBB corporate and the high-yield debt. These numbers are at the very higher end of historical experience (those high-default years following LBO issuance mania). Thus, even in the stressed scenario, the CBO holds up very well relative to the BBB corporate bond.

Defaults on BBB securities are certainly lower than defaults on a portfolio of high-yield securities, but it is not clear how best to make the comparison. Annual default numbers are unfair, as the BBB bond will need much more time to default than a high-yield bond. It is even more difficult to compare BBB rated bonds to a portfolio of 80% bank loans, 20% high yield bonds, as the default patterns on bank loans are not that widely studied. Thus, it really is not crystal clear how to best set up and make a comparison between the BBB corporate and the BBB+ rated CBO.

We essentially set an upper and lower band on the breakeven default rates by assuming that the BBB corporates either (a) do not default at all, or (b) default at the same rate as high-yield bonds. We can try to place a more reasonable number on the breakeven, by juxtaposing actual cumulative default rates over a 10- to 12-year period. Moody's data indicate that the cumulative losses on Baa securities are 4.39% after 10 years, 5.04% after 11 years, and 5.71% after 12 years. By contrast, high-yield bonds (all speculative grades combined) have a cumulative default rate of 28.32%, 30.16%, and 31.96%. Hence it seems reasonable to assume that default rates on the BBB corporate bond are approximately ⅙ as high as those on the CBO. Thus, a 12% default rate on the CBO corresponds to a 2% default rate on the BBBs. The results of this analysis are shown in Exhibit 6. At close to a 21% default rate on the BBB rated CBO and a 3.5% default rate on the BBB-rated corporate bond, the yields on the two securities are nearly identical. (Column 1 shows the default rates on the CBO; Column 4 shows the default rates on the BBB rated security and the horizontal line denotes the approximate crossover point.) At default rates above the crossover (lower default rates), the CBO represents the higher-yielding alternative. Clearly, for all default rates over the past three decades (even assuming that the default rate on the CBO is six times as high as on a BBB rated corporate bond) — the CBO represents the better relative value.

Exhibit 5: BBB CBO versus BBB Corporate with Extreme Recoveries

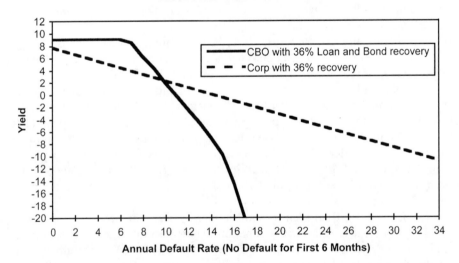

Exhibit 6: BBB CBO versus BBB Corporate Yields

BBB CBO Default*	CBO Yield with 82% Loan Recovery and 45% Bond Recovery	Corp Yield with 45% Recovery	BBB Corp Default*	Which Yields More?
0	9.08	7.76	0.00	CBO
1	9.08	7.68	0.17	CBO
2	9.08	7.60	0.33	CBO
3	9.08	7.53	0.50	CBO
4	9.08	7.45	0.67	CBO
5	9.08	7.37	0.83	CBO
6	9.07	7.29	1.00	CBO
7	9.07	7.21	1.17	CBO
8	9.07	7.14	1.33	CBO
9	9.07	7.06	1.50	CBO
10	9.07	6.98	1.67	CBO
11	9.07	6.90	1.83	CBO
12	9.07	6.83	2.00	CBO
13	9.07	6.75	2.17	CBO
14	9.07	6.67	2.33	CBO
15	9.07	6.59	2.50	CBO
16	9.07	6.51	2.67	CBO
17	9.07	6.44	2.83	CBO
18	8.88	6.36	3.00	CBO
19	8.11	6.28	3.17	CBO
20	7.23	6.20	3.33	CBO
21	6.33	6.12	3.50	CBO
22	5.50	6.05	3.67	Corp
23	4.65	5.97	3.83	Corp
24	3.82	5.89	4.00	Corp
25	3.06	5.81	4.17	Corp
26	2.25	5.73	4.33	Corp
27	1.55	5.66	4.50	Corp
28	0.88	5.58	4.67	Corp
29	0.41	5.50	4.83	Corp
30	−0.20	5.42	5.00	Corp
31	−0.83	5.34	5.17	Corp
32	−1.27	5.27	5.33	Corp
33	−1.87	5.19	5.50	Corp

* Annual Default Rate Expressed as a Percent.

CONCLUSION

The risk-return profile on the mezzanine tranche of a CBO is much more lever-aged than that on the corporate bond. Moreover, the collateral behind a CBO will often be different than on a corporate bond of the same credit rating.

In this chapter, we showed how to make relative value comparisons between CBOs and corporate bonds. We held that the correct approach is to compare "breakeven" default rates on CBO tranches versus corporate alternatives under a range of assumptions. This allows an investor to gauge under what scenarios the CBO tranche will outperform, and determine if those scenarios are likely, particularly given the range of historical experience.

Our results demonstrate that under all default scenarios experienced over the past three decades — the CBO represents better relative value than equivalent-rated corporate bonds. Of course, this will change if CBO spreads tighten relative to equivalently-rated corporate paper.

There is no question that some of the incremental yield on the BBB rated CBO is a function of liquidity. CBO tranches are smaller, and are clearly less liquid than equivalently-rated corporate bonds. The incremental yield is also a function of the fact that the CBO market is relatively new, and investors are usually compensated well for entering a market at the early stages. Indeed, as the CBO market matures, we expect liquidity to improve, and the new product yield premium should erode.

Chapter 11

Relative Value Framework for Collateralized Debt Obligations

Charles Schorin
Principal
Director of ABS Research
Morgan Stanley Dean Witter

Steven Weinreich
Associate
Morgan Stanley Dean Witter

In this chapter, we develop a framework for analyzing relative value both within the collateralized debt obligation (CDO) sector and between CDOs and other asset-backed securities. In analyzing CDOs, we first attempt to genericize the sector by differentiating between balance sheet CLOs on the one hand and arbitrage CDOs on the other. After this initial cut, we can further categorize CDOs as generally belonging to one of the following:

- 100% domestic high yield loans
- 100% domestic high yield bonds
- 80% domestic high yield/20% emerging markets
- 60% domestic high yield/40% emerging markets
- > 80% emerging markets.

The composition of the underlying collateral pool, and its breakdown into high yield and emerging market debt, provide the initial pass at valuing the transaction. Morgan Stanley monitors yield spreads of arbitrage CDOs on a generic basis, with the collateral breakdowns listed above. We also track yield spreads on balance sheet CLOs on a generic basis. (See Exhibit 1.)

Any individual transaction, of course, could deviate from the benchmark in terms of the collateral, manager or structure. These differences would be reflected in the pricing of the tranches.

Exhibit 1: Generic CDO Yield Spreads by Collateral Composition

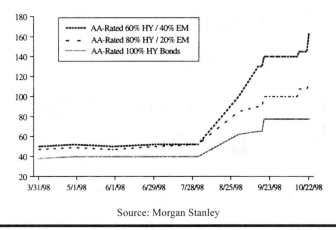

Source: Morgan Stanley

COMPARISON WITH ABS PRODUCT

In comparing CDOs to other asset backed product, investors should

1. first consider the asset backed collateral,
2. then examine the structural overlay and resultant average life and rating, and
3. finally, compare the cash flow similarity.

It sometimes may be difficult to make a direct comparison, owing to the CDO collateral mix, its various restrictions and the trading that may occur within the CDO collateral pool. Analyzing a static pool of collateral is not necessarily appropriate, because the composition can, and generally does, change over time. Nevertheless, there are similarities to other ABS sectors. For example, home equity loan collateral itself is low investment grade, at best; it is only the structural overlay and credit enhancement that provides for the highly rated ABS classes. Also, note that the mechanics of the home equity senior/subordinate structure, with the diversion of cash flow away from the mezzanine and subordinate classes in the event that collateral performance triggers are failed is not dissimilar from the various collateral tests and constraints on CDO collateral. The triggers may actually be more conservative in CDOs because they allow for the redirection of interest to pay principal, in addition to redirecting principal to pay principal. Manufactured housing ABS also could be compared to CDOs, although we would have to make the comparison on a swapped to LIBOR basis, because manufactured housing paper has been almost exclusively fixed rate.

Exhibit 2: Yield Spread Comparison: 80% Domestic High Yield / 20% Emerging Market CDO versus HEL ABS

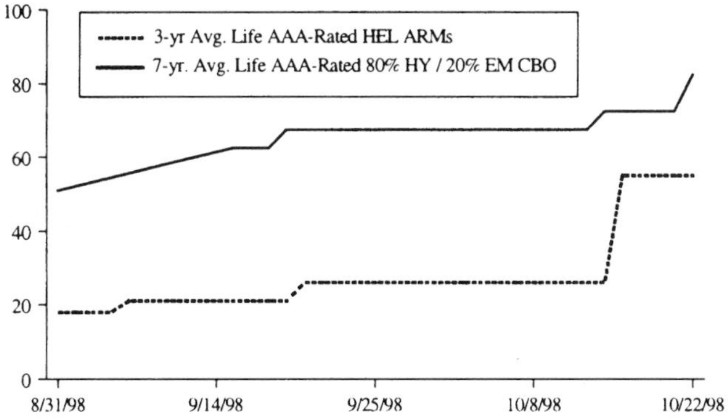

Legend:
- ------- 3-yr Avg. Life AAA-Rated HEL ARMs
- ——— 7-yr. Avg. Life AAA-Rated 80% HY / 20% EM CBO

X-axis: 8/31/98, 9/14/98, 9/25/98, 10/8/98, 10/22/98

Source: Morgan Stanley

Exhibit 2 compares spreads on AAA-rated CDOs with a collateral mix of 80% domestic high yield/20% emerging markets to those on AAA rated 3-yr HEL ABS. In both cases, the bonds are floating rate.[1]

The asset class most similar to any type of CDO is the credit card ABS sector, which closely resembles balance sheet CLOs. Whereas credit card asset backeds are secured by a multitude of consumer credit lines, balance sheet CLOs are backed by large numbers of commercial and industrial loans. Generally, the credit quality of the C&I loans is superior to that of the consumer credit cards, with higher expected recovery rates. Structurally, however, the two types of securities look very similar. The extent to which yield spreads deviate significantly between the two sectors would be the extent of a relative value opportunity. Exhibit 3 shows the historical relationship between credit card ABS and balance sheet CLOs.

We also can compare mezzanine classes of CDOs to similarly rated asset backed securities. Exhibit 4 compares the spreads of a generic BBB rated CDO with a collateral mix of 80% domestic high yield/20% emerging markets to BBB rated floating rate HEL ABS. The average lives are on the order of 12 and 6 years, respectively.

COMPARISON WITH UNSECURED CORPORATE DEBT

CDOs also can be compared with unsecured corporate debt. Most domestic unsecured corporates are fixed rate, but still can be compared to floating rate CDOs by incorporating swap rates.

---

[1] Historical generic yield spreads on ABS products are reported regularly in the Morgan Stanley *ABS Research Weekly*.

Exhibit 3: Yield Spread Comparison: Credit Card ABS and Balance Sheet CLOs

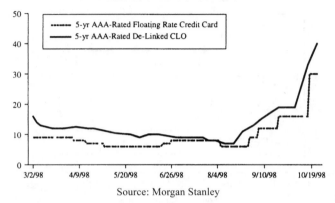

Source: Morgan Stanley

Exhibit 4: Yield Spread Comparison: Mezzanine CDO Class and BBB Floating Rate HEL ABS

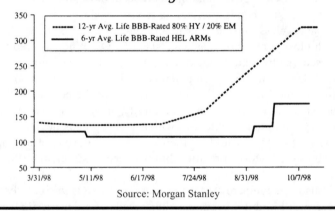

Source: Morgan Stanley

For a given rating category assigned by a rating agency, the risk of loss is normalized across the various bond products. Therefore, the expected loss should be the same on an A rated unsecured corporate bond, an A rated asset backed security and an A rated CDO class. This makes them directly comparable.

Exhibit 5 shows yield spreads from our generic series of AA-rated CDOs, with collateral comprised of 100% domestic high yield bonds. This series is compared to that of an index of A2-rated fixed rate unsecured corporate debt, swapped to LIBOR. Note the spread advantage of the CDO despite its higher rating.

Some of the spread differential clearly is related to technicals, such as the relatively wide sponsorship of the domestic corporate debt market and the relative lack of transparency of CDOs. Nonetheless, the differential in spreads — when put on a common benchmark — makes the CDOs look very compelling.

Exhibit 5: Yield Spread Comparison: AA-Rated High Yield CDO versus A-Rated Unsecured Corporate Debt

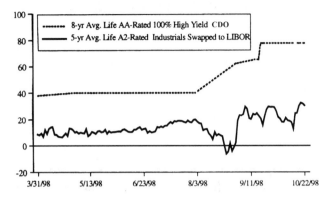

8-yr Avg. Life AA-Rated 100% High Yield CDO
5-yr Avg. Life A2-Rated Industrials Swapped to LIBOR

Source: Morgan Stanley, Bloomberg Financial Markets

DEFAULT ANALYSIS

Determining value in the CDO sector requires understanding and analyzing both credit and structure. Here we present a framework for examining defaults and their impact on the rated notes of a CDO transaction.

One cannot simply examine the maximum amount of defaults a particular structure can withstand before taking a loss, and then determine value through this absolute threshold approach. The timing of defaults and recoveries, along with the probability associated with different default events, must be examined in order to differentiate transactions.

Morgan Stanley has developed a methodology drawing from Moody's default and ratings migration studies.[2] The premise of the analysis is that examining an actively managed portfolio while holding ratings and expected defaults constant over time is inherently a flawed approach. Over time, the ratings, and expected default risk, of the underlying collateral change.

Morgan Stanley's approach is based on the probability distribution of ratings migration over a 1-year period. Ratings migration is characterized by a transition probability matrix. This transition matrix is then applied for successive years, using the resultant ratings composition of the pool from each respective prior period. This methodology is then repeated numerous times by generating multiple default paths in a Monte Carlo simulation. Exhibit 6 shows the probability distribution for the ending rating after a one year period of a bond rated Ba by Moody's at the beginning of the year.

---

[2] Moody's Investors Service, Global Credit Research, *Moody's Ratings Migration and Credit Quality Correlations, 1920-1996*, July 1997.

Exhibit 6: Probability Distribution of Rating After One Year for Ba-Rated Security

Rating at End of Year	Probability of this Event (%)
Aaa	0.01
Aa	0.08
A	0.39
Baa	4.61
Ba	79.03
B	4.96
Caa-C	0.41
Default	1.11
Rating Withdrawn	9.39

Source: Moody's Investors Service

This approach has multiple benefits. Using a rating transition matrix captures the ratings dynamics and allows investors to explore potential scenarios of both default and rating changes over time, and most important, the distribution of a given amount of loss on a pool through time. While a CDO class may be able to withstand a certain level of defaults over its life if defaults were evenly distributed through time, the performance may be weaker if defaults were applied more realistically — i.e., with spikes and drop-offs in default rates. A static pool approach holding ratings — and therefore expected defaults — constant through the life of the transaction fails to account for the potential change in the distribution of ratings within a portfolio.

As an example, consider a portfolio with two bonds, one rated B and the other rated Baa. Moody's transition matrix implies a probability of 3.49% and 0.28%, respectively, that these bonds will default by the end of one year. Examining the possibility of rating migration, however, adds a layer of realism to the analysis. Moody's one-year ratings transition matrix implies a 4.68% chance of the Baa rated bond being downgraded to Ba over a one-year time horizon. If this event occurs, the probability that the now Ba rated bond will move into default in one year is 1.11%, nearly four times as likely. With a probability of 3.08%, the B-rated bond will be downgraded to Caa. At this rating, the probability of defaulting at the end of year 2 is now 12.41%, more than three times that of a B-rated security.

This analysis attempts to answer the basic questions which investors should ask:

- What are realistic default expectations over time?
- How much variance from this expected default curve can the structure absorb?

Step 1 — Condense a large portfolio of correlated bonds to a smaller portfolio of representative, uncorrelated bonds. Examining each issue in the collateral pool independently ignores the correlation of bonds within the pool. To account for this without calculating correlations, we create a portfolio with the number of equal par value bonds equal to its diversity score. The initial rating applied to each of these bonds is determined by the representation of each rating in the underlying pool. Exhibit 7 works through this methodology for a collateral pool with a diversity score of 8.

Step 2 — Generate Ratings Migrations Matrix We next use the cumulative probability distribution in conjunction with a uniform random number generator to create a timeline of events for each representative bond in our portfolio. The random number is matched against the cumulative distribution to determine the rating at the end of a year. Another random number is then drawn from the cumulative distribution of the resultant rating, resulting in a rating at the end of year 2. This process is repeated for each year, for each representative bond in the portfolio. The probability that a bond with a given rating defaults is included in the transition matrix. Exhibit 8 steps through this process for a single bond in the portfolio over a 12-year period.

Exhibit 7: Creating a Representative Portfolio: Diversity Score of 8

Rating	Percent of Total Portfolio Par Value	Number of Bonds in Condensed Portfolio
Baa	12.5	$0.125 \times 8 = 1$
Ba	25.0	$0.250 \times 8 = 2$
B	62.5	$0.625 \times 8 = 5$

Source: Morgan Stanley

Exhibit 8: Ratings Migration of a Single Ba-Rated Bond, 1 Path

Year	Rating at End of Year	Par Value
1	Ba	$100
2	Ba	100
3	Ba	100
4	Ba	100
5	B	100
6	Default	0
7	Ba	40
8	Ba	40
9	Baa	40
10	Baa	40
11	Baa	40
12	Baa	40

Note: Assumes 40% recovery rate for a bond with original par value equal to $100.
Source: Morgan Stanley, Moody's Investors Service

Step 3 — Simulation Step 2 above is repeated multiple times generating a new random number for each iteration. We can then calculate the mean expected default over several paths and apply it to the rated debt. If the rated bonds survive the base case level of defaults, then we can apply stress scenarios next. The stress scenarios we have chosen are based upon examining the distribution of the default observations in each year over the numerous paths. We calculate the level below which a target percentage of observations fall. This target percentage — analogous to a confidence interval — should change relative to the rating of the bond, as well as the spread versus competing products. All else equal, a more highly rated bond must sustain a higher target percentage than a lower rated bond, i.e., survive the level below which a larger percentage of observations fall.

DEFAULT FRAMEWORK APPLIED TO CALHOUN CBO

Exhibit 9 applies this analytical technique to Calhoun CBO, Ltd., the representative cash flow arbitrage transaction that was displayed in Exhibit 8 in Chapter 1. Exhibit 9 works through the steps listed above beginning at the closing date of the transaction.

Exhibit 9: Default Analysis of Calhoun CBO

Step 1 — Condense the Portfolio

The diversity score for the collateral pool at time of closing was calculated to be 46. As such, the 113 bonds in the original portfolio are condensed into 46 representative securities. The composition of the original pool in terms of rating breakdown is listed below.

Moody's Rating	% of Par Value in Rating Bucket	Number of Diversified Bonds in Portfolio
A	0.61%	0
Baa	1.21%	1
Ba	18.98%	9
B	79.20%	36
Total Portfolio	100.00%	46

Step 2 — Generate Ratings Migration Matrix

We generate a transition for each of these 46 representative buckets for a 12 year time horizon. Defaulted bonds are added back into the analysis at the original rating, but with a smaller balance based on the recovery rate assumption. For example, consider a Ba-rated bond migrating to a B rating in year 3 and defaulting in year 4. If this bond represented 2% of the par value of the collateral, then in year 5 the bond would be reintroduced into the pool with a Ba initial rating and a par value equal to the recovery rate times the original par value. Subsequent defaults of this bond would further reduce the balance. All defaults are calculated as a percent of outstanding balance, analogous to a percent CDR (conditional default rate) for use with the cash flow model for the particular transaction.

Exhibit 9 (Continued)

Step 3 — Simulate Defaults

We simulate 10,000 paths and aggregate the defaults in each period to come up with a mean expected default curve. Below are the mean and median default schedules along with the levels below which 80%, 90% and 95% of simulated observations occurred for the Calhoun transaction for each year, assuming a 40% recovery rate on all defaulted securities.

Year	Mean	Median	80% Target Level	90% Target Level	95% Target Level
1	2.90%	2.17%	4.35%	6.52%	6.52%
2	2.70	2.20	4.46	6.52	6.70
3	2.79	2.26	4.53	6.61	6.88
4	2.82	2.29	4.59	6.70	7.02
5	2.79	2.33	4.69	6.71	7.08
6	2.77	2.36	4.75	6.79	7.29
7	2.76	2.39	4.81	6.70	7.39
8	2.77	2.44	4.89	6.04	7.40
9	2.64	2.46	4.89	5.83	7.39
10	2.66	2.49	4.93	6.00	7.48
11	2.66	2.53	5.00	5.90	7.55
12	2.62	2.55	4.98	5.92	7.60

Results

Scenario	Results for Senior Bond	Results for Mezzanine Bond
Mean Defaults	• No coverage tests are breached • No losses	• No coverage tests are breached • No losses
Median Levels	• No coverage tests are breached • No losses	• No coverage tests are breached • No losses
80% Target Level	• No coverage tests are breached • No losses	• No coverage tests are breached • No losses
90% Target Level	• No senior coverage tests are breached • No losses	• Par value test breached in period 5 and recovers in period 18. • No losses
95% Target Level	• No senior coverage tests are breached • No losses	• Second priority par value coverage test is breached in period 5 and does not recover • Incurs $500,000 interest shortfall and $3.4 million principal loss. IRR is reduced 36 bp to 6.85%.

Source: Morgan Stanley

The Morgan Stanley default model predicts that even with 95% confidence, the senior notes from the Calhoun transaction continue to perform extremely well, and the second priority notes are only marginally affected, with a 36 bp reduction in IRR. In fact, the senior notes are unaffected at the 99% confidence level as well; however, the mezzanine securities are detrimentally affected and incur significant losses at this level. Consider, however, the absolute level of losses implied by the 99% confidence level: consistent annual defaults ranging from 9.5% to nearly 11.0% for 12 consecutive years. This is an extremely high level of losses to apply for such an extended period of time.

Also, note that this is a conservative analysis, because it ignores any active role of the collateral manager. In reality, the professional collateral manager is hired to improve upon these simulated results. To the extent that a bond performs well in this default analysis methodology, it should perform even better when the collateral pool is actively managed.

CONCLUSION

In this chapter we present a new methodology for analyzing defaults and their impact on CDO transactions. Rather than simply examine the amount of defaults that a transaction can withstand over its life, we calculate ratings transitions — including defaults — probabilistically on an interim basis and apply these to the transaction. This methodology dynamically updates the ratings distribution of the collateral pool on a probabilistic basis and accounts for changing risk, and therefore, changing default likelihood, on an ongoing basis.

Chapter 12

Pricing Debt and Equity in a Market Value CDO

Luigi Vacca, Ph.D.
Vice President
Structured Credit Products
Banc of America Securities

D ebt and equity in market value CDOs can be priced as derivative instruments whose underlying instrument is the asset portfolio. In this chapter, we present a valuation approach based on the seminal works of Fischer Black, Myron Scholes, and Robert Merton.[1]

FUNDAMENTAL ASSUMPTIONS

The fundamental assumptions are as follows:

- a frictionless market, in which assets can be bought and sold short with no transaction costs
- taxes are ignored
- the risk-less rate r is constant
- the debt and equity tranches are collateralized only by the assets of the fund
- the fund does not pay any fees
- all fund proceeds are reinvested in the portfolio until maturity
- the market value of the fund V follows a lognormal distribution given by the formula:

$$dV = \mu \, V \, dt + \sigma \, V \, dZ$$

where μ is the mean return on the portfolio and σ is the volatility of the portfolio return. In addition, dt is an infinitesimal period of time, dV is an infinitesimal change in the portfolio price, and dZ is a Wiener process.

---

[1] See Fischer Black and Myron Scholes, "The Pricing of Options and Corporate Liabilities," *The Journal of Political Economy* (1973); and Robert Merton, "On the Pricing of Corporate Debt: The Risk Structure of Interest Rates," *The Journal of Finance* (1974).

Exhibit 1: Sample Market Value Deal Structure

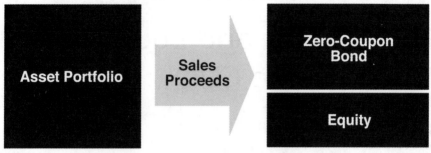

Source: Banc of America Securities LLC.

PRICING DEBT AND EQUITY USING THE BLACK-SCHOLES FORMULA

In our illustration, we consider a simple market value deal structure, using a fund that has issued a zero-coupon bond payable at maturity T and one equity class. (See Exhibit 1.)

At maturity time, the portfolio manager liquidates the fund and pays the zero-coupon bondholders with the sale proceeds (the remaining proceeds are paid to the equity holders). The value of the asset portfolio V at maturity is equal to the sum of the value of the debt and equity tranches, B and E, respectively.

$$V = B + E$$

It is clear that the CDO bond tranche is equivalent to a risk-less zero-coupon bond and a short position on a put option on the assets of the CDO at a strike equal to the face value, F, of the zero-coupon bond. The equity tranche is a call option on the assets of the CDO at a strike equal to the face value of the zero-coupon bond.

Mathematically, $B = PV(F) - P(V, F, r, T, \sigma)$ and $E = C(V, F, r, T, \sigma)$, where P and C are the put and call price, respectively, computed using the Black-Scholes formula and PV stands for present value (see Exhibit 2). Notice that the mean return on the asset portfolio does not enter these formulae.

PRICING DEBT AND EQUITY USING THE BINOMIAL PRICING APPROACH

We add the following features to our simple market value model to make it more realistic:

• The fund pays periodic coupon payments to the CDO bond;

- The CDO bond is a coupon bond priced at a positive spread over the riskless rate; and
- The CDO bondholder will exercise the option of redeeming the fund if the market value of the portfolio falls below a value, $MV = F/AR$, where F is the final principal payment to the coupon bond and AR is a market value averaged advance rate.

We employ a simple and effective method to incorporate these features: the binomial pricing approach, as introduced by John Cox, Stephen Ross and Mark Rubinstein.[2] We give a simple one-period example that describes how this may be implemented numerically in Exhibit 3.

Exhibit 2: Debt and Equity Payoffs as Function of Final Portfolio Market Value

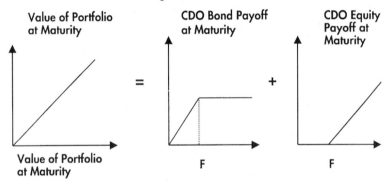

Source: Banc of America Securities LLC.

Exhibit 3: One-Period Binomial Valuation of Debt

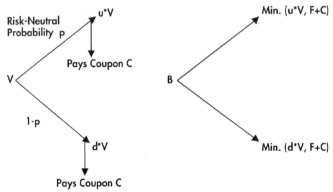

Source: Banc of America Securities LLC.

---

[2] See John Cox, Stephen Ross, and Mark Rubinstein, "Option Pricing: A Simplified Approach," *Journal of Financial Economics* (1979).

The value of the CDO bond is $B = [p \times (\min(u \times V, F + C)) + (1 - p) \times (\min(d \times V, F + C))]/(1 + rT)$, where C is the coupon payment, p is the risk-neutral probability, and u and d are the binomial factors. The equity value is $E = \max(0, V - B)$ at closing and maturity.

A NUMERICAL EXAMPLE OF DEBT AND EQUITY PRICING

The static assumptions are as follows: (1) the size of the deal is $1.2 billion; (2) the risk-less annual rate of return is 6%; (3) the maturity is five years; (4) semiannual coupon payments are made; (5) the blended advance rate is 0.85; (6) the debt par amount totals $1 billion; (7) the debt annual coupon rate is 8%; and (8) volatility of the fund is 20%.

We used a multi-period model to compute the change in price of the CDO bond and equity as the following underlying variables are changed: (1) portfolio volatility; (2) different advance rates; (3) spread between the average coupon paid to the CDO bond and the risk-less rate of return; and (4) leverage while keeping the initial market value of the assets constant (see Exhibits 4-7).

SUMMARY OF RESULTS

We draw the following conclusions from our analysis:

- Bond and equity prices move in opposite directions for a given change in portfolio volatility, with equity significantly more volatile than bonds.
- The equity investment is fundamentally a call on the portfolio assets; therefore, the price of equity will increase with increasing volatility and vice versa. Conversely, the bond price will fall with increasing portfolio volatility and rise with decreasing volatility.
- Lower advance rates can substantially increase a bond's value. The OC test results in the bond price being less sensitive to portfolio volatility.
- The increase of the coupon payment leads to higher bond prices, all things being equal.
- The increase of debt size or leverage increases the equity price with positive acceleration.

CONCLUSIONS

In this chapter, we have introduced an effective derivative approach to pricing market value CDO debt and equity tranches. Equity investors in our analysis purchase a call option on the fund's assets at a strike equal to the face value of the debt. Bond investors in our analysis purchase a risk-less bond and short a put option on a fund's assets at a strike equal to the face value of the debt. The presence of OC tests in a market value CDO is equivalent to a call option owned by the bondholders who can sell the fund's asset portfolio when its market value falls below a given threshold and no cure is found.

Exhibit 4: Bond and Equity Prices Versus Portfolio Volatility: Advance Rate Equals 0.85

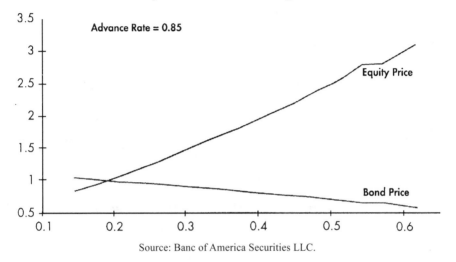

Source: Banc of America Securities LLC.

Exhibit 5: Bond and Equity Prices Versus Portfolio Volatility: Advance Rate Equals 0.5

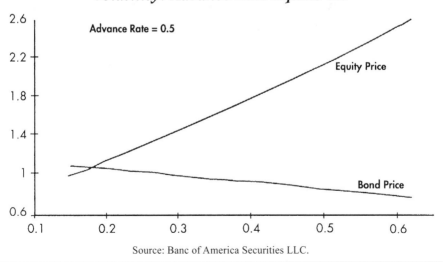

Source: Banc of America Securities LLC.

Exhibit 6: Bond and Equity Prices Versus Portfolio Volatility: Impact of Greater Leverage ($150 Million Equity Versus $200 Million Base Case)

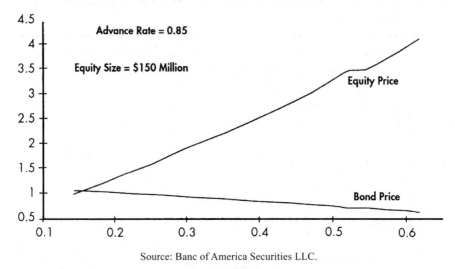

Source: Banc of America Securities LLC.

Exhibit 7: Bond Prices Versus Portfolio Volatility at Different Coupon Rates

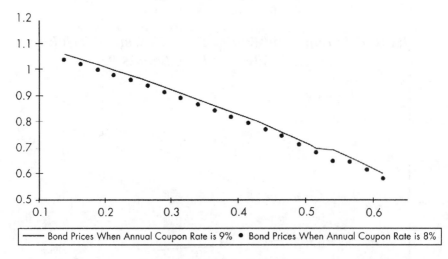

Source: Banc of America Securities LLC.

Chapter 13

Use of Credit Derivatives in CBO/CLO Structures

Meredith Hill
Head of ABS Research
Banc of America Securities

Luigi Vacca, Ph.D.
Vice President, Structured Credit Products
Banc of America Securities

Credit derivatives include a range of instruments designed to transfer credit risk without requiring the sale or purchase of bonds and/or loans. Originally, credit derivatives were designed in the early 1990s by U.S. banks to manage credit risk in their loan portfolios while preserving important customer relationships. The evolution of credit derivatives was prompted by the increased demand for asset-backed deals backed by credit instruments. The credit derivatives market has been growing rapidly since the early 1990s. In particular, the market has witnessed explosive growth over the past two years, reaching $144 billion notional par held by U.S. commercial banks at year-end 1998.

The evolution of credit derivatives allows domestic banks to provide multiple purposes to their clients. We believe that the use of credit derivatives will remain an essential element to inject liquidity into the CBO/CLO market by providing a more accurate asset-liability match in CBO/CLO structures, increasing diversification in CBO collateral portfolios, and repackaging illiquid CBO bonds to tailor risk to investor preferences. The objective of this chapter is to briefly describe the fundamental types of credit derivatives and how they can be used to create synthetic CDOs and repackage CDO debt.

TYPES OF CREDIT DERIVATIVES

The credit derivatives market consists of three basic segments: (1) credit default swaps; (2) total return swaps; and (3) credit-linked notes. In the following, we provide a brief overview of the fundamentals of the credit derivatives market, and

225

we outline how they can be used in conjunction with CBO/CLO asset and liabilities to yield more attractive products.

Credit Default Swaps

The credit default swap market consists of buyers and sellers of credit protection. In its simplest form, the "protection buyer" pays a fixed periodic fee that is a percentage of notional and receives, in turn, a contingent payment in which an event of default occurs on the underlying credit. (See Exhibits 1 and 2.) For default swap transactions, we note that the credit default payment must be clearly defined; thus, it is triggered by a material event such as a scheduled payment delinquency combined with a significant decline in the market value of a higher risk credit.

The contingent payment is usually settled in cash and equals the total market value loss incurred by the protection buyer on the reference asset. An alternative to cash settlement, albeit one rarely used, is the physical delivery of the reference asset for its par value. This solution is not always viable, however, as banks typically prefer not to sell their loans but rather seek to maintain the customer relationship by managing the underlying credits.

Exhibit 1: Credit Default Swaps: Purchase Credit Default Swap

Summary Terms		Summary Results
Reference Asset	XYZ Corp. 8.625% Due 12/01/03	• Credit Default Protection
Notional Amount	$10 Million	
Term	Five Year	• Assets Remain On-Balance-Sheet
Buyer Pays	2.10% Per Annum	
Buyer Receives	Notional Amount x (100% – Market Price) if Credit Event Occurs	

Source: Banc of America Securities LLC.

Exhibit 2: Credit Default Swaps: Sell Credit Default Swap

Summary Terms		Summary Results
Reference Asset	XYZ Inc. Senior Secured Revolver	• Unfunded Investment
Due	04/03/04	• Off-Balance-Sheet
Notional Amount	$25 Million	• Minimal Administration
Term	One Year	• Maturity Flexibility
Investor Receives	2.50% Per Annum	• Seniority Flexibility
Investor Pays	Notional Amount x (100% – Market Price) if Credit Events Occurs	

Source: Banc of America Securities LLC.

Exhibit 3: Total Return Swaps: Single Reference Asset

Summary Terms		Summary Results
Reference Asset	XYZ Loan	• 28.50% Initial Yield
Notional Amount	$30 Million	
Upfront Collateral	$3 Million	• Preserves Capital
Collateral Return	6.00%	
Term	One Year	• Minimal Administration
Initial Price	100.00%	
Investor Pays	LIBOR + 0.75% + Price Depreciation	• Off-Balance-Sheet Financing
Investor Receives	Interest + Fees + Price Appreciation	

LIBOR London Interbank Offered Rate.

Source: Banc of America Securities LLC.

Exhibit 4: A Synthetic CBO Using Total Return Swaps: Total Return Swap Financing

Summary Terms		Summary Results
Reference Asset	High Yield Loan Portfolio	• Participation in Loan Market
Notional Amount	$500 Million	• Protection Against Market Downsides
Collateral Return	LIBOR +3%	• High Returns for Investors
Term	12-Year	• Lower Transaction Costs
Initial Price	100.00%	•Efficient Use of Capital
Investor Pays	Price of Note	
Investor Receives	Interest + Par	

LIBOR London Interbank Offered Rate.

Source: Banc of America Securities LLC.

Total Return Swaps

Total return swaps are bilateral financial transactions in which the total return (which equals the coupon plus price change) of a fixed income security is exchanged for a funding cash flow, usually LIBOR plus a basis spread. (See Exhibits 3 and 4.) Unlike credit default swaps, payments to balance the underlying credit's price depreciation or appreciation are always exchanged without requiring the occurrence of a specific credit event. This swap structure is beneficial to investors as it involves a leveraged participation in a fixed income instrument without the origination cost. Total return swaps are particularly attractive to investment firms that want to diversify their portfolio credit exposure.

Credit-Linked Notes

Credit-linked notes are synthetic securities in which an underlying credit is coupled with a default swap or total return swap. An example of a credit-linked note is a structured note whose cash flow (coupon and/or principal) is generated by a risky credit. (See Exhibit 5.) The issuer of the structured note is usually a special purpose vehicle (SPV), and often has a higher rating than the risky credit. SPVs are trusts that issue securities backed by debt subject to credit risk, such as high yield bonds, loans and emerging market securities. The return of the credit-linked notes is increased by the premium generated by the sale of a credit default swap, where the contingent payment is guaranteed by the collateral. These notes provide investors with exposure to markets which are usually too costly to enter. Typically, these synthetic securities offer good relative value in comparison with their cash market equivalents.

AN APPLICATION OF CREDIT DERIVATIVES: A SYNTHETIC CBO/CLO

Synthetic CBO/CLOs are typically balance-sheet transactions originated by U.S. banks for regulatory capital reduction: for example, J.P. Morgan's *Bistro* which was issued in December 1997 and Swiss Bank's *Glacier*, issued in September 1997. These investment vehicles in the credit fixed income market introduced credit derivatives to structured finance. In a synthetic CBO/CLO, a financial institution sets up an SPV to finance asset purchases. In such transactions, total return swaps are used to pass through underlying security returns to a credit-linked note. These notes, in turn, are placed in an SPV that sells a range of liabilities. The use of total return swaps in these structures allows for the maintenance of client confidentiality and a broad reduction of credit exposure. Unfortunately for issuers, these structures require a higher return than typical balance sheet deals that do not include total return swaps. These high returns are obtained thanks to the leverage offered by total return swaps.

In some cases, synthetic CDOs are cash flow deals. A portfolio manager with a proven track record in the asset class manages the underlying assets (loans and bonds). Unlike typical cash flow deals, however, a third party holds the assets on its balance sheet and passes through the returns to the SPV. On the asset side, the SPV purchases highly rated securities to provide protection in the event of asset price depreciation. On the liability side, the SPV issues a series of structured notes, most of which usually have three or four tranches — namely, senior, senior-subordinated, subordinated, and equity.

Exhibit 5: Credit-Linked Note: Single Reference Asset

Summary Terms		Summary Results
Reference Asset	High Yield	• Adds Liquidity
Notional Amount	$50 Million	
Collateral Return	9.00%	• Reduces Risk
Term	Two Year	
Initial Price	100.00%	• Minimal Administration
Investor Pays	Price of Note	
Investor Receives	Interest + Par	• Off-Balance-Sheet Financing

Source: Banc of America Securities LLC.

Cash Flow Mechanics

To understand the return and risk of a synthetic CBO/CLO, the cash flow stream must be examined. The managed pool of assets consists of high yield securities and/or leveraged loans. For example, using the common case of leveraged loans as an asset class, such loans are written by companies whose rating status is below investment grade and, therefore, require a substantial spread over LIBOR (at least 200 basis points). The advantage of these assets is their senior secured status, which provides for an average 80% recovery rate in cases of default. The notional par amount of such transactions is determined by the total par amount of the managed loan pool. For example, assume a typical par amount of $500 million for a portfolio and a par weighted average coupon of LIBOR + 300 basis points. On the other side of the total return swap, the SPV will pay a debt tranche which pays LIBOR +75 basis points. The proceeds from the sale of the debt tranche will be invested in Treasury securities. The tranche debt will receive the coupon on the Treasury securities plus the net spread of 225 basis points. To achieve high returns on the debt tranche, the issued par amount clearly must be significantly less than $500 million.

At this point in our analysis of the loan structure, leverage becomes a factor as the total par amount of the notes is only a fraction of the total par amount of the loan portfolio. The deal leverage is the ratio between the loan par value and the total par value of the notes. This ratio must be chosen in order to assign a coupon payment to the notes that rewards the investors for the risk present in the structure. For example, assume that the amount of debt sold is $250 million. Now the debt receives the Treasury rate on $250 million plus 225 basis points on a notional of $500 million. This translates into an equivalent rate of a Treasury rate plus 450 basis points to the debt tranche.

This approximation assumes that the SPV collateral interest is not consumed by fees. A series of market value and interest coverage tests exist to determine the degree of prepayment that debt will require for a given default rate. If the collateral portfolio suffers a loss in market value, the proceeds from the deal sale will be used to repay such loss. If default rates are substantial, the deal can be unwound; under this scenario, the most subordinated notes likely would suffer a loss of both principal and interest.

These synthetic CBO/CLO deals are attractive to investors that seek strong exposure to the loan market but lack the infrastructure to originate and/or buy and manage a large, diversified loan portfolio.

AN APPLICATION OF CREDIT DEFAULT DERIVATIVES: MEZZANINE DEBT AND DEFAULT PROTECTION

The subordinated, also called mezzanine, debt in a cash flow CBO is debt protected by an equity layer and excess spread. In a comparative analysis to equity tranches, subordinated bondholders do not have the right to call the deal as the majority of equity holders. Furthermore, the return of an equity tranche in a low default scenario can be 1,000 basis points or more than the return on mezzanine debt. Conversely, mezzanine tranches receive all interest and principal payments before any secondary and incentive management fee is usually paid out. This substantial difference in returns between subordinated debt and equity suggest that the subordinated bondholders are receiving a less attractive cash flow than equity holders on a risk-adjusted basis, especially if secondary management fees are relatively small.

As a result, mezzanine tranches are often perceived as a less advantageous investment than their respective mezzanine debt counterparts in the asset-backed universe, forcing underwriters to offer them at a competitive price on the market to enhance their liquidity.

An alternative method of increasing liquidity of the mezzanine debt is to extract mezzanine cash flows and "wrap" them with a credit derivative. (See Exhibit 6.) These repackaged cash flows, in turn, can be sold as an investment grade security to a wider spectrum of investors. As a simple example, we analyze one single interest payment at a given distribution date to a mezzanine bondholder. Assuming a static pool, we can estimate the expected cash flow to be paid as a function of the default rate suffered by the pool between distribution dates. The cash flow stays constant for a certain range of default rates up to a threshold default rate. For default rates above the threshold rate, the amount of interest received by the mezzanine tranche falls rapidly because prepayments to senior tranches are triggered.

Complicating this example, the amount of paid interest is also a function of the short-term interest rate and prepayment speed of the collateral pool. If trading is allowed, the portfolio turnover can have a substantial effect on the amount of the interest distributions. (For our analysis, we assume that these factors can be estimated to an acceptable level of accuracy.)

Exhibit 6: CBO Equity Wrap: Synthetic IO Bond

Summary Terms		Summary Results
Reference Asset	Right to Receive Interest Payment	• Credit Default Protection
Notional Amount	$100 Million	
Expected Payment	$5 Million	• Creates Liquidity
Buyer Pays	Premium: $1 Million	
Buyer Receives	Interest Shortfall	• Targets Risk-Averse Investors

CBO Collateralized bond obligation. IO Interest-only.
Source: Banc of America Securities LLC.

All other factors being constant, the interest payment on the mezzanine is a contingent claim based on the default rate. A risk-neutral methodology can be used to price the interest distribution. Pricing the interest payment is equivalent to computing the fair value of a premium paid to a triple A rated insurer to guarantee the interest payment. In an arbitrage-free world, a security consisting of the rights on a single interest payment plus the insurance premium must return the risk-free rate and, therefore, can be sold at a price equal to the present value of the future cash flow. This approach can be expanded to a series of cash flows of a CBO; however, the payoff behavior will be even more complex to analyze. It will be, in general, a function of the default rate throughout the life of the cash flows, interest rate volatility and portfolio turnover.

CONCLUSION

We believe the growth of the credit derivatives market will help fuel improved liquidity in the CBO/CLO market, as risk can now be more efficiently allocated to investors according to their risk-return profiles. Going forward, the division between credit derivatives and CBO/CLOs will likely continue to blur as both products provide investors with credit exposure structured to their own specific needs.

Index

A

ABS collateral quality, 126
ABS commercial paper (CP) conduit, 115
ABS pools, 12
Acceleration events, 180
Acceptance of the CDO structure by investors, 116
Accrued interest, 50
on liability tranches, 44
Accumulated reference portfolio loss, 180
Administering collections, 189
Advance amount, 44
Advance funding of protection payment obligation, 192
Advance rates, 20, 22, 25, 36, 43, 44, 47, 67, 70, 71, 73, 75
versus credit enhancement, 71, 74
Adverse event in the life of a market value deal, 45
Aeltus III, 103
AG Capital Funding transaction, 24
Alliance Capital Management, 101
Allowable leverage, 38
Amortization schedules, 59
Amortization, 13, 61
Analytical return volatility model to adjust for issuer and industry concentrations, 75
Analytics, 126
Arbitrage deals, 28
Arbitrage transactions, 2, 6, 152
Arbitrage-motivated CLOs, 122
Asian financial crisis, 73
Asset concentration limits, 38
Asset covenants, 39
Asset liquidity, 22
Asset management
arms of commercial banks, 116
assessment of the asset manager, 71
companies (arbitrage-motivated), 116
Asset transfer, 58
Asset type, 75
Asset type limitations, 70
Asset/liability characteristics, 15, 18
Asset-backed securities (ABS), 101, 115
Asset-backed securities market, 1
Assets with correlated default behavior, 135
Asset-specific default rates, 138
Auto, 19
Automatic deleveraging, 82
Average collateral rating, 63
Average default rates, 53
Average-life stability, 133

B

Balance sheet CLO sector, 30
Balance sheet CLOs, 28
Balance sheet deals, 28
Balance sheet transactions, 2, 28, 150
Balance-sheet management tool, 116
Balance-sheet-motivated CLOs, 122
Banc One, 103
Banca Commerciale Italiana, 162
Banco Bilbao Vizcaya, 162
Bank
balance sheet deals, 153
balance sheet management, 141
loans, 91
problems using CLO structures, 142
Bankruptcy
of the market value CDO issuing entity, 48
outcomes of proceedings, 68
research and market experience, 64
Bankruptcy remoteness, 28, 58
of the issuer, 74
Bankruptcy-remote entity, 63
Barclays, 161
Basic motivations for CDO issuance, 116
Basic purpose of quality tests in CDOs, 12
Basic structure and cash flow waterfall for an arbitrage CDO transaction, 8
Basic structure of a cash flow balance sheet transaction, 29
Basic structure of a market value arbitrage transaction, 20
Basis risk, 62
BBB CBO versus BBB corporate with base case recoveries, 201
BBB CBO versus BBB corporate with stressed recoveries, 202
Bear Stearns, 103
Beers, David T., 92
Behavior of distressed securities, 68
Benchmark cash flow arbitrage transaction, 8
Benchmark transactions in the bank balance sheet CLO sector, 30
Bhatia, Ashok, 92
Bid-ask spread
historical records, 69
on bank loans, 77
Binomial branch method, 55
Binomial default model for default risk, 75
Binomial pricing approach, 220
BIS Accord, 193
BIS guidelines, 148
BISTRO transactions, 149
Black, Fischer, 219

Black-Scholes Formula, 220
Blue Stripe transactions, 180
Bond insurance, 61
Bond spreads, 73
Borrower motivation, 162
Borrower notification, 143
Borrowing base "cushions", 36
Bottom-up analysis, 41
Brady debt, 92
Breakeven default rate, 203

C

C&I loans, 211
Calhoun CBO, Ltd., 14, 216
Call options to hedge the BIS proposals, 173
Call provisions, 13
Callable debt instruments, 37
Capital requirements, 148
Capital structures, 14, 33
external infusion of capital into the structure, 74
of a market value CDO, 40
Capital treatment, 151
Capitalization of any market value CDO structure, 36
Caps, 18, 138
Caribbean issuers, 96
Cash and synthetic European bank CLOs, 157
Cash based structures, 196
Cash collateral/reserve account, 61
Cash flow arbitrage deals, 7
and market value arbitrage transactions comparison, 25
Cash flow balance sheet transactions, 28
Cash flow CBO, 103
Cash flow CDOs, 21
Cash flow model, 137
Cash flow structures, 20
Cash flow transactions, 2, 25
Cash flow waterfall, 8
Cash settlement of the underlying defaulted loan, 179
Cast 2000, 190
CBO rating
how CBO ratings are derived, 109
CBO structures, 91
CDO arbitrage, 79
calculating the "arb", 80
crude arbitrage calculator, 82
crude run, 79
major determinant of deal structure, 90
CDO asset-liability arbitrage, 46
CDO deal's exposure period, 75
CDO debt tranches, 43
CDO senior notes, 2
CDO spreads, 120
CDO structures and mechanics, 3

CDOs versus other ABS, 12
Charter Communications, L.P., 126
Citibank, 161
CitiStar 1, 180
CLN structures, 174
CLO arb, 83
CLO arbitrage, 84
CLO sector, 30
CLOs for balance sheet manage-
    ment, 141
Closing bid price, 42
Collateral 15, 28
    an important determinant of
        structure, 88
    coverage, 130
    evaluation, 71, 72
    event risk, 126
    liquidation, 73
    loan participations, 58
    make-up, 158
    manager, 1, 2, 14
    manager/sponsor, 2
    market value, 2
    performance, 130
    performance triggers, 210
    pool for a market value CDO, 21
    portfolio diversity score for debt
        rating purposes, 56
    yield, 170
Collateralization of the notes and
    credit event settlements, 179
Collateralized bond obligations
    (CBOs), 2, 118
Collateralized debt obligations
    (CDOs), 1
    comparison with ABS product,
        210
    comparison with unsecured cor-
        porate debt, 211
    structuring technology, 115
Collateralized loan obligations
    (CLOs), 2, 118
    types of securitization structures,
        164
    typical structure, 142
Commercial mortgage-backed secu-
    rities (CMBS), 11, 101
    conduit, 115, 131, 132
    conduit deals, 105
    credit tenant lease deals, 105
    market, 16,115
Commercial real estate (CRE), 115
Commitment fee, 49
Concentration limits, 12
    based on issuer, industry, geogra-
        phy and asset quality, 21
    in emerging market regions, 13
    in regions and industries, 31
Concentration risk, 41
Configuration of completed deals,
    79
Conseco's restructuring, 145
Contingent interest, 46
Contingent payment, 226
Contingent perfection structures, 184

Conventional securitizations, 173
Convertible debt, 21
Corporate bonds, 36
    investment-grade downgrades,
        127
Cost of liabilities, 112
Coupon, 75
Covenants, 5, 70
Cover fees, 34
Coverage (early-amortization) tests,
    18
Coverage levels, 11
Coverage tests, 11, 18, 22
Cox, John, 221
CP funded issues, 160
CRE products, 116
    distinguishing CRE CDOS from
        ABS CDOs, 131
Credit
    and time tranching, 29
    and trading expertise, 25
    analysis of the collateral portfo-
        lio, 58
    analysts, 71
    perspective, 182
    protection, 48, 149
    protection premium, 181
Credit card ABS, 172
Credit cards, 19, 130
Credit default payment, 226
Credit default swap, 144, 147, 149,
    153, 170, 176, 225
    mechanism, 170
    premiums, 170
    super senior, 177
Credit derivatives, 4, 6, 164, 225
    application to mezzanine debt
        and default protection, 229
    application to synthetic CBO/
        CLO, 228
    evolution of, 225
    fundamental types, 225
    structures, 174
Credit enhancement, 3, 7, 22, 30,
    42, 63, 70, 185
Credit enhancement levels, 15
Credit events, 144, 145, 146, 152,
    176, 178
Credit exposure, 5
Credit linked notes (CLNs), 6, 166
Credit linked reference notes
    (CLNs), 164, 166
Credit linked structures, 166
Credit linked swaps, 6
Credit loss allocation, 178
Credit Lyonnais Cyber Val, 6
Credit risk, 142
    analysis, 59
    and default correlation, 53
    profile of the issuer's balance
        sheet, 116
    relationship between the seller's
        credit risk and right to the collat-
        eral assets, 63
    transfer mechanism, 159, 177

Credit spread, 175
    risk due to rating migration, 76
    risk from factors other than rating
        migration, 76
Credit Suisse First Boston, 103
Credit swap documentation, 144
Credit tenant lease (CTL), 131
Credit tranched, 142
Cross default
    cross acceleration of an obliga-
        tion, 144
    with another obligation of the
        borrower, 178
Cure period, 45, 47
Current fees, 49

D

Deal monitoring, 71
Deal refinancing, 51
Deal structure, 104
Deal triggers, 82
    common triggers, 29
    comparing triggers, 113
Dealers
    behind the transaction, 126
Debt service coverage ratio, 11
Debt service profiles, 158
Declaration of Trust, 165
Default
    analysis, 213
    compare on CBO collateral to
        those on a BBB corporate bond,
        201
    correlation, 54, 55
    framework applied to Calhoun
        CBO, 216
    liquidation, 49
    model, 62
    neutral scenario, 187
    probabilities, 55, 107
    probabilities and loss severity
        assumptions, 190
    probability, 137
    probability assumptions, 194
    rate, 95
    risk, 76, 77
    scenario, 110
    thresholds, 180
Defaulted assets, 112
Default-rate table, 138
Defaults, 12, 13, 67, 127
Deferred interest, 50
Defined principal and interest
    schedules, 8
De-linked structures, 30
De-linked transaction, 30
De-linking
    notes in transactions, 182
    ratings of the synthetic CLO from
        sponsor bank, 180
Departure of the portfolio manager,
    48
Depression-like scenario, 118
Derivatives, 148

Desired rating, 56, 75
Deutsche Bank, 103, 161
    Blue Stripe deal, 177
    CAST, 172
    GLOBE, 172
    series of CORE and CAST deals,
        194
Deutsche Hypotheken Hannover, 172
Digital pay-out, 179
Digital pay-out structures, 179
Disclosure practices, 126
Distressed debt, 4, 5, 21
Distressed, non-current assets, 4
Distressed securities, 36
Diversification, 39, 70, 105
    of servicing risk, 134
    requirements, 73
    scores, 105
Diversified REIT Trust, 103
Diversity, 15
    of the assets in the pool, 15
Diversity score measures, 55
Diversity scores, 12, 25, 96, 97, 135,
    195
Dividend, 37
Documents, 29
Domestic bank commercial and
    industrial (C&I) loans, 5
Domestic bank loans, 5
Downgrades, 127, 130
Due diligence on the manager's per-
    formance history, 19
Duration, 77
    characteristics between the index
        and the portfolio, 77

E

Early amortization, 30
    concept, 30
    difference between balance sheet
        CLOs and credit cards, 30
    events, 180
    events in synthetic CLOs, 180
    process, 30
    triggers, 30, 196
Early partial, 46
Early prepayment, 73
Early termination, 48
Economic triggers, 180
Economics of issuing a synthetic
    CLO, 175
Ecuador, 92
Eligibility or substitution criteria to
    prevent credit quality migration,
    196
Emerging market
    collateral, 5
    corporate bonds, 98
    investments, 36
    sovereign bond defaults
    market debt, 4
    sovereign bonds track record ver-
        sus sovereign bank loans, 94
Enforcement of party agreements,
    74

Enhanced first loss notes, 173
Enhanced MBS I, 103
Equitable assignment, 165
Equities, 21
Equity, 35
    "first loss" piece, 154
    distributions, 51
    holders, 50
    investors, 3
    levels in mortgage CBO struc-
        tures, 104
    participation, 41
    returns, 37
Erturk, Erkan, 75
Euro/144A, 160
European ABS/MBS, 186
European banks
    treatment will vary jurisdiction
        by jurisdiction, 151
European CDO marketplace, 159
    finding value in European CLOs,
        182
    issuance, 161
    recent developments, 170
European CLO investors, 182
European sponsor-linked CLOs, 166
Evaluating managers, 25
Event of default, 48
Event risk, 129, 135
Excelsior master trust, 185
Excess spread, 19, 30, 182
Excess spread/interest, 61
Expected loss, 55, 136
Expected loss level, 15
Expected probability of default, 53
Expected weighted average advance
    rates, 36

F

Failure
    to comply with any regulations of
        the fund, 48
    to comply with the OC and net
        worth tests within their respec-
        tive cure times, 48
    to meet interest, 48
Falcone, Yvonne, 67
Federal Reserve set of capital inter-
    pretations on synthetic CLOs, 151
Fees, 49
Finance companies, 130
    credit standing, 130
Financial Security Assurance Hold-
    ings Ltd. (FSA), 116
First loss (equity) position, 146
First loss (equity) tranches, 173
First loss position, 177
Fitch, 13, 40
    assumptions for stressed default
        rates, 63
    approach to rating ABS CDOs
        and CRE CDOs, 139
    default curve, 63, 139
    industry classifications, 65

market value CDO rating meth-
    odology, 71
methodology, 63
proprietary information, 63
stress scenarios, 74
Fixed/floating composition, 18
Floating revolving loan, 49
Floating-rate coupons of CBO
    tranches, 200
Floors, 138
Foreign bank loans, 4, 6
Foreign exchange risk, 180
Fortress Investment, 103
Framework for analyzing relative
    value, 209
Frictionless market, 219
Fully funded structures, 176
Fully funded CLOs, 170
Fully funded synthetic CDO, 148
    advantages of the synthetic fully
        funded CDO, 148
Fully funded synthetic transaction,
    175
Fully leveraged, 46
Funding costs, 143

G

Gauging activity levels, 86
GeldiLux 1999-2 transaction, 184
General level of interest rates and
    credit spreads, 68
Geographically diversified commer-
    cial mortgage loans, 131
Glacier Finance Ltd., 145
Global bank balance sheet term
    CLO market, 160
Global fixed income credit markets,
    160
Globe 2000, 180, 190
Gluck, Jeremy, 67
Goldman Sachs, 103
Guarantee fees, 170

H

Healthcare, 133
Hedges, 18, 19
    mark-to-market risk, 181
Hedging agreement, 181
Hedging and arbitrage transactions,
    141, 152
Hedging credit risk, 152
Hedging dealer inventories, 153
Hedging fees, 49
Hedging interest-rate volatility, 138
HEL sector, 19
High yield
    bond deals, 84
    bonds, 91, 112
    bond market, 58
    CBO, 104
    index, 82
    loans, 5
    market, 53
Historical data simulation, 68

Historical default information collected by S&P, 59
Historical default rates, 203
Historical loss patterns, 58
HLT loans, 5
Home equity, 130
  ABS sectors, 22
  loan (HEL) market, 118
  loan ABS senior/subordinate transactions, 10
  equity loan, 19
Hotel and leisure, 133
Hurdle rates, 51
Hybrid transactions, 153
Hybrids, 118
HypoVereins Bank's Geldilux transactions, 177, 181

I

Illiquidity, 68
Indenture, 13, 29
Independent third-party appraisal, 42
Index benchmarks, 41
Industrial, 133
Industry and/or geographic portfolio concentrations, 68
Industry classification, 59
  system, 55
Instituto de Credito Oficial (ICO), 173
Insurance companies, 116
Insurance wrap, 28
Interest, 28
Interest coverage by tranche and par value, 138
Interest coverage ratio test, 11, 29
Interest coverage tests, 30, 112
Interest coverage triggers, 113
Interest debt service, 170
Interest deficiency, 180
  in the capital structure, 175
Interest rate derivatives, 34
Interest-rate hedges, 34
Interest-only (I/O) strip, 130
Interest payments, 50
Interest rate mismatches, 62
Interest rate risk, 18, 76
Interest shortfalls, 62
Intermediary bank, 148
Internal credit enhancements, 18, 19
Internal Revenue Service (IRS) rules, 133
International Swaps and Derivative Association (ISDA), 178
Intex Group, 126
Investment-grade REIT bonds, 131
ISDA (International Swap Dealers Association), 144, 145
Issuance costs, 46
Issuer motivation, 1, 158
Issuer profile, 162
Issuer/sponsor, 6
  post-transaction capital charge, 174

J

Japanese banks, 28
Japanese legal system, 28
JP Morgan's BISTRO, 170, 228

K

KBC's Cygnus Finance, 181
Kingdom of Spain, 173

L

Latin American countries, 92
Latin American issuers, 96
Lease-backed ABS, 186
Legal
  analysis of the transaction, 58
  considerations, 74, 196
  expenses, 49
  risk, 63, 129
  soundness of securitization structure, 18
  state of the issuer, 63
  structure, 71
Lehman, 103
Leverage, 85
  effect of higher leverage, 85
  ratio, 35
Leveraged returns, 3
Liability structure, 104
LIBOR-indexed liabilities, 80
LIBOR-plus portfolios, 200
Limitations on payments, 48
Linked transaction, 29
  versus de-linked, 29
Liquidation, 46, 186
Liquidity, 42
  and credit quality of assets, 73
  haircuts, 69, 71
  in distressed markets, 73
  of the underlying assets, 20
Liquidity risk, 76, 77
  in normal market conditions, 76
Liquidity spread model, 75
Loan yield, 83
Loans to private and public equity, 36
Loan-to-values (LTVs), 132
Long Term Credit Bank (LTCB), 185
Loss, 110
  curves used by all three rating agencies are front-end, middle- and back-loaded, 135
  determination and settlement, 190
  expectations, 195
  for each default path, 136
  severity, 194

M

Macroeconomic
  analysis, 41
  factors, 54
  shocks, 55
Main risk factors, 67
  affecting rated tranches in market value CDOs, 67

Maintenance tests, 138
Make-whole premium, 50
Manager, 19
  of a cash flow transaction, 19
Managing the rating agency covenants, 36
Mandatory redemption
  due to an OC or minimum net worth test failure, 49
Manufactured housing sectors, 19
Margin call provisions, 181
Marginal arbitrage, 90
Marked-to-market discipline, 20
Marked-to-market value, 25
Market downturn, 73
Market driven arbitrage, 134
Market reference interest rate, 49
Market risk, 67, 76
Market value CDO transactions, 2, 20, 21, 25
  versus cash flow transactions, 25
  with preferred equity classes, 46
Market value test, 23
Market volatility, 70
Master trust structure, 28, 29
Maturity, 75
Maturity restrictions, 12, 14
Maximum concentrations of issuers, industries and sectors, 39
Mechanics of synthetic CLOs, 170
Mechanism of risk transfer, 164
Merrill Lynch Cash pay index, 80
Merton, Robert, 219
Mezzanine, 142
  ABS, 116
  classes, 1, 11
  comparing mezzanine classes of CDOs to similarly rated asset backed securities, 211
  debt, 21
  holders, 8
  investments, 34
  tranches of CBOs, 199
  tranches of mortgage deals, 112
  junior notes in SPV-less structures, 184
Microeconomic analysis, 41
Minimum diversity score, 31
Minimum net worth tests, 23, 46, 47, 71, 74
  failure, 50
Minimum standard of diversification, 41
Minimum weighted average rating test, 13, 31
Modeling and stress testing, 71, 73
Monthly standard deviations, 76
Moody's Investors Service, 4, 12, 40
  Binomial Expansion Model (BET), 135
  default and ratings migration studies, 213
  default experience, 106
  default study, 135
  how advance rates are computed, 69

idealized cumulative expected loss rates, 136
market value deal rating methodology, 67
measures portfolio volatility, 68
methodology, 53
monthly default report, 67
Moratorium, 178
Morgan Stanley, 209, 211
Morgan Stanley Dean Witter, 103
Mortgage categories, 105
Mortgage CBO market, 101
Mortgage collateralized bond obligations, 101
Mortgage instruments, 34
Mortgage market value CDOs, 39
Mortgage-related collateral, 87
Mortgage-related securities, 113
Motivation for issuance, 115
Multi-currency asset pool, 180

N

National Westminster Bank, 161
NationsBank Commercial Loan Master Trust, 5
NationsBank, 5
Natix, 180
NatWest ROSE, 162
Negative carry, 19, 37
Negative convexity, 110
Nelson, Soody, 75
Non-market risk, 41
Nonperforming loans (NPLs), 40
Non-systemic price shocks, 68
Non-systemic risk, 41
of the portfolio, 76
Note redemption, 180
Number of rated issuers, 59

O

O/C trigger, 113
Obligation acceleration, 178
OECD bank, 147, 151, 175
Off-balance sheet collateral, 152
Office, 133
Optimal structure in CDOs, 87
Optimize deal structure, 87
Optional redemption, 50, 51
by a majority of equity holders, 49
Originating bank, 142
risk transference between originating bank and SPV, 148
Overcollateralization (OC), 30, 67, 79
Overcollateralization levels, 80
Overcollateralization tests, 44, 47, 70, 71, 74, 112
calculations, 41
test failure, 45
Overcollateralization trigger, 112
Overcollateralization/subordination, 61
Overleveraging, 36

P

Paid in kind (PIK), 50
PaineWebber, 103
Pakistan, 92
Par value ratio test, 29
Par value test, 11, 30
Parametric simulation, 68
Partial early amortization, 30
Partially funded structures, 151, 175, 176
Partially funded synthetic CDOs, 149
leveraging the triple-A tranche in a partially funded structure, 191
Partially funded CLOs, 170
Pattern of CDO issuance, 79
Payment dates, 62
Payment periodicity between the assets and the liabilities, 62
Perfected security interest, 3, 28
Perfection of security interests, 74
Performance of the underlying securities, 1
Performance triggers, 29
Performance-based changes, 129
Pfandbriefe, 172, 175
Phoenix Investment Partners, 103
Platinum Commercial Loan Master Trust, 185
Pledge of the assets as security for the deal obligations, 63
Pooling and servicing agreement, 29
Portfolio approach in estimating the total risk of a market value deal Portfolio, 68
Portfolio credit default swaps, 174
Portfolio credit risk, 58
Portfolio limitations, 39, 41, 73
Portfolio manager's track record, 71
Portfolio's aggregate credit exposure, 53
Potential exposure to collateral credit risks, 187
Potential exposure to sponsor bank risk, 189
PPM America, 103
Predictability of cash flows, 129
Preferreds/convertible preferreds, 21
Prepayment risk, 50
Prepayment sensitive assets, 139
Prepayment tests, 139
Price volatility, 20, 25, 75
Primary coverage tests, 30\
Principal, 28
Principal payments, 37, 49, 50
Principal repayment, 170, 180
Private equity, 34
Private placements, 42
Probability of default, 59, 107, 127
Projected cash flows of the underlying collateral, 8
Prudential, 103
Purchasing participation rights, 168
Pure credit-linked note structures, 172
Put option, 181

Q

Qualitative factors in the rating methodology, 58
Quality credits, 73
Quality tests, 9, 11, 12, 16, 19, 22

R

Ramp-up criterion, 35
Ramp-up period, 34, 35, 39, 58, 82
Ramp-up risk, 58
Ramp-up schedule, 35
Rated second priority senior notes, 14
Rating, 75
analysis, 15
cash flow arbitrage transactions, 15
expenses, 49
factors, 16
migrations matrix, 215
of each issuer, 59
of the underlying assets, 15
process, 62, 63
triggers, 182
Rating agencies, 5, 15, 19, 36, 127
ABS CDO criteria, 118
methodologies, 39
standard industry classifications, 132
stress scenarios for recoveries, 202
Rating methodologies, 105
for cash flow CBOs, 53
for market value CDOs, 66
Real estate investment trust (REIT) securities, 101
Real estate investment trusts (REITs), 131
Realized capital gains and losses, 37
Realized losses, 179
Recovery assumptions, 17, 110, 137, 138
for ABS/RMBS/CMBS, and REIT assets, 108
Recovery rates, 17, 56, 64, 95, 108, 139
associated with different asset classes, 15
assumptions on mortgage deals, 108
Reference assets, 186
Reference loans, 166
Reference pool guidelines, 196
Reference portfolio, 178
Regulatory call options, 193
Regulatory capital, 149
Regulatory capital relief, 166
example, 176
Reimbursement depending on final recovery values, 166
Reinvestment period, 8, 62
REIT sectors, 133
Relative value, 113
Remitting payments, 189
Repeat issuers, 162
Repo agreement, 180
Repo financing, 3

Repo interest, 179
Repudiation, 144, 178
Repurchase agreements, 149
Reset risk, 62
Residential, 133
Residential mortgage-backed securities (RMBS), 101
Residual interest in the fund, 50
Residual negative carry, 179
Restructuring, 144, 145
    of an underlying loan, 178
Retail, 133
Return-on-equity, 82, 84
Returns on a risk-adjusted basis, 72
Revolving facility, 37
Revolving line of credit, 22
Revolving period, 8
Risk components and methodology, 76
Risk factors, 58
Risk weighting of the protection seller, 148
Risk weighting of the underlying assets (the loans), 148
Risk-based capital charge on the swap, 148
Risk-management tools, 41
Risk tranching, 126
Rose Funding, 6, 161
ROSE2, 184
Ross, Stephen, 221
Rubinstein, Mark, 221
Rule 144A investments, 42
Rules of CDO deal structuring, 86
Russia, 92
Russian Federation, 92

S

SBC Glacier transactions, 6, 162
Scala 1, 180
Scheduled repayment changing the percentage composition of the pool, 12
Scholes, Myron, 219
Seasoning curve, 135
Security's structural features, 129
Self-storage, 133
Senior and mezzanine tranches, 29
Senior facility, 44, 49, 50
Senior notes, 1, 50
Senior secured loans, 17
Senior secured note class, 8
Senior to debt service in the cash flow waterfall, 196
Senior/subordinate bonds, 8
Senior/subordinate structure, 28
Seniority level in the capital structure, 44
Senior-subordinated debt, 45
Senior-subordinated notes, 50
Servicing related risks, 189
SFA, 103
Shadow rating, 16, 54, 106
Short duration, high-grade assets, 101

Simulation approach, 68
    versus an analytic approach to measure portfolio volatility, 68
Single B stress scenario, 73
Sizing, 36
    credit enhancement, 195
Snailer, Joseph, 67
Soft bullets, 29
Sovereign emerging markets bonds, 91
Sovereign guaranteed CLOs, 173
Spanish banks, 173
Special purpose CDO vehicle, 5
Special purpose vehicle (SPV), 145
Special situation loans, 4, 5, 6
Special situations investments, 40
Specialty finance companies, 130
Spinnaker, 103
Sponsor bank, 170
    as credit protection buyer, 186
    bank risk, 181
Sponsor, 29
    downgrade, 29
    of arbitrage transactions, 3
    of the CDO, 134
Sponsor-linked CLOs, 164, 166, 172
Spread behavior in the synthetic CLO market, 192
Spread products, 184
    stratification of spreads by product type, 122
Spread sector portfolio, 126
SPV, 18
Standard & Poor's (S&P), 13, 40, 75
    approach to rating ABS CDOs and CRE CDOs, 137
    methodology, 58
    models default risk, 77
    ramp-up risk, 62
Stepdown date, 19
Story bonds, 98
Stress factor, 68, 69
Stress scenarios, 136
Structural
    analysis, 58
    considerations, 196
    covenants, 33
    credit protection, 42
    credit support, 170
    differences between market value and cash flow CDOs, 51
    features of market value CDOs, 34
    priorities, 46
    protections, 97
    provision, 71
    risks, 196
Structure, 18
    impact of CDO arbitrage on, 86
Structure related risks, 189
Structured Credit Partners, 103
Structured finance business, 118
    of the financial guaranty firms, 116
Structured notes, 28

Structuring expenses, 49
Structuring model, 80
Subordinated debt, 45
Subordinated noteholders, 8
Subordinated notes, 50
Subordinated notes/equity of the CDO, 1
Subordinated residential mortgage paper, 112
Subordinated tests, 46
Subordination, 7, 9, 30, 70, 88
    and enforceability, 58
    and excess spread protection, 118
    interest costs drive, 87
Sub-participated structures, 172
Sub-participation, 168
Sub-prime MBS, 186
Substantive consolidation, 58
Sumitomo Bank, 161
Super senior
    credit default swap, 151
    piece, 150
    senior swap, 175
    tranche, 176
    swap counterparty, 177
Surveillance, 71, 75
Swap arrangements, 147
Swap counterparty, 152
Swap curve, 80
Swap rates, 80
Swaps, 18, 138
Swiss Bank's Glacier, 228
Synthetic CDO, 411
    allows banks to reduce regulatory capital charges and reduce economic risk, 141
    allows banks to reduce regulatory capital charges, 141
Synthetic CLOs, 164, 168
    differences between synthetic and conventional CLOs, 187
    disadvantage of a fully funded synthetic CDO, 148
    growth in synthetic CLOs issuance, 170
    key advantages of synthetic CLOs, 174
    key features of synthetic CLOs, 177
    key features that differentiate synthetic CLOs from cash based structures, 187
    return and risk of a synthetic CBO/CLO, 229
    versus cash flow CLOs, 186
Synthetic structures, 197
    identifying the ideal structure, 191
Synthetics/credit derivatives, 63

T

Target asset mix by a fund's portfolio manager, 36
Target mix, 75
Target ratings, 22
Targeted leverage ratio, 35

Threshold level of losses, 149
Top-down analysis, 41
Total portfolio risk, 76
Total return swaps, 225, 227
Track record, 127
  of the manager, 19
Trading activity, 37
Trading by the collateral manager, 29
Trading constraints, 23
Traditional asset-backed transactions, 5
Traditional fully funded securitization, 149
Tranche OC test, 71
Tranche-by-tranche payment window, 134
Transfer through sub-participation, 168
Transition matrix formulation, 67
Transparency and availability of information, 126
Triangle Funding II, 179
Tribeca 1, 103
Trigger, 18
Trigger events, 29
True sale, 5
True sale cash flow CLOs, 164
True sale provisions, 29
Trust Company of the West, 101
Trust fees, 8
Trustee, 46, 71, 191
  fees, 49
  performance, 191

U

U.S. domestic bank loans, 4
U.S. domestic high yield bonds, 4
UBS, 103
UBS Warburg, 103
Ukraine, 92
Underleveraging, 36
Underlying collateral pool, 12
Underwriter, 106
Underwriting criteria for ABS, 127
Underwriting dealer, 80
Underwriting expenses, 49
Undiversifiable correlation, 55
Unrated subordinated classes, 14
Unrealized capital gains, 47
Unscheduled payments of underlying assets, 12
Upfront costs, 48
Upfront fees, 49
Upgrades, 130
  of credit enhancers, 130

V

Variable funding notes (VFNs), 172
Violation of a coverage test, 11
Volatility adjustments, 77
Volatility and correlation assumptions, 68
Volatility model to adjust for duration, 75

W

Waterfall, 29, 50
  payment structure of cash flow CDOs, 36
Weighted average credit rating, 54
Weighted average rating factor (WARF), 106
Weighted average rating, 12
Weighted-average probability of default of a portfolio, 136
West LB, 103
Workout loans, 6

Y

Yield (to worst), 80
York Funding, 184
Yugoslavia, 92

Z

Zero-default corporate bond, 203
Zero-default scenario, 62